International Human Resource Management in South Korean Multinational Enterprises

Haiying Kang • Jie Shen

International Human Resource Management in South Korean Multinational Enterprises

palgrave
macmillan

Haiying Kang
School of Management, RMIT
University, Melbourne, Australia

Jie Shen
Shenzhen Audencia Business School
(SABS), Shenzhen University
Shenzhen, China

ISBN 978-981-10-3092-5 ISBN 978-981-10-3093-2 (eBook)
DOI 10.1007/978-981-10-3093-2

Library of Congress Control Number: 2017932758

Printed on acid-free paper

This Springer imprint is published by Springer Nature
The registered company is Springer Nature Singapore Pte Ltd.
The registered company address is: 152 Beach Road, #21-01/04 Gateway East, Singapore 189721, Singapore

Foreword

I am very pleased to write a Foreword for *International Human Resource Management in South Korean Multinational Enterprises* by Haiying Kang and Jie Shen. This book is one of the first scholarly efforts to outline and examine the international HRM practices used by managers in South Korean multinational enterprises operating in China. Using both interview data and survey data, the authors discuss IHRM policies and practices and provide examples of good and bad outcomes.

This book is underpinned by a strategic approach to HRM, focusing on the linkages between strategy, people, and performance. The South Korean MNEs in this study were operating in China with South Korean expatriate managers and host-country Chinese nationals. A particular contribution of this book is the focus of the authors on the willingness of host-country nationals to assist expatriate managers. There is a lack of research on this issue, and the discussion on this topic is one of the key contributions of this book. Readers will be engaged by the relevant examples that appear throughout the book and by the rigorous intellectual and practical approach that the authors apply to their research findings, linking key IHRM concepts to the outcomes of their empirical research. Professor Jie Shen has published extensively in the field of international human resource management. This book will certainly be appreciated by many researchers and managers.

Peter J. Dowling
International Management & Strategy
La Trobe University
Melbourne, VIC, Australia

Foreword

Dr. Haying Kang and Professor Jie Shen have written a very interesting research book titled *International Human Resource Management in South Korean MNEs.* Both authors have published extensively in the field of international human resource management, and Professor Shen is considered a world-class expert in this field. This book presents an interesting analysis of how South Korean MNEs manage international human resources management in their international subsidiaries. Past IHRM literature has focused on how MNEs based in Western countries have managed IHRM. With the emergence of countries such as China, South Korea, and India, researchers are now interested to know whether MNEs originating in these countries exhibit different IHRM approaches. Hence, this book is very important and relevant.

The book conducts a comprehensive analysis of a range of IHRM policies and practices, including international staffing, international training and development, international performance appraisal, and international compensation. The authors have appropriately chosen China as the host nation. China is now a major force in world markets and is the largest recipient of foreign direct investment. It is the ideal experimental field for understanding how foreign MNEs manage IHRM overseas.

This book analyzes the reasons behind South Korean MNEs' decisions on IHRM policies and practices. For example, the authors argue that the relative strength of the South Korean economy over the Chinese economy is a major reason South Korean MNEs transfer some of their HRM practices to Chinese subsidiaries. Such an analysis enriches the IHRM literature and enables companies across the world to develop effective IHRM strategies.

This book also explores the effects of IHRM practices on host-country nationals' work outcomes. More specifically, this study explores the effects of IHRM on the willingness of HCNs to help expatriates. The book provides a better understanding of organizational contextual effect on HCNs' attitudes and behaviors toward expatriates.

The existing IHRM models focus on strategic integration. This study considers the interests of employees and external stakeholders by exploring the effects of high-commitment IHRM and socially responsible IHRM on HCNs' willingness to help expatriates. This is certainly a pioneering research.

The authors should be commended for writing a book that fills an important gap in IHRM research. Very little is known about the IHRM policies South Korean MNEs adopt in their overseas operations. After reading this book, companies all over the world will be able to deal more effectively with South Korean MNEs and enhance the value of joint venture partnerships.

Brian D'Netto
Curtin Graduate School of Business
Curtin University
Perth, WA, Australia

내 벗이 몇인가하니 수석과 송죽이라
동산에 달 오르니 그 더욱 반갑구나
두어라 이 다섯밖에 또 더하여 무엇하리

You ask how many friends I have?
Water and stone, bamboo and pine.
The moon rising over the eastern hill is a joyful comrade.
Besides these five companions, what other pleasure should I ask?

—*Yun Seondo* (윤선도, *1587–1671*)

Acknowledgment

We wish to thank a number of people who without their contributions to our inspiration and support this book could not have been written. In particular, we thank Professor John Benson who has collaborated with us on non-traditional expatriates. We would like to thank Professor Peter Dowling for working with us on exploring the relationships of international HRM practices with employee outcomes and for endorsing this book. We sincerely thank Professor Brian D'Netto who has been supportive to our research and also endorses this book.

Above all we would like to express our gratitude to our families, Yingai Quan, Changlong Kang, Chengri Quan, Ci Song, and Ben Shen, who have provided tremendous support and encouragement to us. It is to them that we hereby dedicate this work. Last but not least, our research was partially supported by the Chinese National Science Foundation Grant 71572157 and Key Chinese National Science Foundation Grant 71132003.

Haiying Kang
Jie Shen

Contents

Authors

Dr. Haiying Kang, Lecturer of HRM at RMIT, Melbourne, Australia. Her research interest is international HRM. Dr. Kang has published her research in the *International Journal of Human Resource Management*, *Human Resource Management*, *Thunderbird International Business Review*, and *Asia Pacific Business Review*.

Dr. Jie Shen, Professor of HRM at Shenzhen International Business School, Shenzhen University, and Adjunct Professor of HRM at the University of South Australia. Previously, he held positions as Professor of HRM and Associate Professor of HRM at Curtin University, Monash University, and the University of South Australia. His main research interests are HRM, international HRM, and corporate social responsibility. He has published over 70 refereed articles in journals, such as the *Journal of Management*, *Human Resource Management*, *Journal of Business Ethics*, *International Business Review*, *International Journal of Human Resource Management*, and *Group & Organization Management*. His is the author of the following books: *International HRM in Chinese MNEs*, *Human Resource Management Strategic Integration of Indian Organizations*, and *Labour Disputes and Their Resolution in China*.

Abbreviations

BARS	Behaviorally Anchored Rating Scale
BHMC	Beijing Hyundai Motor Company
CCT	Cross-cultural training
CFA	Confirmatory factor analysis
CFI	Comparative fit index
CMV	Common method variance
CSR	Corporate social responsibility
EMBA	Executive Master of Business Administration
FDI	Foreign direct investment
FIE	Foreign-invested enterprise
GFI	Goodness of fit index
GDP	Gross domestic product
HCN	Host-country national
HRM	Human resource management
IHRM	International human resource management
JV	Joined venture
KPI	Key performance indicator
MBA	Master of Business Administration
MBO	Management by objective
MNE	Multinational enterprise
OBOR	One-belt, one-road
POE	Private-owned enterprise
POS	Perceived organizational support
PRP	Performance-related pay
RMSEA	Root mean square error of approximation
SME	Small- and medium-sized enterprise
SOE	State-owned enterprise

SEM	Structural equation modeling
SIHRM	Strategic international human resource management
SPSS	Statistical Product and Service Solutions
SRIHRM	Socially responsible international human resource management
SRMR	Standard root mean square residual
TLI	Tucker–Lewis index
TCN	Third-country national
UniSA	University of South Australia
UK	United Kingdom
USA	United States of America

List of Figures

List of Tables

CHAPTER 1

Introduction

Since the 1960s, while business activities have become increasingly international and interconnected, workforces have become more diverse and mobile. This development has made managing human resources a key challenge for multinational enterprises (MNEs) (Tarique and Schuler 2010). Scullion (1995, p. 352) defined international human resource management (IHRM) as 'the human resource management issues and problems arising from the internationalization of business, and the human resource management strategies, policies and practices that firms pursue in response to the internationalization process'. IHRM has been widely recognized as an important source of organizational competitive advantage and the key to MNEs being successful (Black et al. 1992; Dowling et al. 2013; Scullion and Collings 2006). Empirical research has found there is a significant relationship between MNEs' IHRM practices and business performance (e.g. Ngo et al. 1998; Park et al. 2003; Shen 2011).

The IHRM literature was initially developed in industrialized Western economies, particularly the United States (US) (e.g. Kobrin 1988; Tung 1982). However, in the last few decades, growing research attention has been paid to MNEs originating from emerging and now increasingly powerful market economies, like China (e.g. Shen and Edwards 2004), India (e.g. Rienda et al. 2013), Turkey (e.g. Demirbag et al. 2009), and South Korea (e.g. Zou and Lansbury 2009). This shift reflects the growing importance of outward foreign direct investment (FDI) from

H. Kang, J. Shen, *International Human Resource Management in South Korean Multinational Enterprises*,
DOI 10.1007/978-981-10-3093-2_1

non-Western industrialized economies, and such research has enriched the Western IHRM literature (Dowling et al. 2013; Sheehan et al. 2010). South Korea's economy grew significantly from the late 1950s onward, and 14 South Korean companies were recently listed on the Fortune 500 index in 2015 (Fortune 2016). Like other MNEs from emerging, newly industrialized economies, South Korean MNEs use 'outward investments as a springboard to acquire strategic assets needed to compete more effectively against global rivals and to avoid the institutional and market constraints they face at home' (Luo and Tung 2007, p. 482).

Despite the growing interest in researching IHRM practiced by South Korean MNEs, relatively few studies have been published, and there is a great need to conduct more research in order to better understand how South Korean MNEs manage HRM in their global operations (e.g. Kang and Shen 2013). This book presents the findings of a recent empirical analysis we conducted to investigate how South Korean MNEs manage human resources in their Chinese subsidiaries. Our research involves international recruitment and selection, training and development, performance management, reward and compensation, as well as the impact of IHRM practices on employees' work attitudes and behaviors. More specifically, we investigated the effects of high-commitment HRM and socially responsible HRM on host-country nationals' (HCNs) willingness to help expatriates. Our research has significant theoretical and practical implications. In this book, most chapters have the following three major components: a review of the literature on HRM practices in China and South Korea, the concepts of specific IHRM issues, and the empirical findings.

In this introductory chapter, we first discuss the general IHRM concepts including definitions, characteristics and development of IHRM, approaches to IHRM, and factors determining these approaches. Subsequently, we discuss the HRM practices in South Korea and the development of South Korean MNEs and the HRM practices and the development of inward FDI in China. Next, we explain the methodology of the research. Finally, we outline the structure of the book.

IHRM Concepts

Definition of International Human Resource Management

The development of technology and changes in institutional frameworks following the Industrial Revolution in the nineteenth century stimulated international trade and economy. These processes further increased globalization and the importance of MNEs in the twentieth century (Meyer et al. 2011). Globalization has brought a great degree of complexity and diversity to international business, meaning that for MNEs the formulation of international strategies is very challenging. It is widely recognized that any international strategy needs people to formulate and implement it. As such, managing the global workforce has become an important aspect of international business (Di Cieri and Dowling 2012), which relates to one of the major areas of MNE management—IHRM.

While there are numerous definitions of IHRM, Scullion's has remained the most popular. IHRM is defined by Scullion as 'the human resource management issues and problems arising from the internationalization of business, and the human resource management strategies, policies and practices that firms pursue in response to the internationalization process' (Scullion 1995, p. 352). The last two decades have witnessed a rapid growth in the IHRM field for a number of reasons (Scullion and Linehan 2005). First, the rapid growth of internationalization and intensified global competition have increased the number and significance of MNEs and mobility of the global workforce (Black et al. 2000). Second, there is growing evidence showing that financial costs of international operations, to which IHRM is regarded to be crucial, are greater than domestic operations (Dowling et al. 2013). Third, in general, there is a serious shortage of international managers for MNEs globally (Scullion 1994). Such a shortage is likely to hinder the implementation of global strategies and consequently constrains corporate efforts to expand abroad (Black and Gregerson 1999; Morgan et al. 2003).

Characteristics of IHRM

Human resource functions which are conducted in an international context are very similar to those done in a domestic one, such as recruitment and selection, training and development, performance appraisal, and reward and compensation (Samnani and Singh 2013). However, how those functions are executed reveals important differences between domestic HRM and IHRM. The main factor differentiating domestic HRM from IHRM is that the former deals with a single country and single source of workforce, while the latter operates in different countries (parent country, host country, and third country) and deals with various workforce groups (i.e. expatriates, HCNs, and third-country nationals

[TCNs]) (Scullion and Collings 2006). MNEs often engage in a number of HR activities that are not needed in domestic operations, such as provision of expatriates' cross-cultural training and post-arrival training, and expatriate management. IHRM policies and practices are likely to become more complex than domestic HRM. For example, complexities may arise from expatriates' compensation, and coordination and communication problems between expatriates and HCNs. Furthermore, there are more external factors that influence MNEs managing their HRM systems, such as host-country legal, economic, political, and sociocultural factors. Last but not least, IHRM generates more risks than domestic HRM. For example, MNEs may experience financial losses due to expatriate failure, political risks in the local country, and financial risks caused by volatile exchange rates (Dowling et al. 2013; Stone 2008).

The Development of IHRM

Since the 1960s, IHRM focusing on how MNEs manage HRM in international operations has been recognized as an important competitive advantage for businesses seeking to achieve success. The earliest literature on this subject originated in the US experience (e.g. Perlmutter 1969; Tung 1982). The IHRM literature developed significantly during the 1990s. Researchers explored the rationale of IHRM policies and practices; that is why MNEs adopt certain IHRM practices (e.g. Shen 2005). A number of integrative IHRM models were developed to identify antecedents of IHRM policies and practices, and they have greatly contributed to MNEs building the 'best-fit' IHRM system (Shen 2011). During the same period, research orientation moved from Western-focused, developed economy MNEs to emerging economy MNEs like those in China (e.g. Shen and Edwards 2004) and South Korean MNEs (e.g. Zou and Lansbury 2009).

The current IHRM literature continues to refine and further develop IHRM models (i.e. the relative strength and cultural difference model) to examine the rationale for MNEs adopting particular IHRM approaches. Recent research also extensively focuses on a number of issues such as HR ethics, work–life balance, and diversity management. Because existing IHRM models have failed to address the needs and benefits of internal and external stakeholders, the concept of socially responsible IHRM (SRIHRM) has been recently developed to address this deficiency in the existing IHRM models (Shen 2011). By integrating corporate social responsibility (CSR) into IHRM, the concept of SRHRM extends the macro issues of CSR, for example, strategy and organizational performance, to micro-foundations of CSR (i.e. the effects of CSR on employees).

Approaches to International Human Resource Management

MNEs can adopt a number of approaches to manage human resources in their overseas operations. These include localization, home orientation, globalization, and integration (Dowling et al. 2013; Ferner 1997; Harzing 1999; Perlmutter 1969; Perlmutter and Heenan 1974; Shen and Edwards 2004):

- Localization: MNEs localize HRM systems and fill HCNs in key positions. Australian MNEs typically tend to adopt this approach when operating overseas (Kim and Gray 2005).
- Home orientation: MNEs export home HRM systems abroad. The headquarters make key decisions and send expatriates to control subsidiaries. Research shows that the majority of US and Japanese MNEs adopt this approach in their overseas operations (Kopp 1994; Mayrhofer and Brewster 1996; Tung 1981, 1982).
- Globalization: MNEs adopt universal IHRM policies and practices worldwide. European MNEs tend to adopt the globalization approach (Schuh 2007).
- Integration: MNEs adopt IHRM policies and practices that integrate both home HRM systems and host HRM systems. It is the best-fit approach which MNEs take into account for host-contextual and firm-specific factors in order to achieve the internal fit and external fit. Research suggests that most MNEs strive to achieve the best fit by adopting the integration approach when operating overseas (Budhwar 2012; Muratbekova-Touron 2008).

Each approach has some advantages and disadvantages. One advantage of using the localization approach is that it is relatively easier to formulate and implement localized HRM practices than the home HRM practices in host countries. HCNs tend to accept familiarized HRM practices, and consequently they are likely to be motivated and retained. Moreover, this approach facilitates the adoption of localized international strategies. The major problems associated with the localization approach are that: firstly, expatriates are unable to widen their horizons from working abroad; secondly, it is difficult to coordinate between headquarters and subsidiaries; and thirdly, the headquarters may not be knowledgeable about host regulations and systems (Caligiuri and Stroh 1995; Mayrhofer and Brewster 1996). The advantages for the home orientation approach include the headquarters' control over decision-making and effective communication. However, the home HRM systems may be difficult to implement in host contexts and thus likely to result in strong tension between expatriates and HCNs and high turnover among the latter (Caligiuri and Stroh 1995; Kobrin 1988).

The adoption of the globalization approach facilitates the implementation of global international strategies. While it is easy for the headquarters to formulate globalized HRM practices, it is hard for the headquarters to implement them in diverse host environments (Caligiuri and Stroh 1995; Dowling and Welch 1988; Mayrhofer and Brewster 1996). The main advantage of the integration approach is that MNEs attempt to adopt 'the best' IHRM approaches which achieve internal fit and external fit throughout the organization. As Shen (2005) argued, it is impossible for MNEs to adopt the full home-based or host-based approach, so they tend to adopt the integration approach to some extent. However, it is argued that the 'best fit' is hard to achieve because the transferability and effectiveness of HR best practice are not yet clear and are influenced by a wide range of firm-specific, home-contextual, and host-contextual factors (Janssens 2002; Lertxundi and Landeta 2012; Shen 2005; Osland and Osland 2005).

Factors Determining IHRM Approaches

The most important development in the IHRM literature during the last few decades has been the emergence of a number of theoretical IHRM models which provide the rationale for MNEs adopting their IHRM strategies (Shen 2005). These models have made significant contributions to the IHRM literature by enhancing our understanding of the antecedents to IHRM policies and practices. The major IHRM models include *Two Logistic Approach Model* (Evans and Lorange 1989), *An Integrative Framework of Strategic IHRM* (Schuler et al. 1993), *Two Dimensions of IHRM Model* (Paauwe and Dewe 1995), *An Integrative Model of SIHRM* (Taylor et al. 1996), *A Generic IHRM Model* (Shen 2005), and *Socially Responsible IHRM Model* (Shen 2011). These are explained in more detail below.

The *Two Logistic Approach Model* suggests that product–market and sociocultural factors influence IHRM policies and practices. These factors are subjected to dual pressures for local adaptation and internal consistency (Evans and Lorange 1989). The *Two Dimensions of IHRM Model* suggests that a combination of product, market, and technology factors and another combination of sociocultural and political–legal factors collectively influence IHRM policies and practices (Paauwe and Dewe 1995). The *Integrative Model of SIHRM* (Taylor et al. 1996) examines the determinants of SIHRM at three different levels—the parent, affiliate, and employee levels. The determinants include headquarters' international strategy, senior or executive management's perceptions, subsidiary's strategic role, method of subsidiary's establishments, headquarter–subsidiary's legal and cultural distance, and employees' criticality. Schuler et al.'s (1993) *Integrative Framework of Strategic IHRM* identifies a number of organizational and host-contextual antecedents of SIHRM. Shen's (2005) *Generic IHRM Model* indicates that MNEs' IHRM policies and practices are the interaction of the home/host HRM system, firm-specific factors, and host-contextual factors; their impacts may change over time. There is also interplay between IHRM policies and practices.

The *Two Logistic Approach Model* and *Two Dimensions of IHRM Model* are criticized as not being significantly different to domestic HRM models. Also, they are incomplete due to their failure to categorize factors and neglect some important factors, for instance, the size of operation, type of industry, and so on (Shen 2005). Schuler et al.'s (1993) model ignores country–regional characteristics and some firm-specific factors, for example, size of international operation (Shen et al. 2005). Taylor et al.'s (1996) model overemphasizes subjective factors (e.g. senior management's attitudes to HRM competence) but disregards some important contextual factors like organizational structure or stages of internationalization.

It is recognized that it is impossible for an MNE to completely localize its IHRM, or to fully transfer the home HRM abroad, or adopt a universal IHRM in all subsidiaries due to the fact that home of origin effectively plays a 'push' role, while host countries play a 'pull' role in the transfer/localization process (Shen 2005). To be competitive and efficient, MNEs have to be locally responsive, flexible, adaptable, and fast learning within the shortest of time periods. Furthermore, MNEs should be able to transfer knowledge and learning across their globally dispersed units (Schuler et al. 2002). It is therefore suggested that MNEs strive for the best internal and external fit in order to achieve global integration, local responsiveness, and organizational learning simultaneously (Hartmann et al. 2010).

More recent theories like the strategic alignment view, national cultural view, and dominance effect focus on explaining the 'best-fit' approach. While strategic alignment leads to transfer (Bloom et al. 2003), cultural and institutional similarities between the host and home countries result in localization (Vo and Stanton 2011). As Bloom et al. (2003) argued, 'the strategic alignment model asserts the pre-eminence of organizational contexts; the national cultural model asserts the pre-eminence of local host contexts' (p. 1351). From a different perspective, Pudelko and Harzing (2007) and Smith and Meiksins (1995) argued that international transfer is due to dominance effects, that is, the relative strengths of the host and home economies. Subsidiaries' HRM practices are not shaped in accordance with home (i.e. country of origin) and host (i.e. localization) country, but according to practices originating from dominant economies, which are more likely to be regarded as 'best practice' and therefore transferable (Smith and Meiksins 1995). According to Pudelko and Harzing (2007), when the country of origin is a dominant economy, the MNE tends to transfer HRM policies to international operations. In contrast, when the host country is a dominant economy, the reverse occurs. There is empirical evidence that because the US is a dominant economy, US MNEs tend to transfer HRM policies to international subsidiaries in Germany, Japan (Pudelko and Harzing 2007), Greece (Myloni 2002), and Turkey (Sayim 2010). Dominance effects are logical, especially when receiver countries depend economically or politically on sender countries. When there is no dominant economy, for example, Japan and Germany, Japanese MNEs in Germany or German MNEs in Japan are more likely to adopt more balanced and integrated HRM systems.

The abovementioned models have been developed to address MNEs' strategic needs, but not the needs and interests of internal and external stakeholders (Shen 2011). The concept of socially responsible HRM was initially developed in the general HRM literature (Olitzky and Swanson 2006). According to Olitzky and Swanson (2006), socially responsible HRM practices may include taking into account candidates' attitudes toward CSR in various HRM activities, such as recruitment and selection, training and development, performance appraisal, and reward and compensation. Later, Shen (2011) integrated the concept of socially responsible HRM into the IHRM literature and developed the term 'socially responsible IHRM' (SRIHRM) to address the limitations of strategic

IHRM models. He did this by taking into account the interests and needs of various stakeholders in IHRM. SRIHRM is a two-dimensional construct which includes external CSR-supportive IHRM and employee-oriented IHRM. External CSR-supportive IHRM includes deploying CSR-specific employees, taking into account CSR values of candidates in recruitment and selection, providing CSR training, and taking account of social performance in promotion, appraisal, and reward. For example, the provision of CSR training in MNEs is very important. Through training, employees are more likely to be aware of the effects of CSR policies on themselves, workplace environment, and external social environment (Maon et al. 2009). Research shows that there is a positive relationship between the provision of CSR training and employee organizational commitment because employees identify more with their organization when it actively invests in socially responsible activities (Brammer et al. 2007; Lee and Bruvold 2003). MNEs' training should integrate with the CSR culture so that employees have the opportunity to practice CSR activities (Sharma et al. 2011).

External CSR-supportive IHRM policies and practices are used to implement external CSR initiatives, also known as 'general CSR' (Rupp et al. 2006), and to increase employees' awareness of external CSR and support for corporate external CSR initiatives (Shen 2011). External CSR includes mainly addressing social concerns for poverty (e.g. Jenkins 2005), climate change (e.g. Van den Hove et al. 2002), environmental sustainability (e.g. Basu and Palazzo 2008), helping disaster victims (e.g. Horwich 1993), and corporate community involvement (e.g. Zappalá 2004). The adoption of external CSR-supportive IHRM is critical to the successful implementation of MNEs' CSR initiatives. Hence, HCNs will regard the adoption of external CSR-supportive IHRM as an important signal that the MNE is being socially responsible and committed to CSR.

Employee-oriented SRIHRM is a key component of the internal CSR of MNEs because internal CSR addresses the interests and needs of internal stakeholders, that is, mainly employees (Shen 2011). According to Shen, employee-oriented SRIHRM focuses on personal development, such as training, feedback, mentoring, career and managerial development, employee participation and involvement, work–life balance, job security, health and safety, equality, and legal compliance. The last few decades have witnessed rapid advances in the more general HRM literature in terms of taking account of employees' interests and needs rather than organizational needs for profits in order to motivate employees. Consequently, a range of employee-oriented HRM concepts have emerged, such as high-commitment HRM (e.g. Chiang et al. 2011; McClean and Collins 2011), family-friendly HRM (e.g. Wood and De Menezes 2010), and flexible HRM (e.g. Atkinson and Hall 2011; MacVaugh and Evans 2012). In comparison the IHRM literature has lagged behind in this regard. The development of the concept of employee-oriented IHRM helps to fill this important literature void. As was argued earlier, it is impractical for MNEs to adopt a solely standardized or localized approach; MNEs need to integrate home HRM practices, host HRM practices, and IHRM practices of their counterparts in order to achieve the best internal and external fit. Hence, SRIHRM practices are likely to constitute the integration of home and host SRHRM practices, and other MNEs' SRIHRM practices (Shen 2011).

Changes in the Macroeconomic Context in South Korea

In the early 1970s, South Korea undertook industrial restructuring by emphasizing heavy and chemical industries. Investments in these industries were encouraged by tax and financial incentives. In the 1980s, due to the second oil crisis and unstable political environment, South Korea experienced a decline in its gross domestic product (GDP). The government decided to stabilize the economy, open up investment, and deregulate the relevant policies. In the 1990s, South Korea suffered from sluggish exports and the problem of poor managerial and workplace efficiency and high costs (i.e. high wages, high land prices, and high interest rates). Due to the Asian financial crisis that erupted in 1997, the government stabilized its macroeconomic targets and restructured the finance sector, the labor market, and trade policies (The Bank of Korea 2016). Between 2003 and 2005, South Korea's economic growth stalled. A downturn in consumer spending was offset by the rapid growth in exports, primarily to China. In 2005 the government proposed labor reform legislation and a corporate pension scheme to make the labor market more flexible. In 2006, South Korea's economy recovered its growth rate to 5.1%, and continued to grow steadily in 2007. Currently, the South Korean economy is characterized as experiencing moderate inflation, low unemployment, an export surplus, and relatively equal distribution of income. South Korea continues to strive to maintain its global competitiveness (South Korea Government 2012).

HRM in South Korea

South Korean HRM has experienced substantial changes during the last few decades. Prior to 1987, South Korea adopted a seniority-based HRM system including a lifetime employment, seniority-based promotion, and a compensation system (Bae et al. 2011). From 1988 to 1997, in line with the strong influence of emerging Western HRM practices that reflected a stronger belief in competition and free market economic forces, 'New HRM' (e.g. incentive systems, ability, and performance-based pay) was increasingly implemented in South Korean companies although seniority still plays an important role (Park 2004). In the aftermath of the 1997 Asian financial crisis, seniority-based HRM was criticized as being ineffective. Employment security has declined and individual performance-based incentives increased (Bae et al. 2011). Based on Yu and Rowley (2009), the characteristics of HRM practices at different transitional stages in South Korea are summarized in Table 1.1. The HRM practices in South Korea will be discussed in more detail in the following chapters.

Development of South Korean MNEs

South Korean companies started to operate overseas in the late 1950s (SERI 2008). Since then, they have grown rapidly from being domestic to competitive global players (Kim and Rhe 2009). The growth of South Korean MNEs went through several stages. The first stage was from the 1950s to 1970s, during which time South Korean companies invested mainly in Southeast Asia. For example, textile, clothing, and

Table 1.1 Transition of HRM in South Korea

Stage of HRM	*Period*	*Characteristics*
Seniority-based HRM	Before 1987	* Emphasis on 'harmony' rather than 'competition' * Promotion was based on employment duration, educational background, and age
New HRM	1988–1997	* 'New HRM' (increasingly adopted ability and performance-based payment, recruit and promote irrespective of a person's academic background)
Performance-based HRM	1998–present	* Resourcing flexibility * Performance-based rewards * Recruitment and retention of top talent

footwear companies chose Indonesia as their preferred production site. Labor-intensive products were manufactured overseas and then exported to other countries (Park et al. 2008).

The second stage was between the 1980s and the 1990s. During this period, South Korean MNEs were assembly based, subcontracting dependent, and geared for mass production in foreign markets (Kwon and Oh 2001). They continued to expand the manufacturing sector by focusing on cars, consumer electronics, and semi-conductors (Kwon and Oh 2001; Tolentino 2000). Since the 1990s, in addition to popular destinations in Southeast Asia and North America, South Korean MNEs also invested heavily in Europe. The top three invested destinations were France, the United Kingdom (UK), and Germany, and the major industries were transport equipment, electronics, and textiles (Perrin 1999). The past few decades have seen South Korea become a significant global player in outflow FDI. Its outflow FDI quadrupled from US$ 5.2 billion to more than US$ 20 billion between 2000 and 2012 (United Nations Conference on Trade and Development (UNCTAD) 2012). Table 1.2 shows South Korean outward FDI from 1980 to 2015.

By 2015, South Korean MNEs had invested in more than 100 countries with 14 South Korean MNEs listed on the Fortune 500 (Fortune 2016). Currently, South Korean MNEs mainly invest in the following industries: manufacturing; mining and quarrying; professional, scientific, and technical activities; wholesale and retail; and real estate and renting/leasing (Korea Eximbank 2016b; see Table 1.3).

Since the early 1990s, China has become the most important outward FDI destination for South Korean MNEs. The main motivators for large investment in China are the relatively low labor cost, abundant supply of labor, and large domestic market (Vance et al. 2013). Due to the improvement in the competitiveness of its manufacturing industries, China has already overtaken South Korea in the area of producing low-to-medium-priced goods. It is also much more competent in ensuring that other industries thrive in a competitive marketplace, such as information technology, automobiles, shipbuilding, and iron and steel (Choi 2003).

South Korean outward FDI in China during the last decade increased substantially. A large number of South Korean MNEs have invested in China and these investments increased rapidly once a diplomatic relationship began in 1992 (Lee 2003). Since 1998, over 4000 South Korean factories have moved their production operations from the homeland to China. In 2001, China overtook the US as South Korea's main investment

Table 1.2 South Korean outward FDI (1980–2015) (unit: 1000 US$)

Region	*1980*	*1990*	*2000*	*2008*	*2009*	*2010*	*2013*	*2015*
Asia	49,535	370,864	1,713,921	11,904,097	7,083,184	10,154,315	11,180,509	11,053,409
Middle East	22,608	40,275	34,025	264,368	376,489	342,750	374,443	1,512,995
North America	32,725	454,814	1,474,891	5,274,469	6,018,973	4,686,184	6,389,322	6,167,086
Central and South America	4,878	66,812	1,505,334	2,095,438	989,997	2,225,581	3,372,725	4,589,781
Europe	5,210	81,971	313,849	3,405,273	5,340,143	6,186,467	5,371,650	2,744,791
Africa	25,265	26,520	157,384	320,246	373,603	284,329	222,046	128,278
Oceania	4,975	32,483	90,231	776,493	548,708	778,771	3,282,044	983,770

Source: Korea Eximbank (2016a)

Table 1.3 Overseas investment of South Korean MNEs in different industries in 2015 (unit: 1000 US$)

Industry	*Amount*
Manufacturing	106,881,787
Mining and quarrying	56,474,237
Professional, scientific, and technical activities	18,116,146
Wholesale and retail activities	34,098,900
Real estate and renting/leasing	26,026,848
Financial and insurance activities	30,619,052
Electricity, gas, steam, and water supply	5,991,281
Construction	8,190,940

Source: Korea Eximbank (2016b)

destination (Hart-Landsberg 2004). The number of South Korean MNEs operating in China rose from 1791 in 2001 to 4694 in 2006. By the end of 2012, South Korean investment in China was 39% of its total global investment (Korea Eximbank 2013). South Korean MNEs invested in a wide range of industries in China, such as manufacturing, telecommunications, wholesale, retail, catering, transportation, storage, finance, insurance, real estate, and service industries (Pan and Zhang 2011). In 2007, South Korean investments reached their peak at US$ 5.44 billion. China became South Korea's number one FDI destination in 2012 (OECD 2013). The ensuing global financial crisis meant that the amount of South Korean investment in China decreased gradually from 2008. This investment in other countries also declined accordingly. China, the US, and Vietnam were the three biggest recipients of South Korean investment. As shown in Table 1.4, the investment in China fell by 14% from 2011 to 2012, but this decline was larger in the case of the US by 23% (Korea Eximbank 2016c). Therefore, China is still an ideal laboratory for studying South Korean MNEs' IHRM policies and practices. Table 1.4 summarizes the amount of MNEs' investment in China from 2001 to 2015.

HRM in China and Its Development of FDI

China has changed dramatically from the 'socialist planned economy' to a 'socialist market economy' since the foundation of the People's Republic of China in 1949. Under the planned economy (1949–1978), China adopted a centralized planning and regulatory structure based on Soviet policies. Personnel management and the movement of the

Table 1.4 South Korean direct investment in China (unit: 1000 US$)

Year	*Number of enterprises*	*Amount*
2001	1805	660,910
2002	2567	1,102,096
2003	3163	1,833,067
2004	4015	2,432,272
2005	4672	2,866,773
2006	4708	3,501,862
2007	4614	5,444,819
2008	3328	3,862,256
2009	2127	2,476,927
2010	2297	3,657,766
2011	2211	3,541,844
2012	1866	4,043,478
2013	1881	5,145,567
2014	1613	3,156,950
2015	1647	2,853,662

Source: Korea Eximbank (2016c)

workforce were strictly under the control of the State (Zhu 1997). However, in 1978 the Chinese government began to reduce its role in running business entities (Buckley et al. 2009a) and gradually open up the economy to market forces, allowing enterprises to gain some degree of control of their own HR policies and practices (Cooke 2012). Nonetheless the Chinese government still wields significant influence on the country's SOEs (Buckley et al. 2009a). Fundamental changes occurred in the Chinese HRM system in the 1980s. Enterprise managers were given more autonomy and responsibility in handling HR issues. In 1992, the 'Three Systems Reforms' were implemented involving labor contracts, performance-based compensation systems, and contributory social insurance. More details about HRM practices in China will be discussed in the following chapters. Based on Warner (2010), Table 1.5 summarizes the main stages of HRM in China.

Since the 'Open Door Policy' that emerged in the late 1970s, China has been successful in attracting a substantial amount of global FDI (UNCTAD 2013). Indeed, in 2003, China overtook the US and became the largest recipient of FDI (UNCTAD 2005). This growth in inward FDI is widely believed to be a key factor of China's economic miracle (Buckley et al. 2009c). Based on Buckley et al. (2009b), Fig. 1.1 summarizes the different stages of Chinese inward FDI from 1979 to 1999.

Table 1.5 Evolution of HRM in China

Nascent (1980s)	Labor contracts	Low flexbility of HR
Interim (1990s)	Personnel and labor law	Medium flexbility of HR
Mature (2000s)	Labor contract law	High flextibility of HR

The most recent comprehensive trade and foreign policy—'One-belt, one-road' (OBOR), which was implemented by China's current leader, Xi Jinping—links China to other Asian countries, Europe, and Africa through both land and maritime routes. The new initiative aims to build a close cooperation and mutual trust between Europe, the Middle East, Africa, and the rest of Asia (Thakur 2015). Statistics show that China's outward direct investment jumped from US$ 68.8 billion in 2010 to more than US$ 100 billion in 2014. About 38% of that was invested in OBOR-covered regions (Cheng 2015). It confirms that China is now ready to use its power to create a favorable environment for its own economic and strategic national interests (Thakur 2015).

Methodology

We employed both qualitative and quantitative methodology by conducting in-depth interviews and large-scale surveys to collect the data for the research. The data were collected from ten South Korean MNEs in Beijing, Tianjin, and Yantai. The case companies are of varied sizes and ages, and operate in a wide range of industries, including electronics, telecommunications (mobile phones), online services, automobiles, advertising, and IT. The business structure is consistent with the industry and ownership patterns of South Korean MNEs in China (Korea Eximbank 2016b). Two MNEs, Telecom C and Auto A, are joint ventures (JVs) and others are South Korean-owned enterprises. Hence, the case companies are broadly representative of South Korean MNEs in China. The company profile will be shown in detail in the next chapter.

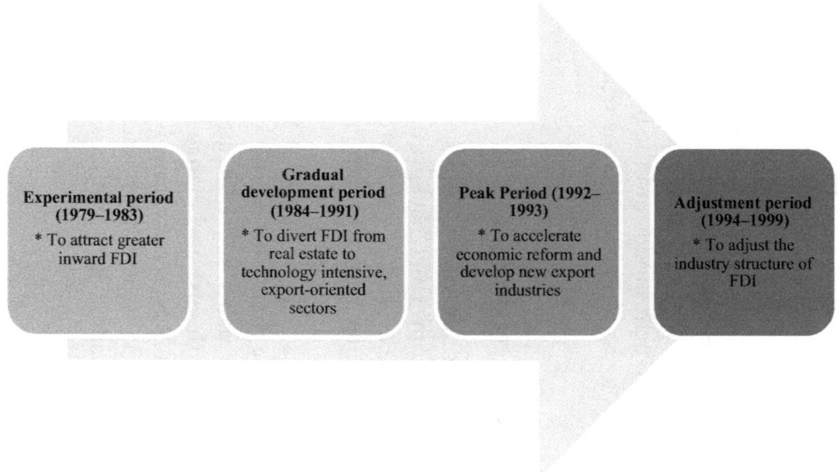

Fig. 1.1 Stages of Chinese inward FDI (1979–1999)

The interviews were conducted in two stages. The first-stage interviews aimed to investigate IHRM policies and practices (i.e. recruitment and selection, training and development, performance appraisal, and reward and compensation) of South Korean MNEs. Twenty semi-structured interviews were conducted with ten HCN and ten expatriate managers during September–October 2011. The second-stage interviews aimed to explore the use and management of non-traditional expatriates working for South Korean MNEs in China. Twenty interviews were conducted between December 2013 and May 2014. A survey was administered involving 485 employees during August–October 2011. Content analysis was performed to examine the qualitative data. Structural equation modeling (SEM) was used to analyze the survey data. The SEM procedure involves testing the measurement model and the hypotheses. More details regarding the methodology used in this analysis will be discussed in the following chapter.

Structure of the Book

This first chapter has introduced the topic and reviewed the existing IHRM literature and contextual background of South Korea and China. The next chapter (i.e. Chap. 2) will provide more detail about the research design, data collection, and data analysis. The subsequent chapters (Chaps. 3, 4, 5, and 6) constitute the core of the book and focus on the IHRM policies and practices of South Korean MNEs in China, with an analysis of the themes of recruitment and selection, training and development, performance appraisal, and reward and compensation. Chapter 7 investigates the use and management of non-traditional expatriates in South Korean MNEs operating in China. In Chap. 8, we examine the impact of IHRM policies and practices on HCNs' willingness to help expatriates. Finally, Chap. 9 discusses the research findings and draws conclusions.

Bibliography

Atkinson, C., & Hall, L. (2011). Flexible working and happiness in the NHS. *Employee Relations, 33*(2), 88–105.

Bae, J. S., Chen, S. J., & Rowley, C. (2011). From a paternalistic model towards what? HRM trends in Korea and Taiwan. *Personnel Review, 40*(6), 700–722.

Basu, K., & Palazzo, G. (2008). Corporate social responsibility: A process model of sense making. *The Academy of Management Review Archive, 33*(1), 122–136.

Black, J. S., & Gregersen, H. B. (1999). The right way to manage expats. *Harvard Business Review, 77*(2), 52–63.

Black, J. S., Gregersen, H. B., & Mendenhall, M. E. (1992). Toward a theoretical framework of repatriation adjustment. *Journal of International Business Studies, 23*, 737–760.

Black, J. S., Morrison, A., & Gregersen, H. B. (2000). *Global explorers: The next generation of leaders*. London: Routledge.

Bloom, M., Milkovich, G. T., & Mitra, A. (2003). International compensation: Learning from how managers respond to variations in local host contexts. *International Journal of Human Resource Management, 14*(8), 1350–1367.

Brammer, S., Millington, A., & Rayton, B. (2007). The contribution of corporate social responsibility to organizational commitment. *The International Journal of Human Resource Management, 18*(10), 1701–1719.

Buckley, J. P., Clegg, J., & Tan, H. (2009a). Cultural awareness in knowledge transfer to China—The role of guanxi and mianzi. In J. P. Buckley (Ed.), *Foreign direct investment, China and the world economy* (pp. 165–191). Basingstoke: Palgrave Macmillan.

Buckley, J. P., Clegg, J., Cross, A., & Tan, H. (2009b). China's inward foreign direct investment success: Southeast Asia in the shadow of the dragon. In J. P. Buckley (Ed.), *Foreign direct investment, China and the world economy* (pp. 239–269). Basingstoke: Palgrave Macmillan.

Buckley, J. P., Wang, C. Q., & Clegg, J. (2009c). The impact of foreign ownership, local ownership and industry characteristics on spillover benefits from foreign direct investment in China. In J. P. Buckley (Ed.), *Foreign direct investment, China and the world economy* (pp. 305–326). Basingstoke: Palgrave Macmillan.

Budhwar, P. (2012). Management of human resources in foreign firms operating in India: The role of HR in country-specific headquarters. *The International Journal of Human Resource Management, 23*(12), 2514–2531.

Caligiuri, P. M., & Stroh, L. K. (1995). Multinational corporation management strategies and international human resources practices: Bringing IHRM to the bottom line. *The International Journal of Human Resource Management, 6*(3), 494–507.

Cheng, M. J. (2015). *One belt, one road, one capital market*. Retrieved April 3, 2016, from http://www.financeasia.com/News/402733,one-belt-one-road-one-capital-market.aspx#reg-popup

Chiang, H. H., Han, T. S., & Chuang, J. S. (2011). The relationship between high-commitment HRM and knowledge-sharing behavior and its mediators. *International Journal of Manpower, 32*(5/6), 604–622.

Choi, C. H. (2003). *The China strategies of Korea's winning companies* (Nomura Research Institute, No. 67, pp. 1–8). Tokyo: Nomura Research Institute.

Cooke, F. L. (2012). *Human resource management in China: New trends and practices*. New York: Routledge.

De Cieri, H., & Dowling, P. J. (2012). Strategic human resource management in multinational enterprises: Developments and directions. In G. Stahl, I. Björkman, & S. Morris (Eds.), *Handbook of international HRM research*. Cheltenham: Edward Elgar.

Demirbag, M., Tatoglu, E., & Glaister, K. W. (2009). Equity-based entry modes of emerging country multinationals: Lessons from Turkey. *Journal of World Business, 44*(4), 445–462.

Dowling, P. J., & Welch, D. E. (1988). International human resource management: An Australian perspective. *Asia Pacific Journal of Management, 6*(1), 39–65.

Dowling, P. J., Festing, M., & Engle, A. D. (2013). *International human resource management*. London: Cengage Learning.

Evans, P., & Lorange, P. (1989). The two logics behind human resource management. In P. Evans, Y. Doz, & A. Laurent (Eds.), *Human resource management in international firms: Change, globalization and innovation* (pp. 144–161). London: Macmillan.

Ferner, A. (1997). Country of origin effects and HRM in multinational companies. *Human Resource Management Journal, 7*(1), 19–37.

Fortune. (2016). *Global 500*. Retrieved March 27, 2016, from http://fortune.com/global500/

Hart-Landsberg, M. (2004). The South Korean economy and US policy. *Asian Perspective, 28*, 89–117.

Hartmann, E., Feisel, E., & Schober, H. (2010). Talent management of western MNCs in China: Balancing global integration and local responsiveness. *Journal of World Business, 45*, 169–178.

Harzing, A. W. (1999). *Managing the multinationals: An international study of control mechanisms*. Cheltenham: Edward Elgar.

Horwich, G. (1993). The role of the for-profit private sector in disaster mitigation and response. *International Journal of Mass Emergences and Disasters, 11*(2), 189–205.

Janssens, M. (2002). Developing a culturally synergistic approach to international human resource management. *Journal of World Business, 36*(4), 429–450.

Jenkins, R. (2005). Globalization, corporate social responsibility and poverty. *International Affairs, 81*(3), 525–540.

Kang, H. Y., & Shen, J. (2013). International recruitment and selection practices of South Korean multinationals in China. *The International Journal of Human Resource Management, 24*(17), 3325–3342.

Kim, Y., & Gray, S. J. (2005). Strategic factors influencing international human resource management practices: An empirical study of Australian multinational corporations. *The International Journal of Human Resource Management, 16*(5), 809–830.

Kim, J. M., & Rhe, D. K. (2009). Trends and determinants of South Korean outward foreign direct investment. *The Copenhagen Journal of Asian Studies, 27*(1), 126–154.

Kobrin, S. J. (1988). Expatriate reduction and strategic control in American multinational corporations. *Human Resource Management, 27*(1), 63–75.

Kopp, R. (1994). International human resource policies and practices in Japanese, European, and United States multinationals. *Human Resource Management, 33*(4), 581–599.

Korea Eximbank. (2013). *Investment statistics by country.* Retrieved April 10, 2013, from http://211.171.208.92/odisas_eng.html

Korea Eximbank. (2016a). *By region.* Retrived March 15, 2016a, from http://211.171.208.92/odisas_eng.html?type=03

Korea Eximbank. (2016b). *By industry.* Retrieved March 15, 2016b, from http://211.171.208.92/odisas_eng.html?type=03

Korea Eximbank. (2016c). *Investment statistics by country.* Retrieved April 10, 2016c, from http://211.171.208.92/odisas_eng.html

Kwon, O. Y., & Oh, I. (2001). *Korean direct investment in Australia: Issues and prospects.* Brisbane: Griffith University: Australian Centre for Korean Studies.

Lee, C. W. (2003). Changing labor relations and human resources management of Korean Businesses in China and future challenges. *e-Labor News*, 21. Retrieved August 21, 2013, from http://unpan1.un.org/intradoc/groups/public/documents/APCITY/UNPAN020894.pdf

Lee, C. H., & Bruvold, N. T. (2003). Creating value for employees: Investment in employee development. *The International Journal of Human Resource Management, 14*(6), 981–1000.

Lertxundi, A., & Landeta, J. (2012). The dilemma facing multinational enterprises: Transfer or adaptation of their human resource management systems. *The International Journal of Human Resource Management, 23*(9), 1788–1807.

Luo, Y. D., & Tung, R. L. (2007). International expansion of emerging market enterprises: A springboard perspective. *Journal of International Business Studies, 38*(4), 481–498.

MacVaugh, J., & Evans, J. (2012). A re-examination of flexible employment practices in Japan. *The International Journal of Human Resource Management, 23*(6), 1245–1258.

Maon, F., Lindgreen, A., & Swaen, V. (2009). Designing and implementing corporate social responsibility: An integrative framework grounded in theory and practice. *Journal of Business Ethics, 87*(1), 71–89.

Mayrhofer, W., & Brewster, C. (1996). In praise of ethnocentricity: Expatriate policies in European multinationals. *The International Executive, 38*(6), 749–778.

McClean, E., & Collins, C. J. (2011). High-commitment HR practices, employee effort, and firm performance: Investigating the effects of HR practices across employee groups within professional services firms. *Human Resource Management, 50*(3), 341–363.

Meyer, K. E., Mudambi, R., & Narula, R. (2011). Multinational enterprises and local contexts: The opportunities and challenges of multiple embeddedness. *Journal of Management Studies, 48*(2), 235–252.

Morgan, G., Kelly, B., Sharpe, D., & Whitley, R. (2003). Global managers and Japanese multinationals: Internationalization and management in Japanese financial institutions. *The International Journal of Human Resource Management, 14*(3), 389–407.

Muratbekova-Touron, M. (2008). From an ethnocentric to a geocentric approach to IHRM. *Cross Cultural Management: An International Journal, 15*(4), 335–352.

Myloni, B. (2002). *The transfer of human resource management practices within multinational companies in Greece—A comparative analysis of human resource management practices in subsidiaries of European and US multinationals and Greek companies.* Unpublished doctoral dissertation, University of Bradford, Bradford.

Ngo, H. Y., Turban, D., Lau, C. M., & Lui, S. Y. (1998). Human resource practices and firm performance of multinational corporations: Influences of country origin. *International Journal of Human Resource Management, 9*(4), 632–652.

OECD. (2013). *FDI in figures.* Retrieved 21, July 2013, from www.oecd.org/investment/statistics.htm

Orlitzky, M., & Swanson, D. L. (2006). Socially responsible human resource management. In J. R. Deckop (Ed.), *Human resource management ethics* (pp. 3–25). Charlotte: Information Age Publishing.

Osland, A., & Osland, J. S. (2005). Contextualization and strategic international human resource management approaches: The case of Central America and Panama. *The International Journal of Human Resource Management, 16*(12), 2218–2236.

Paauwe, J., & Dewe, P. (1995). Human resource management in multinational corporations: Theories and models'. In A. Harzing & J. Ruysseveldt (Eds.), *International human resource management* (pp. 75–98). London: Sage.

Pan, Q. H., & Zhang, X. F. (2011). *New changes and effects of Korean investment in China.* Retrieved March 16, 2014, from http://ieeexplore.ieee.org/stamp/stamp.jsp?arnumber=05998548

Park, W. W. (2004). *Human resource management in developing countries.* New York: Routledge.

Park, H. J., Mitsuhashi, H., Fey, C. F., & Björkman, I. (2003). The effect of human resource management practices on Japanese MNC subsidiary performance: A partial mediating model. *The International Journal of Human Resource Management, 14*(8), 1391–1406.

Park, B. S., Kim, J. W., Park, S. B., Kao, J. S., Liu, Y. J., Lin, H. Y., & Sun, M. T. (2008). *Study on Korean and Taiwanese investment patterns in China*. Seoul: Samsung Economic Research Institute.

Perlmutter, H. V. (1969). The tortuous evolution of the multinational corporation. *Columbia Journal of World Business, 4*(1), 9–18.

Perlmutter, H. V., & Heenan, D. A. (1974). How multinational should your top managers be? *Harvard Business Review, 52*(6), 121–132.

Perrin, S. (1999). The emergence of Korean multinational enterprises in European manufacturing. In S. G. Lee & P. B. Ruffini (Eds.), *The global integration of Europe and East Asia: Studies of international trade and investment* (pp. 187–199). Cheltenham: Edward Elgar Publishing.

Pudelko, M., & Harzing, A. (2007). Country of origin, localization, or dominance effects? An empirical investigation of HRM practices in foreign subsidiaries. *Human Resource Management, 46*(4), 535–559.

Rienda, L., Claver, E., & Quer, D. (2013). The internationalisation of Indian multinationals: Determinants of expansion through acquisitions. *Journal of the Asia Pacific Economy, 18*(1), 115–132.

Rupp, D., Ganapathi, E. J., Aguilera, R. V., & Williams, C. A. (2006). Employee reactions to corporate social responsibility: An organizational justice framework. *Journal of Organizational Behavior, 27*(4), 537–543.

Samnani, A. K., & Singh, P. (2013). Exploring the fit perspective: An ethnographic approach. *Human Resource Management, 52*(1), 123–144.

Sayim, K. Z. (2010). Pushed or pulled? Transfer of reward management policies in MNCs. *International Journal of Human Resource Management, 21*(14), 2631–2658.

Schuh, A. (2007). Regionalization in Central and Eastern Europe: Searching for regiocentric orientations in MNC strategies. *Journal of East-West Business, 13*(2–3), 143–166.

Schuler, R. S., Dowling, P. J., & De Cieri, H. (1993). An integrative framework of strategic international human resource management. *Journal of Management, 19*(2), 419–459.

Schuler, S. R., Budhwar, S. P., & Florkowski, W. G. (2002). International human resource management: Review and critique. *International Journal of Management Review, 4*(1), 41–70.

Scullion, H. (1994). Staffing policies and strategic control in British multinationals. *International Studies of Management and Organization, 3*(4), 86–104.

Scullion, H. (1995). International human resource management. In J. Storey (Ed.), *Human resource management: A critical text* (pp. 352–382). London: Routledge.

Scullion, H., & Collings, D. G. (2006). Introduction. In H. Scullion & D. G. Collings (Eds.), *Global staffing* (pp. 1–13). London: Routledge.

Scullion, H., & Lenihan, M. (2005). *International human resource management: A critical text*. Basingstoke: Palgrave.

SERI. (2008). *Study on Korean and Taiwanese investment patterns in China*. Retrieved May 5, 2010, from http://www.seriworld.org/04/wldBookV.html?mn¼E&natcd¼&mncd¼0301&key¼20080808000001&pPage¼1&listopt¼FL
Sharma, S., Sharma, J., & Devi, A. (2011). Corporate social responsibility: The key role of human resources management. *Human Resource Management: Issues, Challenges and Opportunities, 2*(1), 205–213.
Sheehan, C., Fenwick, M., & Dowling, P. J. (2010). An investigation of paradigm choice in Australian international human resource management research. *International Journal of Human Resource Management, 21*(11), 1816–1836.
Shen, J. (2005). Towards a generic IHRM model. *Journal of Organisational Transformation & Social Change, 2*(2), 83–102.
Shen, J. (2011). Developing the concept of socially responsible international human resource management. *The International Journal of Human Resource Management, 22*(6), 1351–1363.
Shen, J., & Edwards, V. (2004). Recruitment and selection in Chinese MNEs. *The International Journal of Human Resource Management, 15*(4), 814–835.
Shen, J., Edwards, V., & Lee, G. (2005). Developing an integrative international human resource model: The contribution of Chinese multinational enterprises. *Asia Pacific Business Review, 11*(3), 369–388.
Smith, C., & Meiksins, P. (1995). System, society and dominance effects in cross-national organisational analysis. *Work, Employment & Society, 9*(2), 241–267.
South Korea Government. (2012). *Economy*. Retrieved March 30, 2016, from http://www.southkoreagovernment.com/economy.htm
Stone, J. R. (2008). *Managing human resource*. Milton: Wiley.
Tarique, I., & Schuler, R. S. (2010). Global talent management: Literature review, integrative framework, and suggestions for future research. *Journal of World Business, 45*(2), 122–133.
Taylor, S., Beechler, S., & Napier, N. (1996). Toward an integrative model of strategic international human resource management. *Academy of Management Review, 21*(4), 959–985.
Thakur, R. (2015). *One belt, one road: China's new strategic and trade policy*. Retrieved March 30, 2016, from http://www.delhipolicygroup.com/publications-detail/one-belt-one-road- chinas-new-strategic-and-trade-policy.html
The Bank of Korea (2016). A Sixty-Year History. Retrieved on 4 April 2-16, from http://dl.bok.or.kr/viewer/MediaViewer.ax?cid=180415&rid=5&moi=0&infoID=67115
Tolentino, P. E. (2000). *Multinational corporations: Emergence and evolution*. London: Routledge.
Tung, R. L. (1981). Selecting and training of personnel for overseas assignments. *Colombia Journal of World Business, 16*(2), 67–78.
Tung, R. L. (1982). Selection and training procedures of US, European, and Japanese multinationals. *California Management Review, 25*, 57–71.

United Nations Conference on Trade and Development (UNCTAD). (2005). *World investment report 2005*. Geneva: United Nations.

United Nations Conference on Trade and Development (UNCTAD). (2012). *World investment report 2012: Towards a new generation of investment policies*. Retrieved June 20, 2013, from http://www.unctad-docs.org/ files/UNCTAD-WIR2012-Full-en.pdf

United Nations Conference on Trade and Development (UNCTAD). (2013). *Inward and outward foreign direct investment stock, annual, 1980–2011*. Retrieved May 1, 2013, from http://unctadstat.unctad.org/TableViewer/tableView.aspx

Van den Hove, S., Le Menestrel, M., & de Bettignies, H. C. (2002). The oil industry and climate change: Strategies and ethical dilemmas. *Climate Policy, 2*(1), 3–18.

Vance, C. M., Chow, I. H. S., Paik, Y. S., & Shin, K. U. (2013). Analysis of Korean expatriate congruence with Chinese labor perceptions on training method importance: Implications for global talent management. *The International Journal of Human Resource Management, 24*(5), 985–1005.

Vo, A., & Stanton, P. (2011). The transfer of HRM policies and practices to a transnational system: The case of performance management practices of the US and Japanese MNEs operating in Vietnam. *International Journal of Human Resource Management, 22*(17), 3513–3527.

Warner, M. (2010). In search of Confucian HRM: Theory and practice in Greater China and beyond. *The International Journal of Human Resource Management, 21*(12), 2053–2078.

Wood, S. J., & De Menezes, L. M. (2010). Family-friendly management, organizational performance and social legitimacy. *International Journal of Human Resource Management, 21*(10), 1575–1597.

Yu, G. C., & Rowley, C. (2009). The changing face of Korean human resource management. In C. Rowley & Y. S. Paik (Eds.), *The changing face of Korean management* (pp. 29–51). London: Routledge.

Zappalà, G. (2004). Corporate citizenship and human resource management: A new tool or a missed opportunity? *Asia Pacific Journal of Human Resources, 42*(2), 185–201.

Zhu, C. J. (1997). Human resource development in China during the transition to a new economic system. *Asia Pacific Journal of Human Resources, 35*, 19–44.

Zou, M., & Lansbury, R. D. (2009). Multinational corporations and employment relations in the People's Republic of China: The case of Beijing Hyundai Motor Company. *International Journal of Human Resource Management, 20*(11), 2349–2369.

CHAPTER 2

Methodology

Introduction

This chapter explains the methodology used in this research. The research design concerning the nature of the study and justification for using the methods are firstly outlined. This is followed by a discussion of ethical considerations. Subsequently, the sample and data collection procedures are addressed. Next, the data analytical strategies are described in detail. This chapter concludes with a summary of the key points in relation to the methods employed.

Research Design

Methodology refers to 'the blueprint or set of decisions and procedures that governs a study and renders it understandable to others and is subject to inquiry, critique, and replication or adaptation to other settings' (Schensul 2012, p. 70). One of the most important aspects of methodology is the research design because it provides the framework and method for solving research questions (Bryman and Cassell 2006). A research design is 'a plan for collecting and analyzing evidence that will make it possible for the investigator to answer whatever questions he or she has posed' (Ragin 1994, p. 191). A good research design will ensure the evidence is obtained through the data (De Vaus 2001), thereby making the research accurate and reliable (Yin 2011). As this study aims to explore

H. Kang, J. Shen, *International Human Resource Management in South Korean Multinational Enterprises*,
DOI 10.1007/978-981-10-3093-2_2

how South Korean MNEs manage HRM in their overseas operations as well as the relationship between IHRM practices and the willingness of HCNs to help expatriates, the study employed both qualitative and quantitative methods to achieve the dual research purposes.

Qualitative Research

When studying social and cultural phenomena, qualitative research is regarded as the best way to 'understand people's motivations, their reasons, their actions, and the context for their beliefs and actions in an in-depth way' (Myers 2009, p. 6). Qualitative research is 'an approach that enables researchers to explore in detail social and organizational characteristics and individual behaviors and their meanings' (Schensul 2012, p. 69). It can be used to investigate the meaning of people's lives, represent the perceptions of people addressing contextual environments where people live, and contribute to the existing knowledge base to explain particular human behaviors (Yin 2011). Using the interviews with middle/senior managers in the sample companies, the researchers were able to explore the IHRM policies and practices employed by South Korean MNEs and the use and management of non-traditional expatriates in their Chinese subsidiaries.

There are three approaches to conducting a qualitative research study. The first is the 'realist approach', which 'generates knowledge that captures and reflects as truthfully as possible something that is happening in the real world' (Willing 2013, p. 15). This approach could be characterized as discovery orientation because researchers are expected to detect new theories or knowledge by utilizing their existing knowledge, skills, and experiences to uncover what is going on in reality. The second is the 'phenomenological approach', which aims to produce knowledge based on participants' subjective experience. The third is the 'social constructionist approach', which is concerned with 'the social construction of knowledge itself and how people construct versions of reality through the use of language' (Willing 2013, p. 17). The phenomenological approach is relevant to this study because South Korean MNEs' IHRM policies and practices are experienced by employees and their perceptions reflect their experience.

Qualitative research methods include mainly case study, action research, and grounded theory (Yin 2011). The case study method involves 'systematically gathering enough information about a particular person, social setting, event or group to permit the researcher to effectively understand how the subject operates or functions' (Berg 2004, p. 251). There are three types of case study designs: exploratory, explanatory, and descriptive. Explanatory case studies tend to be more deductive, while exploratory and descriptive case studies are more inductive (David and Sutton 2011). Yin (2009) suggested that the exploratory case study approach should be used if the research tests a concept or theory that does not have much literature and mainly answers 'what' and 'how' questions. Explanatory case studies are used to answer how and why events occur in the real world (Yin 2011). Finally, descriptive case studies are employed to describe 'an intervention or phenomenon and the real-life context in which it occurred' (Baxter and Jack 2008, p. 548). This approach allows data to be collected from many different sources that are considered to be appropriate and provide in-depth information. However, the case study approach has been criticized: firstly, it lacks statistical reliability and validity; secondly, case studies can be only used to generate hypotheses rather than test them; and thirdly, generalization can hardly be achieved on the basis of case studies (Van Maanen 2000).

Action research focuses on real-life issues by engaging with groups of researchers and organizations, and it helps to ensure the research is relevant to practical management. However, it is difficult to conduct action research due to the problems of time limitation and high cost (Walsham 2006). Grounded theory is 'an inductive, iterative, interactive and comparative method geared toward theory construction' (Charmaz 2006, p. 41). It provides both a rigorous and a flexible guide for improving data analysis (Charmaz 2006).

Our qualitative study aims to explore IHRM policies and practices of South Korean MNEs and the use and management of non-traditional expatriates in China. Both phenomena are largely unknown due to not much research having been conducted on them (Kang and Shen 2013). According to Shen (2005), MNEs originating from, or operating in, different countries tend to adopt various IHRM practices in order to achieve the best fit. It is therefore appropriate to use the exploratory case study approach in the current research.

Quantitative Research

A quantitative research is defined as:

> One in which the investigatory primarily uses postpositive claims for developing knowledge (i.e., cause and effect thinking, reduction to specific variables and hypotheses and questions, use of measurement and observation,

> and the test of theories), employs strategies of inquiry such as experiments and surveys, and collect data on predetermined instruments that yield statistics data. (Creswell 1994, p. 21)

In quantitative research, numerical data are used to quantify or measure phenomena and generate findings (Johnson and Onwuegbuzie 2004). It tests causal relationships using a deductive procedure from the existing knowledge (Hyde 2000). There are many advantages associated with this method. For example, research findings can be generalized when the data are based on random samples of sufficient size. It also enables researchers to test and validate existing theories about how certain phenomena occur (Johnson and Onwuegbuzie 2004). A survey design provides 'a quantitative or numeric description of trends, attitudes, or opinions of population by studying a sample of that population' (Creswell 2003, p. 153). There are many advantages in conducting surveys. For example, surveys are useful for exposing the current status of a specific variable within a particular group. In addition, survey results are more accurate because the variables are represented by numbers (Murray 2003). The quantitative study is conducted to explore the effects of IHRM policies and practices on the willingness of HCNs to help expatriates. The quantitative approach is therefore appropriate for achieving this research objective. A survey involving 485 HCNs was conducted for collecting the quantitative data.

Ethical Considerations

All research which involves human beings may to some extent bring risks to participants (Marczyk et al. 2005). The researcher submitted an ethics application that was examined and approved by the University of South Australia's (UniSA) Human Research Ethics Committee before the research began. Participants were advised to contact the Human Research Ethics Committee to address any concerns they may have had. A number of documents were submitted to the Committee to obtain ethics approval. These included participant information statement, participating organizational consent forms, interview/survey questions, telephone scripts, letters seeking participants, and a safety protocol if traveling overseas to collect data.

Informed consent is important in research (Myers 2009). As such, the permissions from both managerial and non-managerial employees were obtained from all participating companies. Additionally, approval to tape-record conversations was obtained before all interviews for this study commenced. Respondents were informed that their participation was voluntary and they were free to withdraw from the research project at any stage. Disclosure of the participants' information was explained carefully in both the tape-recorded interviews and surveys. The survey was anonymous and responses to the survey were strictly confidential. The summary of findings would be provided to the participating organizations if requested.

Sample and Data Collection Procedure

Qualitative Study

Sampling considers the selection of a number of items within the specific units used in a study and this procedure is very challenging during the data collection process (Yin 2011). There are different kinds of sampling, for example, purposive sampling, convenience sampling, snowball sampling, and random sampling (Yin 2011). The convenience sampling approach was used in this research to recruit the participating firms. Chinese and South Korean networks were used to recruit South Korean MNEs operating in China to participate. The case companies are of varied sizes and ages, and operate in a wide range of industries, including electronics, telecommunications (mobile phones), online services, automobiles, advertising, and IT. The business structure is consistent with the industry and ownership patterns of South Korean MNEs in China (Export-Import Bank of Korea 2011). Two MNEs, Telecom C and Auto A, are joint ventures (JVs) and others are South Korean-owned enterprises. Hence, the case companies are broadly representative of South Korean MNEs in China. The detailed company profiles are explained in more detail below.

Telecom A

Telecom A is a South Korean owned telecommunication company that was founded in 1997 and began operating in the Chinese market in 2004. The main operations of the company include mobile/internet payment service, online game, and music publishing. The company has acquired some international experiences but it is still at an early stage of internationalization. The company started operations in Taiwan in 2004 and has run a variety of payment services in the local market. Then this company started operations in the US in 2006, where the main emphasis of its business has been on mobile payment service. Again in 2006, Telecom A expanded its operations to Indonesia with the focus there being on ringtone downloading. Currently, the company is planning to cooperate with local IT companies to provide a number of online mobile services.

Chemical A

Chemical A is a large chemical company originally founded in South Korea in 1966, and by 2010, its total assets had reached 1,998,819 million Won (i.e. Korean currency). The main business operations include specialty chemicals (e.g. electrochemicals, polyester binders) and life sciences (e.g. musculoskeletal, antibiotics). The company's sales increased by 17.5% from 2006 to 2010. In 2010, the net income reached 124,457 million Won, which was nearly 2.2 times larger than the net income in 2006. Its overseas subsidiaries are under the management of six regional centers: China, Germany, Japan, the US, Poland, and Indonesia. Chemical A entered the Chinese market in 1992 and currently has five subsidiaries operating in that country.

Telecom B

Originally founded in 1984, Telecom B is now a pioneering company in the mobile industry and is also the leading wireless communications operator serving more than 50% of the local mobile market. The company not only focuses on providing various mobile services to individual consumers but also focuses on providing mobile technologies to enhance productivity for key industry sectors. The current total asset of the company is 18,960 billion Won. The revenue has increased 10.4% from 2007 to 2010. Despite the company still being at an early stage of internationalization, it is presently expanding into global markets, for example, Vietnam, the US, and China. Business emphasis is on forging strategic alliances with other global carriers and IT businesses.

Advertising A

Advertising A is an advertising agency which was founded in South Korea in 2005. Initially, the company had 54 staff to support the main motor manufacturers' global branding strategies. By 2007 the company was employing over 300 staff, and within two years, it had become the third largest agency in South Korea. The company started operating in China in 2005 and then expanded its business to the UK, Germany, the US, and India. The company aims to start operations in more European countries (e.g. Turkey, Czech Republic, France, Russia, Spain, Italy, Austria), Latin America, and Australia in the near future. The main services provided by the company include account services (e.g. account management), marketing services (e.g. brand strategy, market analysis), creative services, and media services (e.g. sports marketing, motor show).

Telecom C

Telecom C is a joint venture company which was founded in China in 2003. The company is in the telecommunications industry and is one of the main telecom value-added service providers. Its major operations include wireless internet value-added services (e.g. information content services, location-based services, download services, and other application services).

Electronics A

Electronics A is a large-scale company which was founded in South Korea in 1958. The main business operations of the company include home entertainment (e.g. flat-panel TVs, home theater), mobile communications, home appliances, and air conditioners and energy solutions. Electronics A is a global corporation with 81 subsidiaries around the world (Europe, Russia and CIS, North America, South and Central America, Asia-Pacific, Middle East, and Africa). The company entered the Chinese market in 1993. In 2009 the company became the second-largest LCD TV provider worldwide and the third-largest supplier of mobile handsets market worldwide.

Electronics B

Electronics B is one of the biggest South Korean conglomerates operating in various industries, for example, electronics, finance, chemical, and heavy industry. Its operations began in 1938, and currently the company has subsidiaries or offices in 68 countries with 680,000 employees around the world. The company started business in China in 1992. By the end of 2009, the company's total investment in China amounted to US$ 8 billion and sales reached US$ 41.8 billion. In China, the company has established 39 operating factories, 36 marketing companies, 6 Research and Development centers, 56 agents, and technical maintenance service offices in various industries with more than 69,000 employees.

Auto A
Auto A is one of the oldest family-owned enterprises in South Korea. The company now has over 60 subsidiaries throughout the world and more than 200,000 employees. The company was established in 1946 as a small auto repair shop. The company formed a JV with a Chinese car manufacturer in 2002 and now has around 7400 employees in total. The plant had a registered capital of US$ 300 million with a contract term of 30 years.

Finance A
Finance A is a financial subsidiary of one of the biggest conglomerates. The main businesses of the company include auto financing, mortgage loans, personal loans, and provision of financial services for sole proprietors. The company leads the field in auto financing and leasing in South Korea and has over 2000 employees. The company was founded in 1993 in South Korea, and it entered the Chinese market in 2005.

Telecom D
Telecom D is a small-size IT company and its main business concerns mobile Internet service. The company has very limited international experiences, and it entered the Chinese market in 2000.

The company details are summarized in Table 2.1.

The data triangulation approach was used to collect the qualitative data because it consolidates the validity of the data (Yin 2011). The interview data were collected together with other data, for example, company documents, company annual reports, papers and brochures on HR initiatives, and website information. Some company documents, such as those regarding turnover rates of repatriates, were also sought from company headquarters in South Korea. The primary data were collected from in-depth interviews, which are considered to be the most common method of data collection in qualitative studies (David and Sutton 2011). The two major forms of interviews are structured interview and semi-structured interview. In this study, semi-structured interviews were conducted to allow flexibility in responses (Punch 2005). The secondary data of this study on South Korean MNEs were collected mainly from analyzing companies' internal documents.

The interviews were conducted with one expatriate manager and a general/HR manager in each subsidiary. Their different nationalities helped to obtain data that reflected different perspectives. Interviews were conducted in Chinese for Chinese managers and in Korean for expatriate managers.

Table 2.1 Company profile

Company	*Year of establishment in South Korea/ China*	*Industry*	*Location in China*	*No. of overseas subsidiaries/ operating countries*	*No. of employees globally/in China*	*Mode of internationalization*
Telecom A	1997/2004	Online services	Beijing	4/4	400/76	FOE
Chemical A	1966/1992	Chemical	Beijing	15/6	10,000/2000	FOE
Telecom B	1984/1987	Mobile phone	Beijing	6/3	4500/350	FOE
Advertising A	2005/2005	Advertising	Beijing	10/5	350/30	FOE
Telecom C	1984/2003	IT	Beijing	1/1	4500/58	JV
Electronics A	1958/1993	Electronics	Yantai	100/44	100,000/36,000	FOE
Electronics B	1938/1992	Electronics	Tianjin	57/65	680,000/69,000	FOE
Auto A	1967/2002	Automobile	Beijing	18/8	68,000/7400	JV
Finance A	1993/2005	Finance	Beijing	2/2	2,375/20	FOE
Telecom D	1999/2000	Mobile phone	Beijing	2/2	100/30	FOE

Note: FOE, foreign-owned enterprise; JV, joint venture

The interview questions focused on the IHRM policies and practices, with particular reference to recruitment and selection, training and development, performance appraisal, and reward and compensation. In addition, questions regarding the use and management of non-traditional expatriates were asked. The interviews which generally lasted between 1 and 1.5 hours were tape-recorded, and the interview summaries were sent back to the interviewees for verification. Follow-up calls were made when issues needed to be clarified. Prior to the interviews, demographic information about the interviewees was sought. The interviews were conducted between September and October 2011 and between December 2013 and May 2014. Tables 2.2 and 2.3 summarize the interviewees' profiles.

Quantitative Study

The quantitative data were collected through large-scale surveys. A survey has been defined as 'a way to collect data from a range of respondents by

Table 2.2 Interviewees' profiles (September–October 2011)

Company	*Position*	*Age*	*Gender*	*Years with company*	*Education*	*Nationality*
Telecom A	Operation Manager	38	M	3	Bachelor	Korean
	General Manager	46	M	5	Master	Chinese
Chemical A	Marketing Manager	41	M	3	Master	Korean
	Marketing Manager	40	M	3	Bachelor	Chinese
Telecom B	Chief Operating officer	44	M	5	Bachelor	Korean
	General Manager	48	M	4	Bachelor	Chinese
Advertising A	Marketing Manager	33	M	3	Bachelor	Korean
	HR Manager	40	F	4	Bachelor	Chinese
Telecom C	Operation Manager	41	M	3	Bachelor	Korean
	General Manager	48	M	4	Diploma	Chinese
Electronics A	Marketing Manager	43	M	3	Master	Korean
	HR Manager	45	M	4	Bachelor	Chinese
Electronics B	Finance Manager	46	M	5	Bachelor	Korean
	General Manager	41	M	4	Bachelor	Chinese
Auto A	Marketing Manager	41	M	4	Bachelor	Korean
	HR Manager	46	M	3	Bachelor	Chinese
Finance A	Finance Director	39	F	4	Bachelor	Korean
	HR Manager	45	M	3	Bachelor	Chinese
Telecom D	Operation Manager	38	M	2	Bachelor	Korean
	HR Manager	46	F	2	Bachelor	Chinese

Table 2.3 Interviewees' profiles (December 2013–May 2014)

Company	*Position*	*Age*	*Gender*	*Years with company*	*Education*	*Nationality*
Telecom A	Operation Manager	38	Male	3	Bachelor	Korean
	General Manager	46	Male	5	Master	Chinese
Chemical A	Research and Development Team Manager	37	Male	3	Bachelor	Korean
	HR Manager	40	Male	3	Bachelor	Chinese
Telecom B	Operation Team Manager	35	Male	4	Bachelor	Korean
	General Manager	48	Male	4	Bachelor	Chinese
Advertising A	Marketing Manager	33	Male	3	Bachelor	Korean
	HR Manager	40	Female	4	Bachelor	Chinese
Telecom C	Operation Manager	41	Male	3	Bachelor	Korean
	General Manager	48	Male	4	Diploma	Chinese
Electronics A	Research and Development Team Manager	35	Male	3	Master	Korean
	HR Manager	45	Male	4	Bachelor	Chinese
Electronics B	Technical Support Team Manager	37	Male	5	Master	Korean
	General Manager	41	Male	4	Bachelor	Chinese
Auto A	Operation Team Manager	40	Male	4	Master	Korean
	HR Manager	46	Male	3	Bachelor	Chinese
Finance A	Finance Director	39	Female	4	Bachelor	Korean
	HR Manager	45	Male	3	Bachelor	Chinese
Telecom D	Operation Manager	38	Male	2	Bachelor	Korean
	HR Manager	46	Female	2	Bachelor	Chinese

asking them questions' (Maylor and Blackmon 2005, p. 182). The advantages of using surveys are their accuracy, and their results are generalizable and easy to administer and manage (Marshall and Rossman 2006). The HR manager firstly identified all the employees who had work relationships with expatriates.

A pilot study refers to 'the specific pre-testing of a particular research instrument such as a questionnaire or interview schedule' (van Teijlingen and Hundley 2001, p. 1). The major benefit in conducting a pilot study is that it gives a warning in advance to researchers that the project may encounter problems due to inappropriate research methods or instruments (van Teijlingen and Hundley 2001). A pilot study involving 20 employees was conducted and the results were content analyzed. The findings of the pilot study showed that the Chinese version of the questionnaire was suitable for Chinese employees despite the need for some changes in wording. Data from this pilot study was not used in the main study. We then distributed questionnaires together with cover letters explaining the research aims, definitions of variables, data collection procedures, and confidentiality issues to these employees (excluding those who had already participated in the pilot study) via the firm's internal mail system. The researchers who are fluent in both Mandarin and Korean also visited the company during the administration of the surveys to answer any queries from participants. Research shows that seven or more response options are more reliable and valid than a five-option response (Weathington et al. 2012); hence, seven-point Likert scales, ranging from 1 = strongly agree to 7 = strongly disagree, were used for all variables.

According to Anderson and Gerbing (1984), a sample size of 150 is required in order to conduct a structural equation modeling (SEM) analysis when the model has three or more indications for each construct. A total of 870 questionnaires were distributed and 485 completed questionnaires were returned, providing a 56% response rate. A total of 475 completed questionnaires were usable. Among the respondents, 49.7% were male and the mean age was 27.6 years (SD = 4.3) (shown in Table 2.4). Most respondents (87.1%) were non-managerial employees and 88.4% of employees had worked for less than five years with the current employer.

Data Analysis

Qualitative Study

Content analysis was conducted to examine the qualitative data. Content analysis is 'a technique for gathering and analyzing the content of text' (Neuman 2003, p. 310) and is suitable for analyzing interview data (Crano and Brewer 2002). Content analysis is 'beneficial to management research in general by providing researchers with a methodology for systematic analysis of the information contained in corporate documents, thus opening a rich data source that has been often neglected' (Morris 1994, pp. 903–904). Coding is an essential approach to content analysis (Bazeley and Richards 2000). Coding is also used to reduce the size of the data and is useful to retrieve and organize data (Myers 2009). One important aspect of coding is to ensure the consistency and reliability of

Table 2.4 Means, standard deviations, reliabilities, and correlations between variables

	M	*SD*	*1*	*2*	*3*	*4*	*5*	*6*	*7*	*8*	*9*	*10*	*11*
1. Age	27.6	4.3	–										
2. Gender	1.5	.50	−.06	–									
3. Education	2.0	.85	−.48**	−.07	–								
4. Position	1.15	.42	.57***	−.09*	.43**	–							
5. Personality	3.9	.21	.02	.09	.07	.03	(.91)-						
6. Social categorization	3.4	.23	.13	.06	.17*	.04	.25*	(.84)					
7. Socially responsible HRM	4.4	1.3	.14	−.10*	−.26**	.36**	.15	.09	(.89)				
8. High-commitment HRM	4.9	1.1	.13	−.05	−.22**	.35**	.07	.04	.36**	(.88)			
9. Organizational identification	4.8	1.2	.26**	−.01	−.23**	.38**	.12	.19	.49**	.43***	(.85)		
10. Perceived organizational support	4.6	1.1	.22*	−.08	−.33**	.30**	.13	.28*	.08	.40**	.27**	(.89)	
11. Willingness to help	5.1	1.7	.21*	−.01	−.26**	.33**	.23*	−.31*	.44**	.36**	.38**	.39**	(.90)

Note: $N = 475$; $*p < .05$. $**p < .01$. Two tailed: gender was dummy coded: female = 1, male = 2. Age was measured by years. Education was coded: 1 = primary school, 2 = high school, 3 = diploma, 4 = bachelor, 5 = graduate. Tenure was measured by working years. Employee position was dummy coded: 1 = non-managerial, 2 = managerial. Cronbach's alphas are reported in the parentheses on the diagonal the contents. In content analysis, many factors will cause reliability problems, such as ambiguity of word meanings or category definitions (Weber 1990). One way to address these problems is to classify contents into categories (Crano and Brewer 2002). Categorizing refers to 'the summary of such concepts into generic concepts and to the elaboration of the relations between concepts and generic concepts or categories and superior concepts' (Flick 2006, p. 125). Interview questions were developed based on the IHRM literature.

Coding Procedure

Tables were drawn in a codebook to conduct the content analysis. In each table, codes, categories, codings, and statements originating from the interview results were listed. Then, interview contents were sorted and put into the tables. The four domains of the IHRM practices, specifically international recruitment and selection, international training and development, international performance appraisal, and international reward and compensation, were treated as the four codes (Dowling et al. 2013; Fisher 1989; Schuler et al. 1993). In addition, the use and management of non-traditional expatriates is another code. Under each code, there are several categories. For example, under the code 'international recruitment and selection', there are five categories: staffing approach, reason to use expatriates, recruitment procedure, recruitment criteria, and repatriation. Under the code of the use and management of non-traditional expatriates, there are six categories: reasons and purposes of using non-traditional expatriates, staffing, training, performance appraisals, and compensation of non-traditional expatriates.

Under each category, there are corresponding codings. For example, under the 'selection criteria' category, the coding is 'expatriate selection'. Under the code 'international training and development', there are four categories: expatriate pre-departure training, expatriate post-arrival training, HCN training, and expatriate/HCN career development. Under the category 'expatriate pre-departure training', there are two codings: training program and training method. Under the code 'international performance appraisal', there are four categories: performance appraisal purpose, performance appraisal method, performance criteria, and performance feedback. Under the category 'performance appraisal method', there are two codings: rater and frequency. Under the code 'international reward and compensation', there are two sub-categories: expatriates' compensation and HCNs' compensation. For the 'expatriates' compensation', there are two codings: expatriates' salary standards and structures and PRP for expatriates. The coding examples are shown in Table 2.5.

Table 2.5 Coding examples

Code	*Category*	*Coding*	*Statement*
International recruitment and selection	Approach	PT (polycentric tendency)	'Three expatriates will go back to Korea because Chinese employees have mastered the technology' (General Manager, Electronics B)
	Reason	Control	'We need someone from headquarters to ensure everything is aligned with headquarters' direction' (HR Manager, Chemical A)
	Recruitment	Procedure	'We attend university job fairs' (HR Manager, Electronics A)
	Criteria	Expatriate selection	'The first criterion for selecting an expatriate is his expertise' (Chief Operating Officer, Telecom B)
	Repatriation	Support	'We normally consider expatriates' spouse careers and children's education as a personal responsibility' (Finance Director, Finance A)
International training and development	Expatriate pre-departure training	Program	'The Headquarters focus heavily on the Chinese culture in expatriate pre-departure training' (HR Manager, Chemical A)
		Method	'Seminars were conducted to discuss cultural differences' (HR Manager, Chemical A)
	Expatriate post-arrival training	Program	'We run workshops to discuss the difficulties expatriates experience in dealing with Chinese colleagues' (General Manager, Telecom A)
		Duration	'We offer three hours of Chinese language lessons to expatriates and their spouses per week' (HR Manager, Electronics A)
	HCN training	Program	'We run English workshops for Chinese managers to improve their communication skills' (General Manager, Electronics B)
	HCN/expatriate management development	Career planning	'There is no career planning for me. My company did not make any promises about what position I will get once I have finished the Chinese assignment' (Operating Manager, Telecom C)
International performance appraisal	Purpose	Compensation	'We rely on performance appraisal results to determine employee promotion opportunities and their compensation' (General Manager, Electronics B)

(*continued*)

Table 2.5 (continued)

	Method	Rater	'Direct supervisors in the subsidiary are supposed to monitor expatriates' performance and comment on expatriates' self-evaluations' (HR Manager, Advertising A)
		Frequency	'We conduct appraisal annually. Normally, self-appraisals take place in mid-December. Interviews with supervisors are conducted in mid-January. Appraisal results are finalized before the Chinese New Year' (HR Manager, Auto A)
	Criteria	Work performance	'We put 50% weight on task completion' (HR Manager, Telecom A)
	Feedback	Feedback form	'My superior is reluctant to provide me written feedback. However, he gives me advice on how to improve my performance' (Marketing Manager, Advertising A)
International reward and compensation	Expatriates' compensation	Expatriates' salary standards and structures	'Expatriates have the same salaries as they had in Korea, plus additional allowance and benefits' (Operation Manager, Telecom C) 'Expatriates' compensation includes base pay, allowances, benefits, and performance-based bonus. The base pay normally constitutes 65% of total compensation' (Finance Manager, Electronics B)
		PRP for expatriates	'The performance pay rate is 8% of base pay for those who achieve the "excellent" level (highest) of performance, 5% for "outstanding", 3% for "normal", and 0% for "unaccepted"' (Marketing Manager, Chemical A)
	HCNs' compensation	HCNs' salaries standards and structures	'All HCNs' compensation is comprised of base salary, allowances, and benefits. Normally, a beginner at the shop-floor level receives RMB 2800–3500 total salary' (HR Manager, Electronics A)
		PRP for HCNs	'The amount of bonus depends on company's profit over the year. Last year, executive level received six months' base salary, middle managers received two months' base salary, and one-month base salary for non-managerial employees' (General Manager, Telecom A) 'The production workers receive bonuses based on the quantity and quality of products. Normally, bonuses are paid biannually with the amount of one-month salary' (HR Manager, Auto A)

The use and management of non-traditional expatriates	Reason of using non-traditional expatriates	Cost reduction	'The use of short-term assignees can save costs on family relocation and accommodation and children education' (HR Manager, Chemical A)
		IT development	'Headquarters can monitor and control subsidiaries' operations remotely. I have to give briefings to my direct supervisor in headquarters on a weekly basis by using teleconferences. Important documentations are also sent through emails to make sure work is done efficiently' (Finance Director, Finance A)
		Career development problems	'Given that most Korean companies do not guarantee a promotion after the assignments and also there is a lack of expatriates' future career planning. It will be a great loss for companies if expatriates start leaving, while using short-term expatriates can avoid this problem' (Research and Development Team Manager in Chemical A)
	Purpose	Problem-solving	'Short-term expatriates are frequently employed for solving problems and transferring knowledge' (General Manager, Telecom C)
		Knowledge transfer	

Quantitative Study

The questionnaire was developed in English, translated into Chinese and back-translated by two bilingual researchers. We used seven-point Likert scales for all study variables, ranging from 1 = strongly disagree to 7 = strongly agree.

Measures

The Willingness of HCNs to Help Expatriates

Help in the workplace was measured through HCNs' reported provision of the five types of 'role information' identified by Morrison (1993). This measure has been used by Varma et al. (2011). Sample items include 'I am willing to provide Korean expatriates with information on what is expected in their jobs' and 'I am willing to provide Korean expatriates with information on the behaviors and attitudes that the organization values and expects'. Help outside the workplace was measured using a four-item scale for 'social support' developed by Caplan et al. (1980). Sample items are 'I am willing to make work life easier for expatriates' and 'I am willing to give Korean expatriates information about local customs'. Help within the workplace was highly correlated to help outside of the workplace ($r = .82$, $p < .001$).

We conducted factor analyses to examine whether the two dimensions of help were distinctive constructs. The exploratory factor analysis using principal axis factoring extracted one factor with an eigenvalue exceeding 1 (4.87) explaining 60.9% of variance. Standardized factor loadings were significant at $p < .001$, ranging from .73 to .88. In support of the result derived from the exploratory factor analysis, the confirmatory factor analyses (CFAs) revealed that the single-factor model was a good fit [$\chi2(27) = 34.2$, $p < .001$, confirmatory fit index (CFI) = .99, Tucker–Lewis index (TLI) = .99, and the root mean square error of approximation (RMSEA) = .011] and fitted better than the two-factor model [$\chi2(26) = 56.7$, $p < .001$, CFI = .94, TLI = .92, RMSEA = .11, $\Delta\chi1 = 22.5$, $p < .001$). As shown in our later analyses, the proposed measurement model with a single-factor dependent variable had the best fit with the data and the hypothesized relationships were significant and in the expected directions. These results provide evidence for convergent and discriminant validity. Hence, it was appropriate to treat HCNs' willingness to help expatriates in and outside of the workplace as a single-dimension construct. Cronbach's alpha for this scale was .90.

High-Commitment HRM

High-commitment HRM was measured using eight items from Collins and Smith (2006). Sample items include 'My company has done whatever it can to keep people employed' and 'Rewards in my company are performance-based and competitive in the industry.' Cronbach's alpha for this scale was .88.

Socially Responsible HRM

Socially responsible HRM was measured using six items developed by Shen and Benson (2014). Sample items are 'My company considers personal CSR values in recruitment and selection' and 'My company provides adequate CSR training to promote CSR as a core organizational value'. Cronbach's alpha for this scale was .89.

Organizational Identification

Organizational identification was measured using three items developed by Kim et al. (2010). The three statements are 'I feel strong ties with my company', 'I experience a strong sense of belongingness to my company', and 'I am part of my company'. Cronbach's alpha for this scale was .85.

Perceived Organizational Support

POS was measured using eight items adapted from Eisenberger et al. (1986). Sample items are 'My company really cares about my well-being' and 'My company strongly considers my goals and values'. Cronbach reliability of this scale was .89.

Control Variables

It is argued that the personalities of HCNs (Caligiuri 2000; Johnson et al. 2003) and social categorization (Toh and DeNisi 2007) influence their attitudes and behaviors toward expatriates. For this reason, we controlled for personality and social categorization. Social categorization was measured using four items adapted from Varma et al. (2011). A sample item is 'I consider Korean expatriates as "them" and other locals in the organization "us"'. Cronbach reliability of this scale was .84. HCN personality was measured using ten items developed by Gosling et al. (2003). A sample item is 'I am extraverted and enthusiastic'. Cronbach reliability of this scale was .91. Previous studies, for example, Schroeder and Graziano (2015), found demographic variables were related to employee helping behavior. Hence, we controlled for gender, age, education, and position in hypothesis testing.

Data Analytical Strategy

The validity and reliability of the data was assessed using Statistical Product and Service Solutions (SPSS) 20. Missing data were replaced by the mean scores and outliers were removed. SEM was utilized to test all hypotheses with the software MPlus 7.2. SEM is 'a statistical methodology that takes a confirmatory approach to the analysis of a structural theory bearing on some phenomenon' (Byrne 2012, p. 3). The advantage in conducting SEM is that it provides the opportunity to estimate the extent of errors in the model, and it tests the structural relationships between variables (William 2006). SEM also makes it possible to identify error variance in the statistical analysis. Moreover, it provides a number of fit indices that assess the overall fit of the complete structural model (Smith and Langfield-Smith 2004).

We used SEM to fit models with maximum likelihood as the procedure. Due to the single-sourced data, we first tested for common method variance (CMV) (Podsakoff et al. 2003), which would be indicated if the fit of the model comprising all latent variables was improved by adding an uncorrelated latent method factor on which all items loaded. Summing the squared loadings, we assessed the variance explained by the common method factor to gauge its influence. Next, we assessed the discriminant validity of the measurement model by comparing the proposed model against other nested models including, the four-factor model combining socially responsible HRM and high-commitment HRM and the one-factor model collapsing all variables. Subsequently, we compared the goodness of fit of the base model with those of the nested alternative models using chi-square differences to test hypotheses. The selection of rival models was based on the literature (Browne and Cudeck 1989; MacCallum 1986). Values of CFI and TLI higher than .90 and values of the RMSEA lower than .80 are regarded as indicating acceptable fit (Browne and Cudeck 1989).

Conclusion

This study has implemented a mixed research methodology. Specifically, the qualitative study investigated the IHRM policies and practices and the use and management of non-traditional expatriates of South Korean MNEs in China. Ten South Korean MNEs with varied company sizes and industries were recruited to participate as case studies. Content analysis was used to analyze the interview contents. The data for the quantitative study were collected through surveys involving 485 HCNs. SEM was employed to test the hypothesized relationships. The next chapter will turn to the international recruitment and selection policies and practices of South Korean MNEs in China.

Bibliography

Anderson, J. C., & Gerbing, D. W. (1984). The effect of sampling error on convergence, improper solutions, and goodness-of-fit indices for maximum likelihood confirmatory factor analysis. *Psychometrika, 49*(2), 155–173.

Baxter, P., & Jack, S. (2008). Qualitative case study methodology: Study design and implementation for novice researchers. *The Qualitative Report, 13*(4), 544–559.

Bazeley, P., & Richards, L. (2000). *The NVIVO qualitative project book.* London: Sage.

Berg, B. L. (2004). *Qualitative research methods.* Boston: Pearson Education..

Browne, M. W., & Cudeck, R. (1989). Single sample cross validation indices for covariance Structures. *Multivariate Behavioral Research, 24*, 445–455.

Bryman, A., & Cassell, C. (2006). The researcher interview: A reflexive perspective. *Qualitative Research in Organizations and Management: An International Journal, 1*(1), 41–55.

Byrne, B. M. (2012). *Structural equation modeling with Mplus: Basic concepts, applications, and programming.* New York: Routledge.

Caligiuri, P. M. (2000). Selecting expatriates for personality characteristics: A moderating effect of personality on the relationship between host national contact and cross-cultural adjustment. *Management International Review, 40*(1), 61–80.

Caplan, R. D., Cobb, S., French, J. R. P., Van Harrison, R., & Pinneau, S. R. (1980). *Job demands and worker health: Main effects and occupational differences.* Ann Arbor: University of Michigan Institute for Social Research.

Charmaz, K. (2006). *Constructing grounded theory: A practical guide through qualitative analysis.* London: Sage.

Collins, C. J., & Smith, K. G. (2006). Knowledge exchange and combination: The role of human resource management practices in the performance of high technology firms. *Academy of Management Journal, 40*(3), 544–560.

Crano, W. D., & Brewer, M. B. (2002). Content analysis. In N. J. Mahwah (Ed.), *Principles and methods of social research* (pp. 245–263). Mahwah: Lawrence Erlbaum Associates.

Creswell, J. W. (1994). *Research design: Qualitative, quantitative and mixed methods approach*. London: Sage.

Creswell, J. W. (2003). *Research design: Qualitative, quantitative and mixed methods approaches*. Thousand Oaks: Sage.

David, M., & Sutton, C. (2011). *Social research: An introduction*. London: Sage.

De Vaus, D. A. (2001). *Research design in social research*. Thousand Oaks: Sage.

Dowling, P. J., Festing, M., & Engle, A. D. (2013). *International human resource management*. London: Cengage Learning.

Eisenberger, R., Huntington, R., Hutchison, S., & Sowa, D. (1986). Perceived organizational support. *Journal of Applied Psychology, 71*(3), 500–507.

Export-Import Bank of Korea. (2011). *Foreign investment statistics by country*. Retrieved May 6, 2011, from http://www.kexim.co.kr/en2/05_fdi/02_statistic/04.jsp

Fisher, C. D. (1989). Current and recurrent challenges in HRM. *Journal of Management, 15*(2), 157–180.

Flick, U. W. E. (2006). *An introduction to qualitative research*. London: Sage.

Gosling, S. D., Rentfrow, P. J., & Swann Jr., W. B. (2003). A very brief measure of the Big-Five personality domains. *Journal of Research in Personality, 37*(6), 504–528.

Hyde, K. F. (2000). Recognising deductive processes in qualitative research. *Qualitative market research: An International Journal, 3*(2), 82–90.

Johnson, R. B., & Onwuegbuzie, A. J. (2004). Mixed methods research: A research paradigm whose time has come. *Educational Researcher, 33*(7), 14–26.

Johnson, E. C., Kristof-brown, A. L., Van Vianen, A. E. M., De Pater, I. E., & Klein, M. R. (2003). Expatriate social ties: Personality antecedents and consequences for adjustment. *International Journal of Selection and Assessment, 11*(4), 277–288.

Kang, H. Y., & Shen, J. (2013). International recruitment and selection practices of South Korean multinationals in China. *The International Journal of Human Resource Management, 24*(17), 3325–3342.

Kim, H. R., Lee, M., Lee, H. T., & Kim, N. M. (2010). Corporate social responsibility and employee–company identification. *Journal of Business Ethics, 95*(4), 557–569.

MacCallum, R. (1986). Specification searches in covariance structure modeling. *Psychological Bulletin, 100*(1), 107–120.

Marczyk, G., DeMatteo, D., & Festinger, D. (2005). *Essentials of research design and methodology*. Hoboken: Wiley.

Marshall, C., & Rossman, G. B. (2006). *Designing qualitative research* (4th ed.). London: Sage.

Maylor, H., & Blackmon, K. (2005). *Researching business and management: A roadmap for success.* Basingstoke: Palgrave Macmillan.

Morris, R. (1994). Computerized content analysis in management research: A demonstration of advantages & limitations. *Journal of Management, 20*(4), 903–931.

Morrison, E. W. (1993). A longitudinal study of the effects of information seeking on newcomer socialization. *Journal of Applied Psychology, 78*(2), 173–183.

Murray, T. R. (2003). *Blending qualitative and quantitative research methods in theses and dissertations.* Thousand Oaks: Corwin Press.

Myers, M. D. (2009). *Qualitative research in business & management.* London: Sage.

Neuman, W. L. (2003). *Social research method: Qualitative and quantitative methods.* Boston: Allyn and Bacon.

Podsakoff, P. M., MacKenzie, S. B., Lee, J. Y., & Podsakoff, N. P. (2003). Common method biases in behavioral research: A critical review of the literature and recommended remedies. *Journal of Applied Psychology, 88*(5), 879–903.

Punch, K. F. (2005). *Introduction to social research: Quantitative and qualitative approaches.* New Delhi: Sage.

Ragin, C. C. (1994). *Constructing social research.* Thousand Oaks: Pine Forge Press.

Schensul, J. J. (2012). Methodology, methods and tools in qualitative research. In S. D. Lapan, M. Y. Quartaroli, & F. J. Reimer (Eds.), *Qualitative research an introduction to methods and designs* (p. 70). San Francisco: Jossey-Bass.

Schroeder, D. A., & Graziano, W. G. (2015). *The Oxford handbook of prosocial behaviors.* Oxford: Oxford University Press.

Schuler, R. S., Dowling, P. J., & De Cieri, H. (1993). An integrative framework of strategic international human resource management. *Journal of Management, 19*(2), 419–459.

Shen, J. (2005). Towards a generic IHRM model. *Journal of Organisational Transformation & Social Change, 2*(2), 83–102.

Shen, J., & Benson, J. (2014). When CSR is a social norm: How socially responsible human resource management affects employee work behavior. *Journal of Management.* p.0149206314522300.

Smith, D., & Langfield-Smith, K. (2004). Structural equation modeling in management accounting research: Critical analysis and opportunities. *Journal of Accounting Literature, 23*(1), 49–86.

Toh, S. M., & DeNisi, A. S. (2007). Host country nationals as socializing agents: A social identity approach. *Journal of Organizational Behavior, 28*(3), 281–301.

Van Maanen, J. (2000). *Qualitative methods in management research.* Thousand Oaks: Sage.

van Teijlingen, E., & Hundley, V. (2001). The importance of pilot studies. *Social Research Update, 35*, 1–4.

Varma, A., Budhwar, P., & Pichler, S. (2011). Chinese host country nationals' willingness to help expatriates: The role of social categorization. *Thunderbird International Business Review, 53*(3), 353–364.

Walsham, G. (2006). Doing interpretive research. *European Journal of Information Systems, 15*(3), 320–330.

Weathington, B. L., Cunningham, C. J. L., & Pittenger, D. J. (2012). *Understanding business research.* Hoboken: Wiley.

Weber, R. P. (1990). *Basic content analysis.* Newbury Park: Sage.

William, N. (2006). *Social research methods.* London/Thousand Oaks: Sage.

Willing, C. (2013). *Introducing qualitative research in psychology.* Maidenhead: Open University Press.

Yin, R. K. (2009). *Case study research: Design and methods.* Thousand Oaks: Sage.

Yin, R. K. (2011). *Qualitative research from start to finish.* New York: Guilford Press.

CHAPTER 3

International Recruitment and Selection Policies and Practices

Introduction

International staffing, one of the key initiatives and responsibilities of global talent management, comprises recruitment and selection, and deals with 'critical issues faced by multinational corporations with regard to the employment of home, host, and third country nationals to fill key positions in their headquarters and subsidiary operations' (Scullion and Collings 2006, p. 3). Through international staffing, MNEs coordinate and control their global operations (Stroh and Caligiuri 1998). Furthermore, international staffing plays a key role in innovation, organizational learning, corporate integration, and staff's retention in MNEs (Collings et al. 2009; Reiche 2007). Consequently, international staffing may influence the performance of subsidiaries as well as the MNE as a whole (Colakoglu and Caligiuri 2008; Colakoglu et al. 2009). This chapter is structured as follows: firstly, we review the literature on the recruitment and selection practices in South Korea, followed by a discussion of the recruitment and selection practices in China. Subsequently, we report our empirical findings on international staffing policies and practices of South Korean MNEs operating in China. The major international staffing issues considered in this chapter include international staffing approaches, reasons for these approaches, recruitment procedures, selection criteria for both expatriates and HCNs, and repatriation management.

H. Kang, J. Shen, *International Human Resource Management in South Korean Multinational Enterprises*,
DOI 10.1007/978-981-10-3093-2_3

Recruitment and Selection Policies and Practices in South Korea and China

Recruitment and Selection in South Korea

South Korean HRM has experienced substantial changes during the last few decades. Prior to 1987, South Korea adopted the seniority-based HRM system including lifetime employment, seniority-based promotion, and a compensation system (Bae et al. 2011). The major source of recruitment for conglomerates (i.e. *chaebols*) is graduates from prestigious universities (Rowley 2005). From 1988 to 1997, with the strong influence of emerging Western HRM practices, the 'New HRM' (e.g. incentive systems, ability, and performance-based pay) system was increasingly implemented in South Korean companies, although seniority still played an important role (Park 2004). However, the situation of resourcing remains unchanged (Rowley and Bae 2002). After the 1997 Asian financial crisis, seniority-based HRM was criticized for being ineffective. Large conglomerates have since then experienced significant restructuring, for example, mergers and acquisitions, and management buyouts (Rowley and Bae 2002). Both economic crisis and changing business environments encourage South Korean firms to actively pursue more flexibility in managing their workforce (Park and Yu 2000). They have already begun to utilize external labor markets as sources of recruitment, which enables them to actively recruit contingent workers. Under these changed institutional and economic circumstances, people's employment security has declined and individual performance-based incentives have been highly emphasized (Bae et al. 2011).

In South Korea, there are two types of recruitment systems: *Yon-go* (i.e. relation-based recruiting) and *Gong-chae* (i.e. open recruitment). *Yon-go* is a kind of social relationship or connection based on family ties, school ties, and birthrights (Lee 2004a). Traditionally, most South Korean firms recruit employees based on *Yon-go* relations. The primary source of recruitment normally includes school alumni and friends from the employer's birth place. In order to meet the demands of fast-growing businesses, companies formalize the employment process based on open competition, which tends to focus more on educational achievement (e.g. exam results). However, *Yon-go* relations are still very important in determining the success in gaining employment; graduates from prestigious universities or candidates from certain regions are largely preferred to others. However, due to the fierce competition that now characterizes the global economy and how business is done, many organizations have realized the importance of attracting talent, and subsequently, the nature of recruitment has changed gradually. It has been found that in South Korean enterprises, the influence of *Yon-go* has diminished when recruiting entry-level positions, while for senior positions, *Yon-go* still plays an important role (Horak 2015). *Gong-chae* incorporates contemporary recruitment and selection practices, which are similar to Western HRM practices (Lee 1998). Many companies, especially large companies, have started to adopt this system to attract talent (Chung et al. 1997). Samsung was the first company to adopt the *'Gong-chae'* system in 1957 (Lee 1998).

Generally speaking, the recruitment of university students takes place in spring and fall each year. Campus recruiting is considered one of the most common and effective recruitment activities in South Korean companies. Normally, companies or corporations send executives who have graduated from universities to recruit potential employees. Managers give briefings to students and send out company brochures to attract job seekers to join the company. Sometimes, company tours are also provided to students so that they can experience real worksites and have a better understanding of how the company works. Another important source of recruitment is recommendations from university professors. Professors are in the best position to recommend students because they know how well they actually perform and what their abilities are (Chung et al. 1997).

Some conglomerates prefer to select applicants especially those who had enjoyed the opportunity of internships in their companies. One of the benefits of the internship system is that companies can observe candidates' behaviors and abilities directly and in this way they can decide whether they have the competence and aptitude for the job (Chang and Chang 1994). TV advertisement is also an effective recruitment method. Potential employees will be easily attracted due to this medium's presentation of the company's favorable image (Chung et al. 1997). On the other hand, small- and medium-sized enterprises (SMEs) tend to rely on the informal recruitment method, such as employee referrals (Koch et al. 1995). This form of recruitment is a less formal hiring process, and is often carried out irregularly whenever companies have vacancies (Park and Yu 2000). When recruiting mid-term career professionals (i.e. 5–10 years' employment), larger firms tend to use recruitment channels like internet recruitment and external recruitment agencies. In particular, the recommendation system (either firm-internal recommendation based on *Yon-go*;

or external recommendation through agencies) is considered to be more effective when selecting the most desirable candidates (Horak 2015).

The major selection procedures in South Korean firms normally include written tests, which assess job-related skills and general knowledge (Kim 1992), and interviews (Lee 1998). During the last decade, some *chaebols* (e.g. Samsung, Hyundai) dropped knowledge tests and replaced them with aptitude tests, which is a type of psychological test including personal aptitude, personality, and personal interests (Kim and Briscoe 1997; Kim 1997; Pucik and Lim 2001). After passing the tests, applicants will be interviewed by senior managers. Many companies are now putting more emphasis on interviews in an attempt to obtain better candidates suited to the company; as a result, the interview procedures are becoming more standardized. The applicants who pass all the screening steps will be asked to take a physical examination before being hired (Lee 1998). For example, Samsung adopts the *Gong-chae* system, which includes the following selection procedures: (1) review the application form, (2) conduct written examinations (e.g. general or technical knowledge, foreign language proficiency, psychological tests), (3) conduct interviews, (4) review recommendation letters, (5) review of internship performance, and (6) conduct physical examination.

Traditionally, the selection criteria in South Korean companies emphasize certain personal characteristics, such as seniority, education, prestige of university, or sometimes personal relationships with managers (Yu and Rowley 2009). Although the *Gong-chae* system has remained stable, employees' skills and competencies have changed to adapt to transformations in economic conditions and the globalized environment. Nowadays, the major selection criteria focus more on job-related competencies, for instance, specific subject knowledge and technical qualifications. In addition, companies emphasize English competence when they are recruiting graduates. Candidates who have better oral communication skills in English are more competitive in the job market (Jang 2015). It should also be stated that education and having good moral or ethical attitudes are also considered relevant (Lee 2004a; Yu and Rowley 2009).

Some problems do exist in the South Korean recruitment and selection system. For example, attracting high-quality female employees is always challenging for South Korean companies. Although more and more females are joining the workforce, the majority of them are still low-educated who only work in sales or service industries (Jang and Merriam 2004), and they have much fewer opportunities to be promoted compared to male workers

(Kim et al. 2008). Additionally, the selection of senior positions is to some extent not open and transparent. It has also been reported that the selection decision regarding senior-level positions, such as chief executive officer and auditing officer, is often influenced by recommendations through *Yon-go* (e.g. from political leaders) (Kim and Rowley 2001).

Recruitment and Selection in China

The Chinese labor market has undergone significant and far-reaching changes during the past six decades. Under the planned economy (1949–1978), a centralized planning and regulatory structure based on Soviet policies (i.e. top-down economic planning) was implemented to support the central labor allocation system and the Marxist collectivist ideology. The old personnel system was characterized by 'three old irons': (1) iron rice bowl (lifetime employment), (2) iron chair (state-controlled appointment and promotion of managerial staff), and (3) iron wage (centrally administered wages). Most firms were state-owned enterprises (SOEs) in which employees were assured lifelong employment (Zhao and Chen 2011), and this system discriminated against residents from rural areas (Hlasny and Jiang 2014). The State not only controlled the number of people employed but also the sources of recruitment. Workers were assigned to enterprises by State labor bureaus (Ng and Warner 2000). At the organizational level, job analysis was rarely conducted, person specifications were implicit, and job instructions were only broadly specified (Cai et al. 2011).

China embarked on changing the fundamentals of its economic system in the late 1970s. Since then, companies in many sectors have been privatized and reorganized, and they have gradually gained some degree of control over HR policies and practices (Cooke 2012). Fundamental changes occurred in the Chinese HRM system in the 1980s, during which time enterprise managers were given more autonomy in handling HR issues. They took advantage of the drive toward deregulation and attempted different ways to hire the best employees (Hlasny and Jiang 2014). In the early 1980s, foreign-invested enterprises (FIEs) started to use short-term labor contracts. In 1986, some SOEs began to use fixed-term contracts for a maximum of four years. Employers also instituted a probation period on workers to assess whether they could do the job (Leung and Smith 2005).

In 1992, the 'Three Systems Reforms' were implemented, and these involved labor contracts, performance-based compensation systems, and contributory social insurance. However, the HR planning was seldom linked to corporate strategies during this transition period (Cai et al. 2011). During the same period, off-farm migrants were allowed to work in urban areas. Most of them were only allowed to work in privately owned township and village enterprises, but not SOEs. Normally, there were no labor contracts for off-farm migrants, and they often encountered unfair dismissals and bad working conditions (Shen et al. 2014).

The labor contract system was widely implemented following the establishment of the Labor Law of the People's Republic of China in 1994 (Warner et al. 1999). The contract system gives both parties (i.e. employers and employees) freedom to enter or terminate their employment relationship. In this time, job security has declined, giving employees the opportunity to learn more skills and knowledge required for the workplace (Cooke 2004). The contract states employment terms and conditions and the employment period in general (Wong and Slater 2011). Labor contracts are generally signed for between one and five years (Warner 2010). In order to control the size of the workforce, some enterprises force employees to retire before the retirement age, which is called 'internal retirement' (*neitui*) (Shen 2007).

Chinese enterprises have been given full authority to recruit employees since the 2000s (Cooke 2011). Many organizations have started to adopt transparent recruitment procedures and sophisticated recruitment methods. Recruitment is more market driven since enterprises recruit potential employees mainly from the labor market (Cunningham 2010). 'Two-way selection' has become prevalent in enterprises and this means free selection of occupations for job candidates and free selection of employees for companies (Shen 2008). Companies can recruit people through various channels, for example, open advertisements, internal recruitment processes, informal referral, and recruitment agencies. The development of the internet has witnessed the rise of online recruitment websites, such as 51job.com, which have become a very popular and effective recruitment tool due to their effectiveness and low cost. More and more companies also set up their own recruitment web pages to uphold the integrity and uniqueness of their brands, and to build resources for their long-term development (Hlasny and Jiang 2014). With reference to selection criteria, enterprises emphasize education, skills, experience, and work performance (Shen 2010). Job interview is the most common method of selecting candidates (Shen 2008).

It should be noted that there is significant variation in staffing practices due to ownership and size of enterprises (Ding et al. 2006). Larger organizations tend to adopt formal recruitment and selection systems, that is, market-oriented recruitment techniques, such as job fairs, advertising, and university campus recruiting (Warner et al. 1999). Privately owned enterprises (POEs) are more likely to recruit employees from job centers and employment agencies (Chen 2006), while small firms tend to rely on informal networks or channels, such as family, relatives, or friends (Kim and Gao 2010). In particular, small POEs generally tend to recruit their workforces mainly through word of mouth and wall posters, and they select people mainly through interviews and on-the-job demonstration (Cooke 2005; Newman and Sheikh 2014).

JVs are more likely to offer individual employment contracts than SOEs, which by contrast, use collective contracts (Wong and Slater 2011). JVs also focus more on written tests plus formal interviews. They follow more rigorous selection procedures: (1) a local HR manager screens candidates' CVs and (2) conducts interviews involving a line manager and a senior expatriate manager. Expatriate managers become involved in an effort to prevent nepotism problems (Bjorkman and Lu 2000). Compared to FIEs, SOEs are less likely to use sophisticated recruitment procedures due to a lack of financial resources to invest in other methods, such as university recruiting and headhunting, and they tend to recruit employees through networks or trusted referrals (Han and Han 2009). Han and Han (2009) further find that network-based recruitment is effective in Chinese enterprises. Other major recruitment channels include job centers, employment agencies, headhunters, online recruitment, and word of mouth (Chen 2006; Cooke 2005; Kim and Gao 2010). In FIEs, headhunters are widely used for recruiting senior managers and high-caliber professions. They are more concerned with candidates' job-related competence, such as analytical skills, while conversely, SOEs tend to value university reputation more (Zhao 2006). Added to these criteria is the fact that political attitude is also considered just as important by SOEs (Hu and Leung 2010).

Chinese enterprises have experienced many staffing-related challenges and problems. During the last few years, due to the shortage of labor, many enterprises, especially POEs, have witnessed difficulties in recruiting high-caliber employees. This has forced many organizations to adopt more sophisticated recruitment strategies to compete for talent from more diverse sources including expatriates and graduates from overseas universities (Cooke 2012). These returnees (also called *sea turtles*) now become an increasingly important labor source in the local labor market. However, they are generally young and lack employment experience, and subsequently, many of them have to work in low-level positions. Many of them who are not willing to take a low-level position then have to wait for employment at home. As a result, they are called *sea weeds* (Tian et al. 2014). With the diminished role of state intervention in recruitment and selection procedures, SOEs have to recruit from external labor markets, which require them to establish transparent staffing policies and formalize their recruitment procedures (Cooke 2004). It is also suggested that SMEs in China should adopt more systematic recruitment and selection approaches to reduce bias and errors. Companies need to consider how they can help employees develop long-term commitment to the company so that skilled workers can be retained. SMEs should also avoid using informal recruitment channels, like word of mouth, to select potential employees (Cunningham 2010).

International Recruitment and Selection of South Korean MNEs

Before we report our empirical findings, we firstly review the existing literature on international staffing practices of South Korean MNEs. Five studies—Glover and Wilkinson (2007), Kim and Slocum (2008), Taylor et al. (2001), Lansbury et al. (2006), and Zou and Lansbury (2009)—have explored the international recruitment and selection issues in South Korean MNEs. Taylor et al. (2001) examined the approaches to staffing and recruitment methods. They found that South Korean companies are more likely to use expatriates to fill senior managerial positions in their overseas operations. However, the employment of local Chinese or ethnic Korean Chinese as low- and middle-level managers is on the rise. In some South Korean MNEs operating in China, Chinese managers are preferred because they have greater cultural understanding of the workforce and better interpersonal skills. Chinese workers are more willing to follow Chinese production managers' instructions than South Koreans, and this is especially important for quality control. Internal promotion and external recruitment are two ways for developing the Chinese management team. The channels for external recruitment include job fairs, local labor exchanges, and job centers. South Korean MNEs are increasingly recruiting skilled and well-educated workers on fixed-term contracts. Lansbury et al. (2006) reported that the selection criteria for HCNs in the Hyundai Motor Company focus on a willingness to do repetitive and monotonous jobs and to work in a team. These criteria align with South Koreans' strong work ethic (Paik and Sohn 1998).

The findings of Taylor et al. (2001) are consistent with Glover and Wilkinson (2007), who reported that South Korean MNEs are changing their staffing approach from an ethnocentric to a polycentric basis. Local managers are increasingly believed to have better knowledge than expatriates in working in the local environment. However, studies also reveal that, although the number of South Korean expatriates has declined, they still wield a strong influence over management due to their close ties with the parent company, which normally exercises tight control over overseas subsidiaries through expatriates (Ahn 1998; Bae 2004).

Kim and Slocum (2008) examined the selection criteria for South Korean expatriates and expatriates' premature return in the US subsidiaries. They reported that English fluency is the most important selection criterion. Moreover, South Korean MNEs are likely to recruit expatriates who have prior overseas experience, which is regarded as being important in reducing expatriate failure rates. South Korean expatriates in general tend not to return home prematurely, even when they experience unsuccessful work adjustment. This is for a number of reasons, including saving face and not wanting to miss positive career development and promotion opportunities upon their return (Dastmalchian et al. 2000). This is also because South Korean culture is prejudiced against disloyal people (Kim and Slocum 2008) and looks favorably on children's education in the US (Bae and Lawler 2000).

The study by Zou and Lansbury (2009) examined how Beijing Hyundai Motor Company (BHMC), a joint venture, recruited and selected employees. BHMC was required by the local government to employ local production workers. The company needed to seek the government's approval if it hired workers from other regions. However, no such constraint was imposed on the recruitment of managerial and engineering people, for whom formal education qualifications were the key selection criterion. Other criteria included personality and work attitude. Moreover, BHMC preferred younger candidates because they were easier to orient and more willing to accept or adapt to the company's organizational culture. Different employees signed different labor contracts. Specifically, production workers were offered one-year contracts, university graduates one- to three-year contracts, and postgraduates three- to five-year contracts.

Based on the discussions above, it becomes clear that despite the international staffing literature having developed significantly during the last two decades (cf. Collings et al. 2009; Dowling et al. 2013; Shen and Edwards 2004; Tharenou and Caulfield 2010), the literature on international recruitment and selection in South Korean MNEs is limited. The extant literature mainly concentrates on recruiting and selecting HCNs in South Korean MNEs; international staffing approaches and how expatriates are recruited and selected by South Korean MNEs are largely unknown. More studies are needed to explore international staffing approaches, reasons for adopting those approaches, recruitment procedures and selection criteria for both expatriates and HCNs, and repatriation management of South Korean MNEs. Such research is important to understand the global staffing practices of South Korean MNEs and therefore has the potential to contribute to the international staffing literature. Hence, the following sections will present our empirical findings on international staffing approaches and associated reasons, recruitment procedure and selection criteria for both expatriates and HCNs, and expatriate repatriation management adopted by South Korean MNEs in China.

International Staffing

International Staffing Approaches

Staffing approaches defined as staffing strategies are central to international recruitment and selection (Ando 2011; Dorrenbacher and Geppert 2010). There are four major international staffing approaches: ethnocentric, polycentric, geocentric, and regiocentric (Perlmutter 1969; Permutter and Heenan 1974, 1979). The ethnocentric approach fills all key positions in subsidiaries abroad with expatriates. This approach is often adopted in three situations. Firstly, there is a lack of HCNs who are qualified in management positions; secondly, when MNEs want to maintain a consistent organizational culture through PCNs; and thirdly, when MNEs aim to use PCNs to transfer knowledge/competencies to local subsidiaries (Tian et al. 2014). The polycentric approach does so with HCNs. The geocentric approach utilizes the best people for senior positions regardless of their nationalities (Dowling et al. 2013). To be consistent with this approach, it is suggested that MNEs should source key talent regardless of their locations so that the talent pools in different locations can be filled, thereby managing the global talent more effectively (Collings 2014). Finally, the regiocentric approach selects the best people but within a particular region (Dowling et al. 2013). Ethnocentric firms emphasize the centralization of

HR policies and are more likely to implement universalistic practices. On the other hand, polycentric firms emphasize decentralization of HR policies and are more likely to implement culture-specific practices. Geocentric and regiocentric approaches will blend these two perspectives (Ployhart and Weekley 2014).

Each approach has some advantages and disadvantages. The advantages of the ethnocentric approach are effective communication, ease of control, and transfer of knowledge. For example, Japanese subsidiaries in Western countries are frequently managed by expatriates, particularly in the initial establishment phase, to increase global integration and stimulate corporate culture within subsidiaries (Van den Born and Peltokorpi 2010). However, this approach is financially costly and limits the development opportunities for HCNs, which may impact on their morale and cause repatriation problems for expatriates. Moreover, expatriates may encounter difficulties in adapting to host working environments, and the use of expatriates is normally more expensive than HCNs. In contrast, HCNs are familiar with local cultures and working environments and have local connections (Bruning et al. 2011; Dorrenbacher and Geppert 2010). While adopting the polycentric approach may result in coordination and control problems, it has a range of advantages. Firstly, it is less expensive to employ HCNs; secondly, there is little language/culture barriers for HCNs; and thirdly, HCNs have more management development opportunities and, hence, are more committed to MNEs (Dowling et al. 2013).

The geocentric approach enables the MNE to develop effective international management teams, and it enhances a subsidiary's learning, innovation potential, and performance by facilitating the knowledge integration process (Gong 2003). Yet, this approach involves high training costs and relocation and increased difficulties in obtaining work permits in host countries. The regiocentric approach makes it easier for international managers to transfer, but limits their career paths within a given region, and has the potential to lead to federalism on a regional basis (Dowling et al. 2013). Based on Dowling et al. (2013), the major advantages and disadvantages of each staffing approach are summarized in Table 3.1.

MNEs' decisions on different international staffing approaches are determined by a range of host-contextual and firm-specific factors (Perlmutter 1969; Tung 1984; Dowling et al. 2013). The host-contextual factors include political, legal, economic, and sociocultural factors. The firm-specific factors include international strategy, structure, size, industry, international experience, entry mode, and country of origin (Shen 2005).

Table 3.1 Advantages and disadvantages of different staffing approaches

Approach	*Advantages*	*Disadvantages*
Ethnocentric	Effective communication	Limits the promotion opportunities of HCNs
	Easy to control	Adaptation time for expatriates is longer, during which expatriates often make poor or incorrect decisions
Polycentric	Employment of HCNs is less expensive	Limited career path for HCNs and TCNs
	Eliminates language/cultural barriers and avoids adjustment problems	Creates gap between HCN subsidiary and expatriate manager at headquarters
Geocentric	Enhances subsidiaries' learning, innovation potential, and performance	High costs of training and relocation
Regiocentric	Allows managers to transfer between the regional headquarters and subsidiaries	Produces federalism on a regional basis

Most MNEs tend to adopt the ethnocentric staffing approach when operating overseas unless there is a cost advantage for employing many HCNs (Dowling et al. 2013). However, a socially responsible MNE should be able to achieve a balance between coordination and control of headquarters and employ the maximum number of HCNs in order to contribute to the local community (Shen 2011).

The numbers of HCNs and expatriates in middle and senior managerial positions in the case companies are shown in Table 3.2. Based on the information provided in the table, it can be concluded that five firms including Telecom A, Telecom B, Telecom C, Electronics B, and Auto A adopted the polycentric staffing approach. The other five companies including Chemical A, Advertising A, Electronics A, Finance A, and Telecom D implemented a mixed approach, integrating both ethnocentric and polycentric staffing orientations.

The staffing approaches in the majority of the case companies changed over time and the number of expatriates dropped significantly. For example, Telecom A had 10 expatriates (6 senior managers and 4 middle managers) when the company first entered China in 2002. In 2006, 6 expatriates remained in the company. When the research was being conducted in September 2011, this company had only 3 expatriates, but 23 HCN middle and senior managers. Similarly, in Telecom C, the company had 10 expatriates (5 senior managers and 5 middle managers) in 2003.

Table 3.2 Nationalities of managers in the case companies in 2011

Company	*Middle managers (Korean/Chinese)*	*Senior managers (Korean/Chinese)*	*Expatriate managers (%)*
Telecom A	2/20	1/3	11.5
Chemical A	10/28	4/6	29
Telecom B	3/32	1/5	9.5
Advertising A	2/4	1/2	33.3
Telecom C	1/7	1/9	10.5
Electronics A	13/29	4/10	37
Electronics B	1/9	1/3	14
Auto A	3/21	1/8	12
Finance A	4/3	2/0	66.7
Telecom D	5/13	1/1	30

Expatriate managers dropped to 8 in 2007 and 2 in 2011. The number of PCN managers rose from 7 to 16 during the same period. The number of expatriates had also dropped significantly in Telecom B, Electronics B, Auto A, Chemical A, Advertising A, Electronics A, and Telecom D during the past decade.

Reasons for Adopting Staffing Approaches

In the 1970s, Edström and Galbraith identified three reasons why companies send expatriates on international assignments: filling skill gaps, management development, and organizational development (Edström and Galbraith 1977). Four decades on, these three reasons are still relevant (Tungli and Peiperl 2009). For example, Japanese subsidiaries in Western countries are frequently managed by expatriates to reinforce coordination, control, and communication (Van den Born and Peltokorpi 2010). It is, however, argued that the emphasis may have shifted somewhat from filling skill gaps to management development due to the growing importance of developing international managers and advances in technology, particularly since technology makes knowledge transfer so much easier and quicker (Kuhlmann and Hutchings 2010). In addition, maintaining control over the implementation of strategies, finance and marketing, enhancing communication between subsidiaries and the parent company, knowledge exchange (both to and from the subsidiary), socialization with local managers, and company representations make the use of expatriates important (Bruning et al. 2011; Dowling et al. 2013; Lasserre and Ching 1997).

It is argued that different MNEs may use expatriates for different reasons. Tungli and Peiperl (2009) indicated that utilizing expatriates in British and American MNEs is to fill skill gaps and help establish new businesses. For Japanese MNEs, in addition to filling skill gaps, coordinating and controlling local operations are also critical factors (Tungli and Peiperl 2009). German MNEs use expatriates for knowledge exchange (both to and from the subsidiary), international team development, socialization of HCN managers, and managing uncertainty (Bruning et al. 2011). Australian MNEs use expatriates mainly for controlling subsidiaries' operations, reducing risks arising from cultural friction, and keeping knowledge asymmetry or mismatch between the headquarters and subsidiaries to a minimum (Tharenou and Harvey 2006). For emerging MNEs such as China and India, control and communication are the major reasons for using expatriates (Nigam and Su 2010).

Trust and control have been repeatedly mentioned in interviews. This was exemplified by the fact that all the case companies appointed expatriates to fill the positions of Director of Finance. General Manager (Chinese) at Telecom A commented, 'anything to do with money, the Koreans want to put their hands on.' The following statement indicates that sending expatriates to China was done to ensure everything was aligned with corporate strategies:

> The headquarters sends lots of instructions over. Of course, they'd better have their own people here to see how things are done. Is it a trust issue? I am not saying that Koreans do not trust Chinese. However, as long as there is someone from Korea, the headquarters can have its mind set at ease. (HR Manager (Chinese) of Chemical A)

Communication was mentioned frequently as a reason. In the words of General Manager (Chinese) at Telecom B:

> Although some HCN managers speak little English and they can manage to communicate in English with Koreans, the headquarters feels more comfortable to speak Korean and think it is a way to avoid misunderstanding. So we leave expatriate managers to talk to the headquarters.

Marketing Managers (Korean) at Advertising A and Electronics A, and Operation Manager (Korean) at Telecom D reported that expatriates possessed some technical skills that HCNs did not have. Most Chinese interviewees did not agree that all the technologies and knowledge their firms employed were 'cutting edge', but agreed that 'the way Koreans doing things is different from the Chinese.' Other commonly reported reasons for using expatriates included 'easy to expatriate due to short flight (about an hour)', 'representing the headquarters', and 'Koreans' willingness to work in China'. Cultural similarity and Koreans' willingness to work in China were also regarded as contributors to low premature return rates among Korean expatriates. Only Auto A reported two cases of expatriate premature return resulting from work conflicts with HCNs.

The major reason for the transition from the ethnocentric to the polycentric approach was that the need for expatriates diminished over time. The communication problems caused by language barriers were effectively sorted out by recruiting or promoting ethnic Korean Chinese. Ethnic Korean Chinese had a number of advantages compared to expatriates in that they speak Korean, are from a Korean cultural background, and understand Chinese culture. It was commonly asserted that Chinese operations are very similar to how operations are conducted in South Korea. Sending someone over on a short-term mission to solve problems was popular in the case companies. Expatriates' roles in control and knowledge transfer also declined over time. The following remark typifies how these changes occurred and consequently how these changes impacted on international staffing approaches in Korean MNEs:

> Trust between the subsidiary and the headquarters has been developed over time. Once there is mutual understanding there is trust. When senior managers in the subsidiary understand and follow instructions control then will not become the headquarters' major concern. Knowledge transfer was relatively intensive at the beginning and becomes intermittent once operations stabilize. In the late stage knowledge transfer can be achieved through training or sending short-term expatriates. This is my understanding why we have reduced the use of long-term expatriates. (Finance Manager of Electronics B)

Recruitment Procedure and Selection Criteria

Effective recruitment and selection contributes significantly to expatriate performance (Cheng and Lin 2009; Harrison and Shaffer 2005; Mol et al. 2005). MNEs deal with recruitment and selection for both HCNs and expatriates, and most MNEs recruit expatriates internally (Shen and Lang 2009). It is suggested that expatriate selection should consider multiple factors which include technical competencies, personality characteristics, and interpersonal skills (Caligiuri 2000; Rieche and Harzing 2009). The following selection criteria are commonly used when selecting expatriates (Anderson 2005; Caligiuri 2000; Rieche and Harzing 2009; Templer 2010; Tung 1981):

- Job expertise;
- Technical competence;
- Personal traits/interpersonal abilities;
- Cultural openness;
- Ability to adjust to new environments and family issues;
- Previous international working experience (Culpan and Wright 2002; Tsang 2001).

These criteria are regarded as critical to expatriate performance on international assignments (Tungli and Peiperl 2009). In practice, however, most MNEs still use technical competence and knowledge of company systems as the major selection criteria (Harris and Brewster 1999; Morley and Flynn 2003; Sparrow et al. 2004). A review of the literature shows that South Korean MNEs have focused heavily on English fluency in selecting expatriates (Kang and Shen 2014). The primary selection criterion in Australian MNEs is technical competence (Santoso and Loosemore 2013). US MNEs have been more focused on expatriates' technical/professional skills, experience in the company, and willingness to accept assignments (Tungli and Peiperl 2009). Japanese MNEs believe that expatriates' experience in the company, technical skills, personal factors, and language proficiency are the most important selection criteria. Portuguese MNEs mainly recruit expatriates internally and heavily focused on trust from managers, technical and language competence, organizational knowledge, years of service, and availability of candidates (Martins and Diaconescu 2014). For Germany MNEs, candidates' availability is the major selection criterion (Tungli and Peiperl 2009). Research also shows that a company's social performance is critical when attempting to attract high-caliber employees (Behrend et al. 2009), and hence comparatively, these companies should also recruit employees who have positive attitudes toward CSR activities and CSR awareness (Shen 2011). It is necessary for a socially responsible MNE to recruit people who have expertise in CSR initiatives or legislation and are able to monitor MNEs' social performance overseas (Shen 2011; Shen and Zhu 2011). However, other criteria like leadership or alignment between personal and corporate values are largely overlooked (Cerdin and Brewster 2014).

Inappropriate expatriate selection criteria can lead to expatriate failure (Shen and Edwards 2004), which is broadly defined as expatriates returning home prematurely before their assignments are completed (e.g. Harzing and Christensen 2004; Tung 1981, 1984). A number of scholars have called for broadening the definition of expatriate failure from merely early return from assignment to include underperformance and maladjustment to the foreign environment, which has implications for both individuals' psychological adjustment as well as their workplace performance (Dowling and Welch 2004; Harzing and Christensen 2004; Kuhlmann and Hutchings 2010). Expatriate failure will cause problems for expatriates as well as MNEs as a whole. The costs related to expatriate failure are not only the direct costs such as flight tickets and relocation costs; they also include bad relationships with local government personnel and customers (Dowling and Welch 2004). This sort of failure can be detrimental to the effective worldwide operation of MNEs. For this very important reason, selection criteria should be more carefully designed and more comprehensive in areas such as self-selection, and involving the applicant's whole family in the selection process (Caligiuri and Colakoglu 2007).

Referring to the sample MNEs, the most common recruitment channels for HCNs included recruiting websites, company online recruitment, job centers, headhunter agents, and university job fairs. Using headhunters was regarded as the most effective way to recruit high-caliber employees by managers from Telecom A, Telecom B, and Auto A. A common statement that emerged was on the lines of: 'Once head-hunters know what kind of people we are looking for and they know where to find them, they make our recruitment job much easier' (Marketing Manager (Korean) at Auto A). All interviewees reported that they recruited HCNs, especially for lower positions, through the internet extensively. Typically, General Manager (Chinese) in Electronics B said:

> We publish recruitment information mainly on public recruiting websites, for example, 51job.com, zhaopin.com. The main reason we use these websites is that we want more applicants to access our recruiting information. The traditional recruitment channels, such as newspapers, are expensive. Nowadays, you cannot expect young graduates to read newspapers very often.

South Korean MNEs were also generally interested in recruiting fresh Chinese university graduates. Typically, General Manager (Chinese) in Electronics A stated: 'We conduct presentations at prestigious university to attract top graduates. I think these activities are really good opportunities for our company to be known to graduates. We have recruited a number of top graduates through this method.' Chief Operating Officer (Korean) at Telecom B commented: 'We believe that businesses have the social responsibility to recruit employees from universities. This would encourage students to go to university and study hard at university. We do so in Korea and we do the same here.'

All the case companies followed similar recruiting procedures in recruiting HCNs, as described by General Manager (Chinese) in Telecom B:

> After HR Team has screened resumes and supporting documents, qualified applicants will be required to take a language test (Korean/English for managerial positions), EQ/IQ test and psychological test. Applicants who pass written tests will then go through interviews. In our company, we have two rounds of interviews. The first interview will be conducted by the Operation Director to assess applicants' professional knowledge and potentials. The second interview focuses on personality, which is conducted by the HR manager and relevant line managers. I would say procedures are rather rigorous.

All HCNs signed labor contracts with Korean MNEs and contract durations ranged from one to five years depending on positions. Expatriates are normally assigned rather than openly recruited. The following statement was generally supported by the interviewees:

> Generally, management will decide who will be chosen for expatriation. We don't openly advertise for expatriation because we think it is unnecessary. We consider a number of factors to see whether the person is suitable or have the potential to work effectively in China. Employees can decline the appointment, but, in our company, most employees are willing to accept assignments in China. (Marketing Manager (Korean) in Electronics A)

Once an employee was chosen for an international assignment, the person was normally asked to get ready and leave fairly quickly. This is indicated in the statement, 'I got the expatriation notice only 2 weeks before the departure. It was very sudden for me. I wish I had more time to sort out family issues' (Operation Manager (Korean) in Telecom C). The period of working in an expatriate scenario generally lasted between three and five years. South Korean MNEs also recruited Korean students who studied and Koreans who worked in China. Chemical A recruited two

Koreans who were employed in China and Auto A, Chemical A, Finance A, Telecom A, B, and D all recruited a number of Korean students who studied in China. According to one statement, 'They are hired because they have lived in China for many years, speak Chinese fluently, understand the Chinese culture well, and have qualifications in particular areas.' Using this method, these Koreans were recruited normally to fill technical and low managerial positions.

All case companies had written selection criteria and job descriptions for recruiting HCNs. Criteria included education, technical certificate, age, and *hukou* (household registration) for non-managerial employees. HR Manager in Electronics A, General Manager in Electronics B, and HR Manager in Auto A explained that local governments required them to give priority to local residents in order to help solve local employment problems. For managerial positions, language (Korean or English) fluency, working experience, and social network appeared to be more important, as indicated in the comments of HR Manager (Chinese) in Finance A: 'We prefer Chinese managers who have years of experience working in Western MNEs. These people normally have established good relationships with locals.'

Selection criteria for expatriates were similar across all case companies, and mainly included expertise, job performance, communication skill, age, and personality. According to one comment:

> Expatriates are selected based on job performance. To be an expatriate, you must be an expert in your field, and have outstanding performance record. Working experience will help you come up with new ideas to solve problems in a new environment. (Chief Operating Officer (Korean) at Telecom B)

Chief Operating Officer at Telecom B had worked in the company for ten years before being assigned to China. His department won 'the Best Sales and Operation' award for three consecutive years. All other Korean managers had similar successful stories. With regard to communication, a typical statement was made by Marketing Manager (Korean) at Auto A:

> Communication is not only about the language ability, but also the way you communicate with HCNs, which is something to do with cultural empathy. In Korea, subordinates must follow whatever the orders managers give. Here in this country, if a manager does not build up guanxi with Chinese subordinates they will not cooperate. Consequently, there will be no harmony and the expatriate's performance as well as the whole department's performance would be affected.

It was widely suggested that personality and age were considered seriously when it came to selecting expatriates. For instance, Marketing Manager (Korean) at Electronics A said:

> Personality may be often ignored by some companies, but that is not the case in our company. The headquarters prefer someone who is extrovert and easy-going which is regarded as helpful in establishing interpersonal relationships. The age limit for expatriates in my company is 45.

Other companies, for example, Telecom A, Telecom B, and Finance A, set the age limit at 55. The interviewees generally agreed that their firms were effective in recruiting and selecting expatriates, as evidenced by low expatriate failure rates among expatriates assigned to China. Although there was no gender restriction on expatriation, coincidently, all expatriates in Chinese operations were males. The family issue was not considered as a selection criterion. A statement that encapsulated this state of affairs was as follows:

> Family is not an issue for Koreans as they love working overseas. Once a person is selected for an international assignment, his or her family is normally supportive. The company does not encourage families to go with expatriates. However, if they do go the company provides assistance, such as relocation, children's schooling and accommodation.

Repatriation Management

Repatriation is 'the activity of bringing the expatriate back to the home country' (Dowling et al. 1999, p. 204). Repatriation is often seen as a final stage of the expatriation process. However, the way to handle repatriates also impacts on them and MNEs' ability to attract future expatriates (Welch 1994). Effective repatriation is important in retaining employees and enhancing global management transfer (Furuya et al. 2008; Scullion and Collings 2006); hence, it is crucial in managing the key talent who work at MNEs (Cerdin and Brewster 2014). Without formal and systematic repatriation processes, talented repatriated managers are more likely to leave their workplace and potential candidates will be reluctant to accept international assignments. All this could impact adversely on the supply of talent or key global managers (Farndale et al. 2010). Santoso and Loosemore (2013) found that only a few Australian MNEs have developed formal repatriation plans.

The lack of repatriation strategy not only adversely affects expatriates' retention but also undermines the attractiveness of future expatriates accepting overseas assignments. According to the statistics, 26% of repatriates leave their organization within two years of completing their assignment, compared to 13% of expected annual turnover (Brookfield 2012). Ineffective repatriation could result in career stagnation and displacement for repatriates and costs for organizations due to the fact that employees are underutilized (Riche and Harzing 2009; Yan et al. 2002). Therefore, repatriation should receive equal attention, as much as expatriation does (Kulkarni et al. 2010; Lazarova and Cerdin 2007). Scholars have argued that repatriation can be more complex and difficult than expatriation (Forster 2000). In general, repatriation can be divided into the following four phases (Dowling et al. 2013):

- Preparation: involves developing plans for repatriates' future and gathering information about new positions;
- Physical relocation: refers to removing personal effects, breaking ties with colleagues and friends, and traveling to the next posting;
- Transition: this is a period of finding a new position and reestablishing social and work networks;
- Readjustment: involves coping with reverse culture shock and career demands that are followed by the re-entry.

It has been found that MNEs usually provide assistance to relocation but pay less attention to transition (Kulkarni et al. 2010; Newton et al. 2007), career planning (Pattie et al. 2010), and psychological adjustment (Pattie et al. 2010; Shen and Edwards 2004). Specifically, global career planning and development could help identify return on investment for both organizations and individuals (Cerdin and Brewster 2014). However, research suggests that companies find it difficult to retain their expatriates and, thus, lose a valuable source of global competence compared to their competitors (Stroh and Caligiuri 1998). To facilitate repatriation, it is suggested that during the assignment, MNEs should provide expatriates with continuous communication opportunities with the home office. MNEs should also assign mentors to expatriates because mentors can help repatriates generate accurate work expectations, reduce stress, and guide expatriates' future careers within the organization (Lazarova and Caligiuri 2001; Sanchez Vidal et al. 2007).

All the interviewees reported that their firms provided sufficient repatriation assistance in relation to relocation and organizing farewell functions. Normally, HR departments coordinated all relocation issues. A typical remark was that 'the company wants to make sure that repatriation is as smooth as possible to expatriates.' When asked whether the company helped repatriates in handling reverse culture shock, almost all interviewees said that they did not realize there was a reverse culture shock problem given that the two national cultures are similar. However, expatriates were normally given a certain period of time off at the end of expatriation to deal with personal and family issues. Having time off ranged from two weeks to two months, for example, 'In the last month we do not expect them to come to work. They can either take their families for a tour or deal with family or job issues back in Korea.' Most expatriates did not bring their spouses and children with them, and therefore did not need to worry about family issues upon repatriation. South Korean MNEs helped expatriates with family issues in China, for instance, paying tuition fees for children to study in international schools.

Career-wise, most interviewees believed that organizational policies were vague. Chinese managers were not aware of whether there was a career plan for expatriates. Expatriates revealed that there was in general no career planning for them and this concern is reflected in the following two statements:

> There is no career planning for me. My company did not make any promises about my future position. Even now I will complete this assignment in half a year and I have no idea what kind of position I will get back home. The only words I heard were like 'you should not have a problem to be promoted' or 'it really depends'. But I am not worried about my future job. At least I will get the same position as I had before. (Operation Manager (Korean) at Telecom C)
>
> In my opinion the future promotion is not only dependent on the overseas experience. The promotion in my company normally takes four years from one position to a higher one. In addition there are too many complicated factors, for example, position availability, relationship with the big boss. So no one can guarantee promotion for me at this stage. (Operation Manager (Korean) at Telecom D)

However, all South Korean managers agreed that although overseas performance was not the only factor affecting promotion, it is essential for future career development. A commonly held fear was the possibility of

Table 3.3 Expatriate turnover rate from 2007 to 2011

Company	*No. of current expatriates in China*	*No. of repatriates*	*No. of expatriates who left the company*	*Turnover rate (%)*
Telecom A	5	4	1	20
Chemical A	37	5	2	5
Telecom B	33	8	4	12
Advertising A	4	2	0	0
Telecom C	6	4	1	17
Electronics A	45	11	4	9
Electronics B	6	4	2	33
Auto A	5	3	1	20
Finance A	3	1	0	0
Telecom D	3	2	1	33

Source: Company documents from the headquarters of the sample MNEs

failure and what it implied: 'Basically speaking, if I did anything wrong here I am finished.' There was a strong sentiment among expatriates that they were open to joining another company or running their own businesses once their Chinese assignments were completed. Such a sentiment was indicated in the words of Finance Manager (Korean) in Electronics B: 'You will be extremely embarrassed if your colleagues who were your subordinators have become your boss when you are back in Korea.' According to Finance Manager (Korean) in Electronics B, four expatriates in his company went back to South Korea between 2007 and 2011, and only two remained at headquarters. Most of them started their own businesses or joined another company. The turnover rates of repatriates who were assigned to China are shown in Table 3.3.

Discussion

Generally speaking, in our sample, South Korean MNEs in China tended to be polycentric in international staffing. This finding is very different to the findings reported in previous studies, including Paik and Sohn (1998), Kang and Shen (2013), Taylor et al. (2001), and Yang and Kelly (2009), where South Korean MNEs were normally found to adopt the ethnocentric staffing approach.

The major reasons for using expatriates were control, communication and technology, and knowledge transfer. These reasons are consistent with the prevailing international staffing literature (cf. Dowling et al. 2013; Edstrom and Galbraith 1977; Shen 2006). There are two critical reasons why South Korean MNEs use HCNs in China. First, there is a large South Korean Chinese population in China and it is sensible and cost-effective to hire Korean Chinese who understand both Korean and Chinese cultures and languages. Second, China is geographically close to South Korea, making it convenient to send assignees over on short-term contracts to solve problems or convey messages from the headquarters when such a need arises. This finding supports the literature, for example, Schuler et al. (1993), where it is argued that skills availability, labor costs, and cultural similarity are major factors for using HCN managers. The current study also lends some support to Collings et al. (2007), Mayerhofer et al. (2004), and Shen and Lang (2009) who contend that there is a trend for MNEs to use more short-term assignees—so-called flexpatriates (Mayerhofer et al. 2004)—because they are more cost-effective and encounter no repatriation problems. Management development, which has been regarded as a common reason for using expatriates in Western MNEs (Adler and Bartholomew 1992), is not considered very important by South Korean MNEs. This is a significant limitation in South Korean MNE's staffing practices, and to a certain degree, it may result in international assignments becoming a form of career hindrance for expatriates (Dickmann et al. 2008; Suutari and Makela 2007).

South Korean MNEs adopted the 'one-way' selection approach in recruiting expatriates in which potential expatriates were approached by managers and offered international assignments. This finding is consistent with Cho et al.(2013) who stated that expatriates accepting international assignments due to the cultural values of high power distance. They have to accept the assignments due to the demands of company loyalty and job security. This practice is different from the open recruitment method that has been widely practiced in Western firms (Dowling et al. 2008). This practice has a range of disadvantages, the most important being that employees who are not suitable for international assignments may be reluctant to turn down an offer as they are worried that such a refusal may have a negative impact on their future careers. In addition, South Korean MNEs normally did not allow sufficient time for employees to prepare for expatriation and did not consider family situations when recruiting and selecting expatriates. These limitations may have a significant impact on South Korean expatriates' performance in international assignments despite the overall expatriate premature return rates being low.

The major criteria for South Korean MNEs selecting expatriates were job expertise, job performance, communication skills, cultural empathy, and personality, which are commonly used by other Western and emerging MNEs (cf. Dowling et al. 2013; Kim and Slocum 2008; Shen and Edwards 2004). However, previous overseas experience is considered important in expatriate selection by MNEs in general (Dowling et al. 2013; Shen and Lang 2009), but not by South Korean MNEs. The major criteria for selecting HCNs focused on education, age, and technical qualifications rather than political outlook and moral attitudes. It is in this context that South Korean MNEs, other foreign MNEs in China, and local Chinese enterprises converge (Braun and Warner 2002; Li 2003; Shen 2010).

South Korean MNEs focused on helping repatriates with relocation and transition but paid inadequate attention to repatriates' career development, readjustment, and personal and family issues. This practice is similar to the approach of their Australian and Chinese counterparts when managing repatriation (Newton et al. 2007; Shen and Edwards 2004), but different from that of European MNEs (Lazarova and Caligiuri 2001). It is recognized that a lack of emphasis on career development, readjustment, and personal and family issues in repatriation is more likely to contribute to high repatriate turnover (Lazarova and Caligiuri 2001; Shen and Edwards 2004). This study provides evidence that there are high turnover rates of South Korean repatriates from MNEs operating in China. Due to a lack of research on how South Korean MNEs manage international recruitment and selection practices (Kang and Shen 2013), there is limited research conducted to investigate the staffing approach in non-Western MNEs; hence, the current research fills an important literature gap and, therefore, contributes to the international staffing literature.

Conclusion

This chapter has addressed international staffing policies and practices of South Korean MNEs in China, including international staffing approaches, reasons for adopting the staffing approaches, recruitment and selection procedures and criteria, and repatriation management. The international recruitment and selection policies and practices that South Korean MNEs employ in China can be characterized as polycentric in international staffing, 'one-way selection', localized HCN recruitment and selection, and a lack of emphasis on cultural adjustment and career development in expatriation and repatriation management. These characteristics can, to a great extent, be explained by existing IHRM models (e.g. Schuler et al. 1993), which argue that IHRM practices are influenced by host-contextual and firm-specific factors. The next chapter will discuss international training and development practices of South Korean MNEs operating in China.

Bibliography

Adler, N. J., & Bartholomew, S. (1992). Managing globally competent people. *The Executive, 6*(3), 52–65.

Ahn, Y. D. (1998). *Traditional Korean management systems as impediments to localization strategies on United States' subsidiaries*. Claremont: The Claremont Graduate University.

Anderson, B. A. (2005). Expatriate selection: Good management or good luck? *The International Journal of Human Resource Management, 16*(4), 567–583.

Ando, N. (2011). Isomorphism and foreign subsidiary staffing policies. *Cross Cultural Management: An International Journal, 18*(2), 131–143.

Bae, J. S. (2004, June 23–26). *Globalization of human resource management: The cases of Korean MNCs in the UK and Thailand*. The IIRA Asian Regional Congress, Seoul.

Bae, J. S., & Lawler, J. J. (2000). Organizational and HRM strategies in Korea: Impact of firm performance in an emerging economy. *Academy of Management Journal, 43*(3), 502–517.

Bae, J. S., Chen, S. J., & Rowley, C. (2011). From a paternalistic model towards what? HRM trends in Korea and Taiwan. *Personnel Review, 40*(6), 700–722.

Behrend, T. S., Baker, B. A., & Thompson, L. F. (2009). Effects of pro- environmental recruiting messages: The role of organizational reputation. *Journal of Business and Psychology, 24*(3), 341–350.

Björkman, I., & Lu, Y. (2000). Local or global? Human resource management in international joint ventures in China. In M. Warner (Ed.), *Changing workplace relations in the Chinese economy* (pp. 117–138). London: Palgrave Macmillan.

Braun, W., & Warner, M. (2002). Strategic human resource management in western multinationals in China. *Personnel Review, 31*(5), 553–579.

Brookfield Global Relocation Services. (2012). *Global relocation trends 2012 survey report*. Retrieved March 10, 2014, from http://espritgloballearning.com/wp-content/uploads/2011/03/2012-Brookfield-Global-Relocations-Trends-Survey.pdf

Bruning, N. S., Bebenroth, R., & Pascha, W. (2011). Valuing Japan-based German expatriate and local manager's functions: Do subsidiary age and managerial perspectives matter? *The International Journal of Human Resource Management, 22*(4), 778–806.

Cai, Z., Morris, J. L., & Chen, J. (2011). Explaining the human resource management preferences of employees: A study of Chinese workers. *The International Journal of Human Resource Management, 22*(16), 3245–3269.

Caligiuri, P. M. (2000). Selecting expatriates for personality characteristics: A moderating effect of personality on the relationship between host national contact and cross-cultural adjustment. *Management International Review, 40*(1), 61–80.

Caligiuri, P. M., & Colakoglu, S. (2007). A strategic contingency approach to expatriate assignment management. *Human Resource Management Journal, 17*(4), 393–410.

Cerdin, J. L., & Brewster, C. (2014). Talent management and expatriation: Bridging two streams of research and practice. *Journal of World Business, 49*(2), 245–252.

Chang, C. S., & Chang, N. J. (1994). *The Korean management system: Cultural, political, economic Foundations.* Westport: Quorum.

Chen, H. A. (2006). *Recruitment and selection in China: An application to the case of Lenovo.* School of Management, University of Nottingham, Semenyih. http://citeseerx.ist.psu.edu/viewdoc/download?doi=10.1.1.458.7488&rep=rep1&type=pdf

Cheng, H. L., & Lin, C. Y. Y. (2009). Do as the large enterprises do? Expatriate selection and overseas performance in emerging markets: The case of Taiwan SMEs. *International Business Review, 18*(1), 60–75.

Cho, T., Hutchings, K., & Marchant, T. (2013). Key factors influencing Korean expatriates' and spouses' perceptions of expatriation and repatriation. *The International Journal of Human Resource Management, 24*(5), 1051–1075.

Chung, K. H., Lee, H. C., & Jung, K. H. (1997). *Korea management: Global strategy and cultural transformation.* Berlin/New York: Walter de Gruyter.

Colakoglu, S., & Caligiuri, P. (2008). Cultural distance, expatriate staffing and subsidiary performance: The case of US subsidiaries of multinational corporations'. *The International Journal of Human Resource Management, 19*(2), 223–239.

Colakoglu, S., Tarique, I., & Caligiuri, P. (2009). Towards a conceptual framework for the relationship between subsidiary staffing strategy and subsidiary performance. *The International Journal of Human Resource Management, 20*(6), 1291–1308.

Collings, D. G. (2014). Toward mature talent management: Beyond shareholder value. *Human Resource Development Quarterly, 25*(3), 301–319.

Collings, D. G., Scullion, H., & Morley, M. J. (2007). Changing patterns of global staffing in the multinational enterprise: Challenges to the conventional expatriate assignment and emerging alternatives. *Journal of World Business, 42*(2), 198–213.

Collings, D. G., Scullion, H., & Dowling, P. J. (2009). Global staffing: A review and thematic research agenda. *The International Journal of Human Resource Management, 20*(6), 1253–1272.

Cooke, F. L. (2004). *HRM, work and employment in China*. Oxon: Routledge.

Cooke, F. L. (2011). The role of the state and emergent actors in the development of human resource management in China. *The International Journal of Human Resource Management, 22*(18), 3830–3848.

Cooke, F. L. (2012). *Human resource management in China: New trends and practices*. New York: Routledge.

Culpan, O., & Wright, G. H. (2002). Women abroad: Getting the best results from women managers. *The International Journal of Human Resource Management, 13*(5), 784–801.

Cunningham, L. X. (2010). Managing human resources in SMEs in a transition economy: Evidence from China. *The International Journal of Human Resource Management, 21*(12), 2120–2141.

Dasmalchian, A., Lee, S., & Ng, I. (2000). The interplay between organizational and national cultures: A comparison of organizational practices in Canada and South Korea using the competing values framework. *The International Journal of Human Resource Management, 11*(2), 388–412.

Dickmann, M., Doherty, N., Mills, T., & Brewster, C. (2008). Why do they go? Individual and corporate perspectives on the factors influencing the decision to accept an international assignment. *The International Journal of Human Resource Management, 19*(4), 731–751.

Ding, D., Akhtar, S., & Ge, L. G. (2006). Organizational differences in managerial compensation and benefits in Chinese firms. *The International Journal of Human Resource Management, 17*(4), 693–715.

Dorrenbacher, C., & Geppert, M. (2010). Subsidiary staffing and initiative-taking in multinational corporations: A socio-political perspective. *Personnel Review, 39*(5), 600–621.

Dowling, P. J., & Welch, D. E. (2004). *International human resource management. Managing people in a multinational context*. London: Thomson.

Dowling, P. J., Welch, D. E., & Schuler, R. S. (1999). *International human resource management*. Cincinnati: South-Western.

Dowling, P. J., Festing, M., & Engle, A. D. (2008). *International human resource management* (5th ed.). Stamford: Cengage Learning.

Dowling, P. J., Festing, M., & Engle, A. D. (2013). *International human resource management*. London: Cengage Learning.

Edström, A., & Galbraith, J. R. (1977). Transfer of managers as a coordination and control strategy in multinational organizations. *Administrative Science Quarterly, 22*, 248–263.

Farndale, E., Paauwe, J., Morris, S. S., Stahl, G. K., Stiles, P., Trevor, J., & Wright, P. M. (2010). Context-bound configurations of corporate HR functions in multinational corporations. *Human Resource Management, 49*(1), 45–66.

Forster, N. (2000). Expatriates and the impact of cross cultural training. *Human Resource Management Journal, 10*(3), 63–78.

Furuya, N., Stevens, M. J., Bird, A., Oddou, G., & Mendenhall, M. (2008). Managing the learning and transfer of global management competence: Antecedents and outcomes of Japanese repatriation effectiveness. *Journal of International Business Studies, 40*(2), 200–215.

Glover, L., & Wilkinson, A. (2007). Worlds colliding: The translation of modern management practices within a UK based subsidiary of a Korean-owned MNC. *The International Journal of Human Resource Management, 18*(8), 1437–1455.

Gong, Y. (2003). Toward a dynamic process model of staffing composition and subsidiary outcomes in multinational enterprises. *Journal of Management, 29*(2), 259–280.

Han, J., & Han, J. (2009). Network-based recruiting and applicant attraction in China: Insights from both organizational and individual perspectives. *The International Journal of Human Resource Management, 20*(11), 2228–2249.

Harris, H., & Brewster, C. (1999). The coffee-machine system: How international selection really works. *The International Journal of Human Resource Management, 10*(3), 488–500.

Harrison, D. A., & Shaffer, M. A. (2005). Mapping the criterion space for expatriate success: Task- and relationship-based performance, effort and adaptation. *The International Journal of Human Resource Management, 16*(8), 1454–1474.

Harzing, A. W., & Christensen, C. (2004). Expatriate failure: Time to abandon the concept? *Career Development International, 9*(7), 616–626.

Hlasny, V., & Jiang, M. (2014). *Discrimination in recruitment in China: An employer-level analysis of applicant screening*. Available at SSRN 2226238.

Horak, S. (2015). The informal dimension of human resource management in Korea: Yongo, recruiting practices and career progression. *The International Journal of Human Resource Management*, 1–24. doi:10.1080/09585192.2015.1089062.

Hu, F., & Leung, C. M. (2010). *Top management turnover, firm performance and government control: Evidence from China's listed state-owned enterprises*. http://papers.ssrn.com/sol3/papers.cfm?abstract_id=1532724

Jang, I. C. (2015). Language learning as a struggle for distinction in today's corporate recruitment culture: An ethnographic study of English study abroad practices among South Korean undergraduates. *L2 Journal, 7*(3), 57–77.

Jang, S. Y., & Merriam, S. (2004). Korean culture and the reentry motivations of university-graduated women. *Adult Education Quarterly, 54*(4), 273–290.

Kang, H. Y., & Shen, J. (2013). International recruitment and selection practices of South Korean multinationals in China. *The International Journal of Human Resource Management, 24*(17), 3325–3342.

Kang, H. Y., & Shen, J. (2014). International human resource management policies and practices of South Korean MNEs: A review of the literature. *Asia Pacific Business Review, 20*(1), 42–58.

Kim, C. S. (1992). *The culture of Korean industry: An ethnography of Poongsan Corporation*. Tucson: The University of Arizona Press.

Kim, L. (1997). The dynamics of Samsung's technological learning in semiconductors. *California Management Review, 39*(3), 86–100.

Kim, S., & Briscoe, D. R. (1997). Globalization and a new human resource policy in Korea: Transformation to a performance-based HRM'. *Employee Relations, 19*(4), 298–308.

Kim, Y., & Gao, F. Y. (2010). An empirical study of human resource management practices in family firms in China. *The International Journal of Human Resource Management, 21*(12), 2095–2119.

Kim, J. W., & Rowley, C. (2001). Managerial problems in Korea-Evidence from the nationalized industries. *International Journal of Public Sector Management, 14*(2), 129–149.

Kim, K. H., & Slocum, J. W. (2008). Individual differences and expatriate assignment effectiveness: The case of US-based Korean expatriates. *Journal of World Business, 43*(1), 109–126.

Kim, H., Kwon, D. B., & Pyun, C. (2008). Korean corporate HRD in transition: Issues and challenges. *Human Resource Development International, 11*(1), 81–89.

Koch, M., Nam, S. H., & Steers, R. M. (1995). Human resource management in South Korea. In L. F. Moore & P. D. Jennings (Eds.), *Human resource management on the Pacific Rim* (pp. 217–242). New York: De Gmyter.

Kuhlmann, T., & Hutchings, K. (2010). Expatriate assignments vs localization of management in China: Staffing choices of Australian and German companies. *Career Development International, 15*(1), 20–38.

Kulkarni, M., Lengnick-Hall, M. L., & Valk, R. (2010). Employee perceptions of repatriation in an emerging economy: The Indian experience. *Human Resource Management, 49*(3), 531–548.

Lansbury, D. R., Kwon, S. H., & Suh, C. S. (2006). Globalization and employment relations in the Korean auto industry: The case of the Hyundai Motor Company in Korea, Canada and India. *Asia Pacific Business Review, 12*(2), 131–147.

Lasserre, P., & Ching, P. S. (1997). Human resources management in China and the localization challenge. *Journal of Asian Business, 13*(4), 85–99.

Lazarova, M., & Caligiuri, P. (2001). Retaining repatriates: The role of organizational support practices. *Journal of World Business, 36*, 389–401.

Lazarova, M. B., & Cerdin, J. L. (2007). Revisiting repatriation concerns: Organizational support versus career and contextual influences. *Journal of International Business Studies, 38*(3), 404–429.

Lee, H. C. (1998). Transformation of employment practices in Korean businesses. *International Studies of Management & Organization, 28*(4), 26–39.

Lee, Y. I. (2004a). South Korean companies in transition: An evolving strategic management style. *Strategic Change, 13*(1), 29–35.

Leung, A., & Smith, C. (2005, December 4–7). *Chinese human resource practices at the firm level: The migrant worker issue*. Asia-Pacific Researchers in Organization Studies, 11th International Colloquium, Melbourne.

Li, J. (2003). Strategic human resource management and MNEs' performance in China. *International Journal of Human Resource Management, 14*(2), 157–173.

Martins, D., & Diaconescu, L. M. (2014). Expatriates recruitment and selection for long-term international assignments in Portuguese companies. *Tékhne, 12*, 48–57.

Mayerhofer, H., Hartmann, L. C., Michelitsch-Riedl, G., & Kollinger, I. (2004). Flexpatriate assignments: A neglected issue in global staffing. *The International Journal of Human Resource Management, 15*(8), 1371–1389.

Mol, S. T., Born, M. P., & van der Molen, H. T. (2005). Developing criteria for expatriate effectiveness: Time to jump off the adjustment bandwagon. *International Journal of Intercultural Relations, 29*(3), 339–353.

Morley, M. J., & Flynn, M. (2003). The relationship between work-role characteristics and intercultural transitional adjustment domain patterns among a sample of US and Canadian expatriates on assignment in Ireland. *Cross Cultural Management: An International Journal, 10*(3), 42–57.

Newman, A., & Sheikh, A. Z. (2014). Determinants of best HR practices in Chinese SMEs. *Journal of Small Business and Enterprise Development, 21*(3), 414–430.

Newton, S., Hutchings, K., & Kabanoff, B. (2007). Repatriation in Australian organisations: Effects of function and value of international assignment on program scope. *Asia Pacific Journal of Human Resources, 45*(3), 295–313.

Ng, S. H., & Warner, M. (2000). Industrial relations versus human resource management in the PRC: Collective bargaining 'with Chinese characteristics'. In *Changing workplace relations in the Chinese economy* (pp. 100–116). London: Palgrave Macmillan.

Nigam, R., & Su, Z. (2010). Climbing up the performance ladder: A conceptual framework for emerging country multinationals. *International Journal of Business and Management, 5*(4), 13–25.

Paik, Y. S., & Sohn, J. D. (1998). Confucius in Mexico: Korean MNEs and the maquiladoras. *Business Horizons, 41*(6), 25–33.

Park, W. W. (2004). *Human resource management in developing countries*. New York: Routledge.

Park, W. S., & Yu, G. C. (2000). *Transformation and new patterns of HRM in Korea*. Michigan: Citeseer.

Pattie, M., White, M. M., & Tansky, J. (2010). The homecoming: A review of support practices for repatriates. *Career Development International, 15*(4), 359–377.

Perlmutter, H. V. (1969). The tortuous evolution of the multinational corporation. *Columbia Journal of World Business, 4*(1), 9–18.

Perlmutter, H. V., & Heenan, D. A. (1974). How multinational should your top managers be? *Harvard Business Review, 52*(6), 121–132.

Perlmutter, H. V., & Heenan, D. A. (1979). *Multinational organizational development.* Reading: Addison-Wesley.

Ployhart, R. E., & Weekley, J. A. (2014). Recruitment and selection in global organizations. In D.G. Collings, G.T. Wood & P.M. Caligiuri (Eds.), *The Routledge companion to international human resource management* (pp. 155–171). Oxon, UK: Routledge.

Pucik, V., & Lim, J. C. (2001). Transforming human resource management in a Korean Chaebol: A case study of Samsung. *Asia Pacific Business Review, 7*(4), 137–160.

Reiche, B. S. (2007). The effect of international staffing practices on subsidiary staff retention in multinational corporations. *The International Journal of Human Resource Management, 18*(4), 523–536.

Reiche, B. S., & Harzing, A. W. (2009). International assignments. In A. W. K. Harzing & A. Pinnington (Eds.), *International human resource management.* London: Sage.

Rowley, C. (2005). Context, developments and interactions in the HRM system in South Korea: Between rigidity and flexibility. *Journal of Comparative Asian Development, 4*(1), 105–133.

Rowley, C., & Bae, J. S. (2002). Globalization and transformation of human resource management in South Korea. *International Journal of Human Resource Management, 13*(3), 522–549.

Sanchez Vidal, E. M., Sanz Valle, R., Barba Aragon, I. M., & Brewster, C. (2007). Repatriation adjustment process of business employees: Evidence from Spanish workers. *International Journal of Intercultural Relations, 31*(3), 317–337.

Santoso, J., & Loosemore, M. (2013). Expatriate management in Australian multinational enterprises. *Construction Management and Economics, 31*(11), 1098–1109.

Schuler, R. S., Dowling, P. J., & De Cieri, H. (1993). An integrative framework of strategic international human resource management. *Journal of Management, 19*(2), 419–459.

Scullion, H., & Collings, D. G. (2006). Introduction. In H. Scullion & D. G. Collings (Eds.), *Global staffing* (pp. 1–13). London: Routledge.

Shen, J. (2005). Towards a generic IHRM model. *Journal of Organisational Transformation & Social Change, 2*(2), 83–102.

Shen, J. (2006). Factors affecting international staffing in Chinese MNEs. *International Journal of Human Resource Management, 17*(2), 295–315.

Shen, J. (2007). *Labour disputes and their resolution in China.* Oxford: Chandos Publishing.

Shen, J. (2008). HRM in Chinese privatised enterprises. *Thunderbird International Business Review, 50*(2), 91–104.

Shen, J. (2010). Employees' satisfaction with HRM in Chinese privately-owned enterprises. *Asia Pacific Business Review, 16*(3), 339–354.

Shen, J. (2011). Developing the concept of socially responsible international human resource management. *The International Journal of Human Resource Management, 22*(6), 1351–1363.

Shen, J., & Edwards, V. (2004). Recruitment and selection in Chinese MNEs. *The International Journal of Human Resource Management, 15*(4), 814–835.

Shen, J., & Lang, B. (2009). Cross-cultural training and its impact on expatriate performance in Australian MNEs. *Human Resource Development International, 12*(4), 371–386.

Shen, J., & Zhu, C. J. (2011). Effects of socially responsible human resource management on employee organizational commitment. *The International Journal of Human Resource Management, 22*(15), 3020–3035.

Shen, J., Tang, N., & D'Netto, B. (2014). A multilevel analysis of the effects of HR diversity management on employee knowledge sharing: The case of Chinese employees. *The International Journal of Human Resource Management, 25*(12), 1720–1738.

Sparrow, P., Brewster, C., & Harris, H. (2004). *Globalizing human resource management*. London: Routledge.

Stroh, L. K., & Caligiuri, P. M. (1998). Increasing global competitiveness through effective people management. *Journal of World Business, 33*(1), 1–16.

Suutari, V., & Ma kela, K. (2007). The career capital of managers with global careers. *Journal of Managerial Psychology, 22*(7), 628–648.

Taylor, R., Cho, D. Y., & Hyun, J. H. (2001). Korean companies in China: Strategies in the localisation of management. In C. Rowley, T. W. Sohn, & J. Bae (Eds.), *Managing Korean business: Organisation, culture, human resources and change* (pp. 161–181). London: Frank Cass.

Templer, K. J. (2010). Personal attributes of expatriate managers, subordinate ethnocentrism, and expatriate success: A host-country perspective. *The International Journal of Human Resource Management, 21*(10), 1754–1768.

Tharenou, P., & Caulfield, N. (2010). Will I stay or will I go? Explaining repatriation by self-initiated expatriates. *Academy of Management Journal, 53*(5), 1009–1028.

Tharenou, P., & Harvey, M. (2006). Examining the overseas staffing options utilized by Australian headquartered multinational corporations. *The International Journal of Human Resource Management, 17*(6), 1095–1114.

Tian, X., Harvey, M., & Slocum, J. W. (2014). The retention of Chinese managers: The Chinese puzzle box. *Organizational Dynamics, 43*(1), 44–52.

Tsang, E. W. K. (2001). Adjustment of mainland Chinese academics and students to Singapore. *International Journal of Intercultural Relations, 25*(4), 347–372.

Tung, R. L. (1981). Selecting and training of personnel for overseas assignments. *Colombia Journal of World Business, 16*(2), 67–78.

Tung, R. L. (1984). Strategic management of human resources in the multinational enterprise. *Human Resource Management, 23*(2), 120–143.

Tungli, Z., & Peiperl, M. (2009). Expatriate practices in German, Japanese, UK, and US multinational companies: A comparative survey of changes. *Human Resource Management, 48*(1), 153–171.

Van den Born, F., & Peltokorpi, V. (2010). Language policies and communication in multinational companies. *Journal of Business Communication, 47*(2), 97–118.

Warner, M. (2010). In search of Confucian HRM: Theory and practice in Greater China and beyond. *The International Journal of Human Resource Management, 21*(12), 2053–2078.

Warner, M., Goodall, K., & Ding, D. Z. (1999). The 'myth'of human resource management in Chinese enterprises. *Asia Pacific Business Review, 5*(3–4), 223–237.

Welch, D. (1994). Determinants of international human resource management approaches and activities: A suggested framework. *Journal of Management Studies, 31*(2), 139–164.

Wong, L. Y., & Slater, J. R. (2011). Executive development in China: Is there any in a Western sense? *International Journal of Human Resource Management, 13*(2), 338–360.

Yan, A., Zhu, G., & Hall, D. T. (2002). International assignments for career building: A model of agency relationships and psychological contracts. *Academy of Management Review, 27*(3), 373–391.

Yang, I., & Kelly, A. (2009). Assumptions in Korean organizations and their implications in a cross-cultural setting. *Advances in Global Leadership, 5*, 297–320.

Yu, G. C., & Rowley, C. (2009). The changing face of Korean human resource management. In C. Rowley & Y. S. Paik (Eds.), *The changing face of Korean management* (pp. 29–51). London: Routledge.

Zhao, H. (2006). Expectations of recruiters and applicants in large cities of China. *Journal of Managerial Psychology, 21*(5), 459–475.

Zhao, S. M., & Chen, W. S. (2011). Human resource management and employment relations in state-owned enterprises. In P. Sheldon, S. Kim, Y. Li, & M. Warner (Eds.), *China's changing workplace* (pp. 163–179). Oxon: Routledge.

Zou, M., & Lansbury, R. D. (2009). Multinational corporations and employment relations in the People's Republic of China: The case of Beijing Hyundai Motor Company. *International Journal of Human Resource Management, 20*(11), 2349–2369.

CHAPTER 4

International Training and Development Policies and Practices

Introduction

International training and management development is important to MNEs because it improves human capital and the motivation of both expatriates and HCNs. In turn, this influences international business performance (Dowling et al. 2013; McPherson and Roche 1997). This chapter firstly discusses the training and development practices commonly adopted in South Korea and China, and reviews the existing literature on international training and development practices of South Korean MNEs. The chapter then addresses the major international training and development practices, which include expatriate pre-departure and post-arrival training, HCN training, management development of expatriates and HCNs, and factors influencing these policies and practices in South Korean MNEs.

Training and Development Policies and Practices in South Korea and China

Training and Development in South Korea

Enterprise training in South Korea is classified into three categories: pre-employment training, on-the-job training, and retraining. Pre-employment training is provided to those who are first-time job seekers (Lee 2005).

H. Kang, J. Shen, *International Human Resource Management in South Korean Multinational Enterprises*,
DOI 10.1007/978-981-10-3093-2_4

One important part of on-the-job training is company orientation training. Research shows that South Korean companies emphasize the importance of new employee orientation, and consider it as one of the key business strategies to achieve success (Kim et al. 2015). Orientation programs in large conglomerates are extensive, and most have their own training centers with boarding facilities provided to hundreds of trainees (Kearney 1991). For example, Hyundai has a 4-week program lasting 184 hours and covering 62 subjects. The program covers moral education, organizational life and physical fitness, visiting workplaces, and basic job knowledge. They may send new employees to remote areas to test employees' sales ability. Simulation is also popular in the orientation program. In LG, they run a 2-week orientation followed by 1-week computer education and 3 weeks of group education (Chang and Chang 1994). Retraining is provided to those who want to change jobs or are unemployed, and is usually provided by outside training institutes or other education facilities (Lee 2005).

Pohang Iron and Steel Company (POSCO) is a good example providing different training programs to different levels of employees. New employee orientation, basic management training, and field practices are provided to new employees: middle management is offered performance management training, career development training, and operation/marketing management training; while for senior level, leadership training and advanced management programs are offered (POSCO 2008). Korean Air has also established a mature training system. For example, non-managerial employees are provided an orientation program, fundamental air transportation knowledge; for managerial level employees, leadership management and advanced air transportation training are highly emphasized (Korean Air 2014).

In South Korea, vocational training schools play an important role in providing industry training. In the 1960s and 1970s, the industrial need for vocational training was to produce manpower in large quantities, but since the 1990s, this has shifted to highly skilled workers. Vocational schools provide a series of training programs for industries. They offer both initial vocational education that is conducted mainly in the classroom and workshop and field practice to help students find jobs after graduating from school. However, this form of education has been criticized for a lack of direct link to industry needs. In order to address this problem, many approaches such as training on industrial work sites, internships, cooperative training through both training institutes and working places, visiting factories, inviting master craftsmen as instructors or lecturers, and contract-based training have been taken in the process of industrialization since the 1960s. In particular, the '2 + 1 system' has been very popular—students need to attend normal school education (i.e. course work) in the first two years and apprenticeship in the third year. The reason why the system is popular is because it combines both 'school learning' and 'workplace learning' (Lin 2009). Training for technical employees is provided by community colleges. The aim of such training is to train high-class technicians for the green and high-tech industries (Rowley and Yoo 2013).

A challenge for South Korea's human resource development is 'to make the successful transition from conventional trainers to performance specialists' (Cho et al. 1999, p. 98). Hence, it is challenging for enterprises to develop both effective and efficient training programs (Cho et al. 1999). The criticism has also been made that training provided by enterprises is overly theoretical, rather than practical or technical. The training courses are not well designed so in fact they failed to improve employees' skills (Kim and Rowley 2001). In addition, the role of universities and community colleges is becoming increasingly important, due to that the role of vocational education while training at secondary educational level has been reduced (Rowley and Yoo 2013).

Promotion is considered to be an important reward for employees from the company (e.g. Kerr and Slocum 1987). The traditional Korean culture is characterized by authoritarianism, high power distance, and being achievement orientated. Therefore, in such a culture, promotion has been essential to measure one's power, success, and self-actualization. In most South Korean firms, promotion criteria broadly include seniority, job-related skills, work performance, and personality traits. In particular, seniority has been the most critical criterion. However, the relative importance of the promotion criteria varies depending on level of positions. Specifically, seniority is the most important factor in lower-level promotions, while seniority becomes less important in higher-level promotions. At the executive or higher level, past performance and work attitudes are as important as seniority. In most cases, promotion to executive level requires complete loyalty and dedication to work along with a proven track record. Other important promotion criteria also include educational achievements and job-related qualifications, such as graduate degrees, special awards and certificates, technical licenses, foreign language proficiency, and attending an 'in-house Master of Business Administration (MBA)' program; all these will certainly help in a positive evaluation for promotion. Personality traits such as attitudes, harmony, cooperation, and loyalty are highly valued. Although a variety of criteria are considered, promotion decisions especially at the directorate level tend to favor education in prestigious universities. Graduates from prestigious universities hold a high proportion of chief executive positions in large South Korean companies (Chung et al. 1997).

A promotion ladder exists in South Korean firms, which means people have to work for a certain length of time at a rank before being promoted. In most large firms, fresh graduates need to work 4–5 years to be eligible for promotion to the next level, such as 'Assistant Section Manager'; another 3–5 years are needed before being considered for promotion to 'Deputy Department Manager'; and another 4–7 years to be eligible for promotion to 'Department Manager'. Generally speaking, it will take 12–17 years to reach the department manager level. The average age of a department manager in most South Korean firms is 44 (Chung et al. 1997).

In recent years, promotion practices have changed in many South Korean firms. Companies now put less emphasis on seniority, and employees with proven track records are being promoted even before they would have been eligible for promotion under the old system. Large *chaebols*, like Samsung and LG, have all begun to promote exceptional middle managers to the executive level regardless of age and length of their service. They have also been extending performance-based promotion to middle management levels. The number of young executives has increased as greater emphasis is being placed on performance rather than on seniority (Chung et al. 1997).

Training and Development in China

In China, the major forms of workforce training are vocational education and enterprise training. In most cases, vocational education is carried out after high school (Cooke 2005). The main student cohorts for vocational education include self-funded individuals before employment and trainees sent by enterprises. Institutions provide qualifications ranging from vocational certificates to university degrees. Vocational education is normally provided by vocational schools and technical colleges, and they can be classified into three categories. The first category is schools providing training in a variety of subjects like nursing, nursery teaching, and banking and accounting. These schools are normally controlled by regional education bureaus. The second category mainly focuses on providing technical training, and these schools are normally established by large SOEs. The third category specializes in skills in light manufacturing and service industries. These schools are originated from some secondary schools which aim to provide occupational skills to students who are not eligible for universities (Cooke 2005).

Under the heavily centralized and planned economy, vocational training in China was controlled by the government. Since the mid-1980s to early 1990s, however, vocational education has undergone substantial reforms and changes. The government has given some freedom to training institutions and technical colleges, and consequently, the number of training schools has been growing ever since. However, the number of vocational training schools has fallen considerably since the late 1990s due to the difficulty in recruiting students and reduced educational funding. It is also advocated that enterprises, non-profit organizations, and the government should participate to improve Chinese vocational educational training (Li et al. 2011).

Enterprise training has changed significantly in the past six decades. Under the planned economy, enterprise training for blue-collar workers was a form of compulsory apprenticeship upon gaining employment. The training programs focused on working skills. Only cadres who were regarded as potential leaders in SOEs had the opportunity to be sent for training in Chinese Communist Party schools (Shen and Darby 2006). The training for cadres was not compulsory; however, it was an important opportunity to develop networks. The training contents emphasized political ideology, and normally, enterprises covered the training costs (Shen 2007).

Since the economic reforms began, apprenticeship has been replaced by on-the-job training; however, it is seldom provided in enterprises due to the lack of resources and commitment to employee development (Cooke 2005). On-the-job training is mainly used for giving briefings to new employees (Shen 2007). Employee training has become the top priority since the early 1980s. Enterprise training seems more comprehensive because it covers many areas not limited to technical skills (Li et al. 2011). The provision of training has been at the full discretion of enterprises in China since the 1990s (Wang et al. 2007). However, the provision of enterprise training is still inadequate in terms of quality and quantity (Cooke 2005). The limited training is only used to remedy skill deficiencies rather than to develop skills (Li et al. 2011). In the mid-1990s, a number of regulations on employee training were introduced, for example, the Education Law (1995), the Enterprise Employee Training Regulations (1996), and the Enterprise Management Training Plan (1996). Employees have to undertake positional training and obtain vocational competency certificate(s) in order to be employed (Cooke 2005).

The implementation of training varied in different types of enterprise ownership. Large FIEs and SOEs tend to provide structured and systematic training. In contrast, smaller enterprises (e.g. POEs) are less likely to establish their own training systems. They are more likely to use external, private training providers (Jaussaud and Liu 2011). In order to comply with legislative requirements and solve the skill shortage problem, SOEs have actively taken skill training initiatives (Cooke 2011; Nguyen et al. 2011). Most Chinese enterprises provide in-house training aiming to develop employees' skills. Attending conferences facilitated by academics is a major form of training in SOEs (Jaussaud and Liu 2011). Many SOEs also provide continuous training to shop-floor workers to improve their work skills. Normally, one-month skill training is provided to workers every year. The purpose to provide such training is to 'standardize their performance, raise their quality of service and market awareness and develop their potential' (Cooke 2005, p. 47). For example, Lenovo has done well in providing training to different levels of employees. New employees are provided 'new-hire training' to understand company culture and history. Internal courses are also provided through 'professional training' conducted by senior managers. Pre-management training is provided for outstanding employees who have the potential to be promoted. Senior managers are also provided various training, such as post-management training, on-the-job MBA training, and mini-MBA training programs run by outside education institutions (Yeung et al. 2011).

Small POEs also provide some induction training to new employees. Training normally focuses on company policies, tasks and responsibilities, and work-related information (Cooke 2005). In MNEs and JVs, employee training is the key to human resource strategy, and training provision is more formal and systematic (Cooke 2005). For example, in JVs, employee training focuses on basic operational and technical skills and management concepts; training is very extensive if the company is in the technology industry. Some JVs even send employees overseas to attend corporate training programs. Nevertheless, there are some problems concerning training provided in JVs. When providing English-language training to employees, Western training techniques such as discussions and role plays are not effective due to employees' language deficiency and the influence of the traditional Chinese education lecturing style. Also, instructors are not sure about whether participants are satisfied about the training because there is a distinct lack of training feedback after the session (Björkman and Lu 2000). In FIEs, both internal and external training are provided to employees. Internal training consists of in-house training, on-the-job training, classroom training, and short-term assignments abroad (Braun and Warner 2002; Li et al. 2011). External training includes specialized courses run by universities and training institutions, such as leadership development courses and support for individual career development (Hartmann et al. 2010).

Management training in enterprises includes in-house training, mentoring and coaching, regional training centers, local outsourced training programs, and overseas training (Wang and Wang 2006). Some large FIEs actively develop their own managers by setting up corporate universities or sending them to overseas secondments, job rotations, and development programs (Qiao and Wang 2009). According to Warner and Goodall (2009), the Chinese government has been actively seeking to improve management education and training over the last few decades. Nowadays, MBA and executive MBA (EMBA) programs are very popular in terms of workplace training. Joint and international EMBA programs play a role in promoting business education and training in China. At the same time, executive development programs are also booming in some prestigious universities (Li et al. 2011).

Although most enterprises have recognized the importance of training and have actively made some changes in their current training schemes, there are some problems in the current training system. Firstly, the training program is often conducted without considering strategic planning, costs of training, and training needs. Enterprise training is considered to be more of a separate procedure or requirement, rather than addressing the training needs of the employees and the organization. Secondly, training contents are often not well designed and relevant to employee needs. Subsequently employees often feel bored and not motivated to attend training. They are less motivated to learn because training is compulsory and only used for considering promotion and pay increases (Cooke 2005).

The promotion system has been changed due to a series of institutional transformations in China. In 1982, the government implemented the retirement system which forced older managers to retire so that enough vacancies for managerial positions could be retained. In addition, the market economy stimulated competition in the HRM system. In large SOEs, the appointment of senior executives is still under state control (Zhao and Zhou 2004). Non-SOEs are more likely to retain workplace talent through internal promotion (Gong and Chang 2008). For instance, in Lenovo, the promotion for middle-level managers and top executives is conducted by the HR department and senior management. They evaluate the candidate's potential and performance together to ensure the promotion procedure is fair and transparent (Yeung et al. 2011). In JVs, general managers have the power to promote the most capable employees; however, conflicts may occur. For example, the candidates who are competent and recommended by senior expatriates may be seen as 'aggressive' by locals (Björkman and Lu 2000). Managerial capabilities and skills are important for promotion in both SOEs and FIEs (Akhtar et al. 2008). Nevertheless, political loyalty, positive attitude to work, diligence, moral standards, and '*guanxi*' (i.e. personal relationships) are still considered critical in determining promotion in SOEs (Tsai and Wang 2013). In SOEs, management training and qualifications also become a prerequisite for promotion (Cooke 2005).

Existing Literature on International Training and Development of South Korean MNEs

Four studies, namely, Taylor et al. (2001), Gamble (2000), Lansbury et al. (2006), and Zou and Lansbury (2009), have examined training and development policies and practices in South Korean MNEs. Taylor et al. (2001) found that South Korean companies provide three categories of training to HCNs: on-the-job training, secondment to overseas partner companies, and training offered and implemented by local governments. For example, line managers from a shoe manufacturing company attend regular training sessions on practical and technical subjects in relation to quality control in production and HRM (once a month). A rubber company sent 20 employees every year to South Korea from 1998 to 2000. A telecommunications company held an exchange program with an American partner, besides a training operation in South Korea. Generally, promotion from workers to lower-level managers is based on three criteria: education, seniority, and performance. Increasingly, performance and achievement have become the most important criteria (Taylor et al. 2001).

Gamble (2000) discussed language training provided to South Korean expatriates in China. South Korean MNEs put great emphasis on language training for expatriates. South Korean expatriates are generally assigned to China for four or five years and most of them are urged to learn Chinese. The potential expatriates are provided with opportunities to study the Chinese language in South Korea either on a full-time (two or three months) or part-time basis (two hours per day for about six months), or are sent to Beijing for one-year language training. Lansbury et al. (2006) reported that the Hyundai Motor Company provided training for HCNs and the training programs focus on loyalty, motivation, and team spirit. Promotion procedures are slow except for employees who performed outstandingly and they will be granted rapid promotion.

Zou and Lansbury (2009) examined HCNs' training in BHMC. The training programs in BHMC for new production workers consisted of a two-day orientation and two weeks of on-the-job training supervised by senior workers. There was a notable difference in training for production workers and white-collar workers in terms of content and duration. University graduates were offered off-the-job orientation in the first two months with an emphasis on developing interpersonal relationships and teamwork skills. The on-the-job training was provided for four months so workers would understand overall production operations. Those white-collar employees who were the top performers received the opportunity for six- to eight-week training at headquarters in South Korea every year. In addition, there were also some job-specific development programs for executives and managers, shop-floor supervisors, and clerical staff.

It is clear that most international training and development studies focus mainly on expatriates' pre-departure training in Western MNEs. A number of important issues have not been adequately studied, especially in non-Western MNEs. Specifically, the extant South Korean-specific literature mainly concentrates on HCNs' training, while other important international training and development issues including expatriates' pre-departure and post-arrival training, and management development of expatriates and HCNs, are under-researched. Consequently, there is a significant research gap in the international training and management development literature, and hence, further research into the topic is urgently required.

International Training for Expatriates

International training for expatriates includes pre-departure and post-arrival training. The main purpose of pre-departure training is to enhance expatriates' ability to work and live in a new environment (Wang and Tran 2012). Expatriates' pre-departure training programs may be wide ranging, including, for example, cross-cultural training (CCT), language training, skill training, and leadership training (Wang and Tran 2012). While different programs have different emphases, CCT is designed to enhance the individual expatriate's awareness of cultural differences and sensitivity in dealing with cultural issues (Wang and Tran 2012). It is argued that CCT is the most important pre-departure training because it can assist expatriates in reducing culture shock (i.e. a state of distress experienced by an individual who is suddenly exposed to a foreign social and cultural environment), appreciating different cultures, and adapting better to new environments (Harris and Kumra 2000; Morris and Robie 2002). Kim and Slocum (2008) discovered a positive relationship between host-country language fluency and expatriate work performance. Pre-departure training can be provided using a range of methods, such as self-initiated training, briefing, lecture, interview with expatriates or repatriates, simulation, and field experience (Dowling et al. 2013). CCT rigor is defined as the degree of a trainee's cognitive involvement in training (Black et al. 1992; Shen and Darby 2006). As shown in Table 4.1, training rigor is determined by training programs, methods, and durations as these factors influence the degree of a trainee's cognitive involvement

Table 4.1 A model of training rigor

Length of stay	*Length of training*	*Cross-cultural training approach*	*Level of training rigor*
1 month or less	Less than a week	Information-giving approach (e.g. area briefings; films, books, and videos; survival-level language training)	Low
2–12 months	1–4 weeks	Affective approach (e.g. role play, critical incidents, stress reduction training, moderate language training)	Moderate
1–3 years	At least 1–2 months	Immersion approach (e.g. field experiences, simulations, sensitivity training, extensive language training)	High

in training (Black et al. 1992). It is argued that the more rigorous the training is, the more efficient the expatriate's adjustment and work performance will be (Littrell and Salas 2005).

In general, European and US MNEs recognize the benefits of expatriates' training and pay great attention to pre-departure training and provide a variety of programs including look-see visits and shadowing for expatriates (Mitrev and Culpepper 2012). US MNEs generally emphasize pre-departure training, especially CCT, which lasts for 1–2 years in some businesses (Eschbach et al. 2001; Yamazaki and Kayes 2007). The Brookfield Global Relocation Report (2015) shows that only 19% of participating MNEs do not offer any training to expatriates, and 44% of the MNEs offer training to the entire families. At least 36% of Scandinavian MNEs provide job-related training to their expatriates (Björkman and Gertsen 1993). Vance and Paik (2002) argued that on-site training through long-term planning of expatriate assignments can be an important way to increase expatriate competence. In most European MNEs, cultural awareness training remains the most common form of pre-departure training for expatriates.

Nevertheless, other forms of preparation such as look-see visits, shadowing, and briefings are implemented more often than formal training programs due to cost efficiency (Mitrev and Culpepper 2012). Despite the importance of pre-departure training to expatriates, many Australian MNEs (Clegg and Gray 2002; Hutchings 2005; Mehegan 2003; Shen and Lang 2009), Chinese MNEs (Shen and Darby 2006), New Zealand MNEs (Seak and Enderwick 2008), and Taiwanese MNEs (Lin and Wei 2005) only provide limited training. Australian MNEs tend to provide in-country lecture-style CCT, which is normally regarded as a low or median level of rigor training (Shen and Lang 2009). Chinese MNEs tend to provide limited or ad hoc pre-departure training for expatriates (Shen and Darby 2006). New Zealand MNEs provide very little pre-departure training to expatriates as they tend to select expatriates who have previous expatriate experience and have spent significant time in China (Seak and Enderwick 2008). Taiwanese MNEs provide limited pre-departure training to expatriates due to resource constraints (Huang 2002). Taiwanese MNEs pay more attention to expatriate safety and life adjustment training in the mainland operations because culture is not a major issue with expatriates who have the same language and cultural background (Chu 2003; Lee 2004b; Wu et al. 2000). The most common reasons for MNEs not providing enough pre-departure training include lack of time, no warranted budget expenditures for training, no need for training because technical skills are most important for international assignments, lack of training experts and expertise, and the right people do not need to be trained (Baumgarten 1995; Shen 2005; Shen and Lang 2009; Tung 1982; Welch 1994).

Post-arrival training for expatriates is conducted after expatriates have started working in overseas subsidiaries to minimize the problems associated with cultural adjustment (Wang and Tran 2012). Although many MNEs believe that post-arrival training is ineffective and costly, empirical research shows it is not the case: sometimes it is more effective than pre-departure training (Mendenhall et al. 2002; Selmer et al. 1998). Post-arrival training is critical to expatriate adjustment due to the fact that expatriates may have trouble applying pre-departure training to their unpredicted expatriate experience (Gudykunst 2004). Some Australian MNEs believe that overseas subsidiaries have more responsibilities to provide local cultural training to expatriates (Santoso and Loosemore 2013). Post-arrival training provides essential social support and on-site mentoring while expatriates are adjusting (Mendenhall and Wiley 1994). Post-arrival personal coaching is very helpful for expatriates in overcoming problems during their adjustment (Selmer 2002). Different from pre-departure training, post-arrival training gives expatriates an opportunity to evaluate any emerging stressors and problems (Sanchez et al. 2000). It also enables expatriates to combine explicit knowledge and information from their prior knowledge with real experience (Mendenhall et al. 2002; Selmer et al. 1998).

Nevertheless, empirical research reveals that most MNEs provide very limited post-arrival training to expatriates (Wood 2011). Australian MNEs provide very limited relocation assistance and language training in China (Hutchings 2003). US and European MNEs seldom provide post-arrival or follow-up training to the expatriates (El Mansour and Wood 2010). According to Shen and Darby (2006), Chinese MNEs do not have a corporate-level policy concerning post-arrival training for expatriates. Instead, they leave it to managers in subsidiaries to decide if there is a need to provide such training. Normally, systematic post-arrival training is not provided in Chinese MNEs. They mainly provide ad hoc post-arrival training focusing on work safety and government or industry product regulations. It should be noted that the extant international training literature had largely neglected the expatriates' post-arrival training issue (Wood 2011).

All sample South Korean MNEs except for Advertising A and Finance A provided CCT, leadership training, and language training to expatriates prior to departure, although expatriates were chosen mainly from people who had learned Chinese. The longevity of the training programs varied from one to two months depending on the training intensity. On average, the training duration was 2–3 hours per week, which the interviewees regarded generally regarded as too short. In the words of Operation Manager in Telecom D:

> I have received a very short notice for my posting in China-only one month before the expatriation. My language training was only for a few days. Although previously I learned some Chinese, I felt I needed more language training before I took on the Chinese assignment. Some other expatriates said the same thing to me.

CCT was often combined with leadership training. For example, a focus on leadership training at Chemical A, Electronics A, and Electronics B aimed to build trust in the Chinese culture. Marketing Manager at Electronics A commented, 'Through the training, I learned how to be trusted by Chinese subordinates.' Training methods included online learning, workshops, discussions with repatriates, simulation, and on-site visits. Marketing Manager at Chemical A commented, 'We invite repatriates to conduct CCT training so that they can reflect some of their experience.' HR Manager at Chemical A mentioned that the company had online training materials so that expatriates can learn in their own time after they had attended the workshops.

Electronics A, Electronics B, and Auto A arranged one week or so pre-visits for expatriates before departure. General Manager in Electronics B commented that the purpose of a pre-visit is for expatriates to look at their new working and living environments so that they will not be surprised when they have been relocated. No case company provided any pre-departure training to expatriates' family members. Typically, Operation Manager at Telecom C commented, 'Spouses normally do not work in the same company. It is understandable to me that my company would not think it necessary to include my wife in pre-departure training.'

Advertising A and Finance A had briefings on international assignments, but did not provide other formal pre-departure training to expatriates. According to the Marketing Manager at Advertising A and Operation

Manager at Finance A, their companies recruited expatriates from people who could speak Chinese or had lived in China previously. These two interviewees are South Korean expatriates, fluent in Chinese and had lived in China for many years before they joined these companies. Hence, these two companies believed that their expatriates did not have serious cultural and language issues to overcome and, consequently, CCT and language training were not necessary.

Five firms—Telecom A, Telecom D, Chemical A, Electronics A, and Auto A—continued to provide language training to expatriates or provided financial support to those who took language courses after they had arrived in China. Typically, HR Manager at Telecom D commented, 'In my company, financial assistance is always available if someone (expatriate) wants to study the local language.' The duration of language training organized by the sample MNEs was generally 2–3 hours per week, lasting from one month to one year. Electronics A and Auto A also allowed expatriates' families to attend language training. Marketing Manager at Auto A remarked, 'My wife and kids have enjoyed the Chinese language training and have found the training useful for improving their communication skills.' No further CCT was provided except for orientation provided to newly arrived expatriates. Expatriates were often sent back to headquarters for technical training and professional training. For example, Marketing Manager at Electronics A usually went back to South Korea twice a year for professional training. Expatriates who worked in the research and development departments were sent back more often to South Korea for training.

HCN/TCN Training

It is suggested that CCT and language training should be provided to HCNs and TCNs in order for them to be more effective in interacting with expatriates and implementing MNEs' business strategies (Caligiuri 2000; Paik and Sohn 2004; Suutari et al. 2002). The HCN/TCN workforce is important to the success of expatriate assignments. Firstly, HCN/TCN training could enhance HCNs/TCNs' understandings of the expatriates' messages as well as their communication styles. Secondly, HCNs and TCNs may improve their abilities in coping with uncertainty in deal with expatriates through effective training (Vance and Ring 1994).

Vance and Paik (2005) suggested that HCNs and TCNs should be provided with more individually tailored training programs. For example, senior HCN/TCN managers should know the parent company's culture, business strategy, and technical systems. Hence, training programs for senior HCN and TCN managers should cover these issues. For operation-level employees, four major categories of training should be provided: new employee orientation, entry job skills, parent company's predominant language, and cross-cultural awareness. However, research shows that MNEs usually do not provide adequate training to HCNs and TCNs. For example, in Swedish MNEs, training programs are provided to expatriates, yet training to HCNs and TCNs is not provided to the same extent (Eriksson and Kobin 2007). Japanese and South Korean MNEs tend not to provide parent company's language training to HCNs and TCNs (Kang et al. 2015). Lansbury et al. (2006) reported that the training programs provided by South Korean MNEs for HCNs in Canada and India mainly focus on loyalty, motivation, and team spirit, rather than improving skills and ability for career and management development. Zou and Lansbury (2009) reported that the training programs provided by Hyundai Motor Company to Chinese employees are mainly about production operational procedures and how to improve team work. Hartmann et al. (2010) found that Western MNEs sometimes provide temporary overseas training to talented HCNs in China before they are assigned to managerial positions. A lack of training for HCNs and TCNs, as argued by Feely and Harzing (2003), affects the absorptive capacity of HCNs and TCNs and knowledge flow between expatriates and HCNs and TCNs. Relatively speaking, HCN/TCN training has received less research attention. As such, how HCN/TCN training is provided by MNEs remains not entirely clear and consequently requires further studies.

Overall, in the case companies, there is not much training provided to HCNs and TCNs. Most interviewees agreed that the purpose of HCN/TCN training is to improve HCNs' and TCNs' skills (especially production workers) and to reward their good performance. Generally, for office workers, companies provided three- to five-day orientation before they started working. The senior management would organize the training for new employees. The orientation mainly focused on company history, the organizational culture, business operations, and people. According to the General Manager in Telecom B:

> We do not provide much training to the local employees. Especially for office workers, we assume they have enough professional knowledge and abilities to complete their tasks. We select employees strictly to ensure they have such abilities to handle the jobs. There is no need to provide them with more trainings relating to their jobs.

Electronics A, Electronics B, and Auto A provided HCNs and TCNs with work skills and safety training, normally two-week on-site training for new workers, in the production sections. During these two weeks, workers would learn about the major policies and rules of the factory, the specific tasks they needed to complete online and become familiar with the overall work environment. Line managers and experienced workers led the training during these two weeks. On-the-job technical training was provided every month. On-the-job training aimed to improve productivity and techniques of production. The line manager and technicians from headquarters conducted on-the-job training.

Telecom A, Telecom B, Chemical A, Electronics A, and Electronics B provided training to selected HCN/TCN middle-level managers and high performers at the South Korean headquarters. Such training combined headquarters visits, technical and cultural training, and sightseeing, and, according to General Manager at Telecom A, had two purposes. One was to provide an opportunity for HCN managers to update their technical knowledge and learn about organizational cultures and management. The other was to reward those who achieved outstanding performance in their work.

International Management Development

International management development that involves promotion of both expatriates and HCNs is critical for both MNEs and individual employees. It may directly relate to company growth and even to a company's ultimate survival in a very competitive marketplace. As for individuals, it provides directions to their careers and enables them to accomplish their personal goals (Selmer 1999). International management development is a key to attracting, retaining, and developing top international managers (Shen and Darby 2006). The perception of the lack of management advancement opportunities is a major reason for high expatriate turnover (Dowling and Welch 2004). The retention of repatriates is important in that it enables them to transfer their acquired knowledge and skills from international assignments to organizations (Mezias and Scandura 2005). In addition, Feldman and Thomas (1992) found that organizational career development is vital for expatriates' success. For example, a career development plan should be provided to assignees to increase the probability that expatriates will advance more quickly when they return to their home country. Hence, MNEs should provide a well-developed, systematic repatriation system and career planning in such a way that they are committed to individual management development (Bolino 2007; Dowling and Welch 2004).

Many MNEs, typically those of China (e.g. Shen and Darby 2006) and the US (e.g. Tung 1998), do not have formal international management development schemes for expatriates. According to Tung (1998), 60% of American expatriates are not guaranteed a position in their company's headquarters after expatriation, and only one third of expatriates are promised a position at the same organizational level before their expatriation. UK MNEs have a short-term focus and pay less attention to training and development (Lane 1998). Many European MNEs, however, provide written guarantees that their positions will still be there when they return (Scullion and Brewster 2002). Most Finnish MNEs guarantee at least similar-level positions for repatriates, and some of them agree to provide specific jobs on repatriation before the international assignment (Suutari and Brewster 2001). US MNEs do not have long-term career planning before expatriation and do not guarantee future positions upon return (Bossard and Peterson 2005).

It is suggested that HCNs and TCNs should be included in the global leadership program (Debrah and Rees 2011). Otherwise, there will be difficulties in attracting non-parent national talent (Shen and Darby 2006). There are some advantages for promoting HCNs and TCNs in managerial roles. For example, it will enhance the morale of HCNs and TCNs and overcome language and cultural differences easily with other local colleagues (Wong and Law 1999). However, trust is important when MNEs grant authorities to their non-expatriate managers. Without trust, the localization progress may be disrupted (Harvey et al. 1999; Herrmann and Werbel 2007). It is suggested that talented HCN/TCN managers should not only be appointed in subsidiaries in host countries but also transferred to headquarters (i.e. inpatriation) (Shen 2005). Research shows that US MNEs offer HCNs and TCNs opportunities to advance their leadership careers at the regional as well as global level (Vo 2009). Japanese MNEs, however, tend to be more ethnocentric by not promoting HCNs and TCNs to senior management positions (Vo 2009). This is due to the fact that Japanese MNEs are heavily focused on an expatriate-based system and, consequently, HCNs and TCNs experience limited promotion opportunities (Legewie 2002). Research also shows that German MNEs are more likely to promote HCN and TCN subordinates if clear exchange of benefits are made with their supervisors or they have support mechanisms throughout the organization to achieve their objectives (Herrmann and Werbel 2007).

Only Chemical A, Electronics A, and Electronics B formulated career plans for expatriates, although these plans were regarded as vague due to a lack of commitment to management development. Marketing Manager at Advertising A (which had not instituted an expatriate career plan) commented:

> In Korea, an employee's career ladder is normally relatively fixed. It takes several years (normally four years) for a person to be promoted to a higher position. Although international experience and work performance are important there are many factors, such as qualifications, relationship with senior managers, and seniority. So, it is unrealistic to set a career plan for an expatriate. A lack of career planning has resulted in high turnover among expatriates and repatriates.

Operating Manager of Telecom C said:

> Some of my colleagues left the company upon repatriation, and some left the company while they were in China to start their own businesses here. Since my future position is uncertain, I am open to all options including seeking a job in another company.

All interviewees reported that HCNs and TCNs were included in management development schemes, but these were confined to Chinese subsidiaries. HCNs' and TCNs' promotion mainly depended on their qualifications, experience, and job performance. However, because there were limited senior managerial positions, promotion among HCNs and TCNs was rare and difficult to achieve. Promotion was even harder in Electronics A, Finance A, and Advertising A, which adopted an ethnocentric approach to staffing. These MNEs appointed expatriates to fill most senior managerial positions. A lack of opportunities for promotion was a major reason for high-caliber HCNs and TCNs leaving South Korean MNEs. A statement often expressed was as follows: 'It becomes common for HCN/TCN employees to leave after working for two years due to a lack of development chances.'

Factors Influencing International Training and Development Policies and Practices of South Korean MNEs in China

Expatriates' pre-departure training was provided by the headquarters and mainly included CCT, leadership training, and language training. Expatriates' post-arrival training is mainly focused on language training. The results showed that South Korean MNEs provided limited pre-departure and post-arrival training for two reasons. First, there are cultural and institutional similarities between South Korean and China, which made CCT less important. In addition, the sample South Korean MNEs preferred to recruit expatriates who either had previously lived in China or had some degree of knowledge in the Chinese language and culture, which made their adaptation much easier.

The results also showed that the sample South Korean MNEs tended to adopt an integrated approach to managing HCNs' training and development. The orientation program provided for HCNs (both office and production workers) emphasized educating or instilling company culture and company history so that local employees remained loyal to the company and believed 'we belong to one family'. This finding is consistent with relative strength theory, which posits that when the home economy is stronger than the host economy, MNEs tend to adopt the home-based approach. On the other hand, the training duration and methods for production workers tend to be localized. This finding is also consistent with the national cultural view, which suggests that cultural (including institutional) differences between home and host countries do result in the adoption of the host-based approach.

Discussion

Our study reveals that the South Korean MNEs provide extensive pre-departure language training, but only little CCT and leadership training to expatriates. Overall, the rigor of pre-departure training measured by programs, methods, and duration is generally low. More specifically, while no formal pre-departure training is provided in Advertising A and Finance A, training durations are generally of a brief nature in the other sample MNEs. Workshops and lectures, widely deemed to be low-rigor training in the international training literature, are the major training methods used by the sample MNEs. Only three companies, specifically Electronics A, Electronics B, and Auto A, provide pre-visits to the host country. Leadership training tends to be combined with CCT and is only provided by the abovementioned three MNEs. This finding lends some support to Gamble (2000), Lansbury et al. (2006), and Taylor et al. (2001), who reached a similar conclusion, in that MNEs only offer limited, low-rigor pre-departure training. Our study shows that the inadequacy of pre-departure CCT and leadership training is due to managerial perceptions of low training needs because expatriates were chosen from candidates who had already worked or lived in the host country, and pre-departure training being of little use. This finding is consistent with the literature (i.e. Gamble 2000) arguing that MNEs in general pay more attention to choosing the right expatriates than to pre-departure training. Furthermore, studies such as Feely and Harzing (2003) and Gamble (2000) reported that MNEs tend to provide expatriates with language training. Consistent with this literature, our research reveals that the majority of the sample South Korean MNEs put a strong emphasis on language training both prior to departure at home and post arrival in the host country.

The sample South Korean MNEs do not provide expatriates with post-arrival CCT, but with regular language, technical, and professional training. While post-arrival language training takes place in the host country, expatriates are sent back to their headquarters for technical and professional training. Given that published research on post-arrival training is scarce, our study adds to the knowledge base of the international training literature. The case study South Korean MNEs pay significant attention to on-the-job skills and safety training for HCN production workers in order for them to work effectively and safely. However, little of such training is provided to non-production workers because of its perceived irrelevance. No CCT or language training is provided to HCNs and TCNs either. Some high-performance HCN/TCN managers and employees are chosen to be sent to headquarters for training on organizational systems and cultures. As such, training is normally focused on sightseeing and networking with managers at headquarters; it is regarded as a kind of reward for good performance, not employee career development. Our research therefore does not support past studies, such as Lansbury et al. (2006), Taylor et al. (2001), and Zou and Lansbury (2009), arguing that South Korean MNEs provide considerable training to HCNs in foreign operations.

The sample South Korean MNEs have not developed formal career development plans for expatriates. Although international experience is one criterion for promotion in South Korea, other factors such as qualifications, seniority, and relationships with leaders are more important in promotion (Taylor et al. 2001). A lack of management development opportunities is significantly associated with high turnover among Korean expatriates and repatriates. While HCNs are included in management development schemes, managerial positions available to them are restricted in the host country, and chances for promotion are rare. Ineffective international management development has a negative impact on employee organizational commitment and significantly increases turnover and intention to leave among high-caliber HCNs in the sample MNEs. Reviewing the literature, our findings concerning international management development are consistent with the study by Lansbury et al. (2006), who report that, firstly, promotion opportunities provided to HCNs are rare; and secondly, procedures are normally slow and long within the sample MNEs. In comparison, in our study, the sample South Korean MNEs' international management development practices are similar to those of Chinese and US MNEs (Shen and Darby 2006; Tung 1998). That is, they lack formal schemes for expatriate management development, and HCNs are rarely promoted to senior managerial positions. In contrast to this scenario, Kim and Slocum's (2008) study reveals that US-based Korean expatriates have great opportunities for career development and promotion. This finding appears not to be supported by our study.

This research provides some insights into the importance of pre-departure training. It suggests that the case study MNEs provide inadequate, low-rigor pre-departure CCT for expatriates, and this finding is consistent with the existing literature (e.g. Shen and Darby 2006). However, the pre-departure CCT is critical and should not be ignored. Therefore, we suggest it is necessary to re-examine the practices and relative impact of such training to expatriates' adjustment and MNEs' performance overall. Moreover, our study helps to better understand the link between expatriation and management development. There is a lack of expatriates' career development planning in the sample MNEs, which is not consistent with the previous literature (i.e. Kim and Slocum 2008). This finding could be Korea specific and needs to be further investigated in future studies.

Conclusion

International training and management development is an under-researched topic in the IHRM literature. This chapter aims to contribute to the literature by exploring the international training and management development policies and practices that are implemented by South Korean MNEs in their Chinese subsidiaries. It first reviews the literature on training and development practices in both South Korea and China. It then discusses what past studies have contributed on the topic of how South Korean MNEs manage training and development in their overseas subsidiaries. It is suggested that the existing literature is very limited on the topic. Next, the chapter reviews the literature regarding the definitions and purposes of international training and development, international training programs, rigor and provisions in MNEs, the reasons for not providing adequate cross-cultural training, and international development practices. Subsequently, the chapter reports the empirical findings on how South Korean MNEs manage international training and development in their Chinese subsidiaries. Finally, the study's theoretical contributions are discussed. The next chapter will turn to the issue of international performance appraisal practices.

Bibliography

Akhtar, S., Ding, D. Z., & Ge, L. (2008). Strategic HRM practices and their impact on company performance in Chinese enterprises. *Human Resource Management, 47*(1), 15–32.

Baumgarten, K. E. E. (1995). Training and development of international staff. In A. W. K. Harzing & J. van Ruysseveldt (Eds.), *International human resource management* (pp. 205–228). London: Sage.

Björkman, I., & Gertsen, M. (1993). Selecting and training Scandinavian expatriates: Determinants of corporate practice. *Scandinavian Journal of Management, 9*(2), 145–164.

Björkman, I., & Lu, Y. (2000). Local or global? Human resource management in international joint ventures in China. In M. Warner (Ed.), *Changing workplace relations in the Chinese economy* (pp. 117–138). London: Palgrave Macmillan.

Black, J. S., Gregersen, H. B., & Mendenhall, M. E. (1992). Toward a theoretical framework of repatriation adjustment. *Journal of International Business Studies, 23*, 737–760.

Bolino, M. C. (2007). Expatriate assignments and intra-organizational career success: Implications for individuals and organizations. *Journal of International Business Studies, 38*(5), 819–835.

Bossard, A. B., & Peterson, R. B. (2005). The repatriate experience as seen by American expatriates. *Journal of World Business, 40*(1), 9–28.

Braun, W., & Warner, M. (2002). Strategic human resource management in western multinationals in China. *Personnel Review, 31*(5), 553–579.

Brookfield. (2015). Retrieved March 15, 2015, from http://globalmobilitytrends.brookfieldgrs.com/assets/downloads/Full-Report-Brookfield-GRS-2015-Global-Mobility-Trends-Survey.pdf

Caligiuri, P. M. (2000). Selecting expatriates for personality characteristics: A moderating effect of personality on the relationship between host national contact and cross-cultural adjustment. *Management International Review, 40*(1), 61–80.

Chang, C. S., & Chang, N. J. (1994). *The Korean management system: Cultural, political, economic Foundations*. Westport: Quorum.

Cho, Y. J., Park, H. Y., & Wagner, S. (1999). Training in a changing Korea. *Training & Development, 53*(5), 98–100.

Chu, C. M. (2003). *The study on related expatriate cross-cultural training and expatriate success: The example of Taiwanese enterprises in China*. National Science Council Project Research Planning Report. National Science Council in Chinese.

Chung, K. H., Lee, H. C., & Jung, K. H. (1997). *Korea management: Global strategy and cultural transformation*. Berlin/New York: Walter de Gruyter.

Clegg, B., & Gray, S. J. (2002). Australian expatriates in Thailand: Some insights for expatriate management policies. *International Journal of Human Resource Management, 13*, 598–623.

Cooke, F. L. (2011). The role of the state and emergent actors in the development of human resource management in China. *The International Journal of Human Resource Management, 22*(18), 3830–3848.

Debrah, Y. A., & Rees, C. J. (2011). The development of global leaders and expatriates. In A. W. Harzing & A. H. Pinnington (Eds.), *International human resource management* (3rd ed., pp. 377–414). London: Sage.

Dowling, P. J., & Welch, D. E. (2004). *International human resource management. Managing people in a multinational context*. London: Thomson.

Dowling, P. J., Festing, M., & Engle, A. D. (2013). *International human resource management*. London: Cengage Learning.

El Mansour, B., & Wood, E. (2010). Cross-cultural training of European and American managers in Morocco. *Journal of European Industrial Training, 34*(4), 381–392.

Eriksson, S., & Kobin, U. (2007). *International human resource training in Swedish MNCs*. Master's thesis, Department of Business Administration and Social Sciences, University of Technology, LuLea.

Eschbach, D. M., Parker, G. E., & Stoeberl, P. E. (2001). American repatriate employees' retrospective assessments of the effects of cross-cultural training on their adaptation to international assignments. *International Journal of Human Resource Management, 12*, 270–287.

Feely, A. J., & Harzing, A. W. (2003). Language management in multinational companies. *Cross Cultural Management: An International Journal, 10*, 37–52.
Feldman, D. C., & Thomas, D. C. (1992). Career management issues facing expatriates. *Journal of International Business Studies, 23*(2), 271–293.
Gamble, J. (2000). Localizing management in foreign-invested enterprises in China: Practical, cultural and strategic perspectives. *International Journal of Human Resource Management, 11*, 883–903.
Gong, Y., & Chang, S. (2008). Institutional antecedents and performance consequences of employment security and career advancement practices: Evidence from the People's Republic of China. *Human Resource Management, 47*(1), 33–48.
Gudykunst, W. B. (2004). *Bridging differences: Effective intergroup communication*. Thousand Oaks: Sage.
Harris, H., & Kumra, S. (2000). International manager development—Cross-cultural training in highly diverse environments. *Journal of Management Development, 19*, 602–614.
Hartmann, E., Feisel, E., & Schober, H. (2010). Talent management of western MNCs in China: Balancing global integration and local responsiveness. *Journal of World Business, 45*, 169–178.
Harvey, M., Speier, C., & Novicevic, M. M. (1999). The role of inpatriation in global staffing. *International Journal of Human Resource Management, 10*, 459–476.
Herrmann, P., & Werbel, J. (2007). Promotability of host country nationals: A cross cultural study. *British Journal of Management, 18*, 281–293.
Huang, S. C. (2002). *The overseas adaptation of Taiwanese expatriates working at Taiwanese subsidiary companies in Malaysia*. Nantou: National Chi Nan University.
Hutchings, K. (2003). Cross-cultural preparation of Australian expatriates in organisations in China: The need for greater attention to training. *Asia Pacific Journal of Management, 20*(3), 375–396.
Hutchings, K. (2005). Koalas in the land of the pandas: Reviewing Australian expatriates' China preparation. *International Journal of Human Resource Management, 16*, 553–566.
Jaussaud, J., & Liu, X. (2011). When in China… The HRM practices of Chinese and foreign-owned enterprises during a global crisis. *Asia Pacific Business Review, 17*(4), 473–491.
Kang, H. Y., Shen, J., & Xu, G. (2015). International training and management development policies and practices of South Korean MNEs in China. *Thunderbird International Business Review, 57*(3), 229–240.
Kearney, R. P. (1991). *The warrior worker: The history and challenge of South Korea's economic miracle*. New York: Henry Holt & Co..
Kerr, J. L., & Slocum, J. W. (1987). Managing corporate cultures through reward systems. *Academy of Management Executive, 1*(2), 3–15.

Kim, J. W., & Rowley, C. (2001). Managerial problems in Korea-Evidence from the nationalized industries. *International Journal of Public Sector Management, 14*(2), 129–149.

Kim, K. H., & Slocum, J. W. (2008). Individual differences and expatriate assignment effectiveness: The case of US-based Korean expatriates. *Journal of World Business, 43*(1), 109–126.

Kim, M., Chai, D. S., Kim, S., & Park, S. (2015). New employee orientation: Cases of Korean corporations. *Human Resource Development International, 18*(5), 481–498.

Korean Air. (2014). *Who we are*. Retrieved April 13, 2016, from https://www.koreanair.com/global/zh_cn/about/who-we-are2.html

Lane, C. (1998). European companies between globalization and localization: A comparison of internationalization strategies of British and German MNCs. *Economy and Society, 27*(4), 462–485.

Lansbury, D. R., Kwon, S. H., & Suh, C. S. (2006). Globalization and employment relations in the Korean auto industry: The case of the Hyundai Motor Company in Korea, Canada and India. *Asia Pacific Business Review, 12*(2), 131–147.

Lee, T. Z. (2004b). *A study on related factors expatriate human resource management affecting cross-cultural adjustment and organizational involvement*. National Science Council Project Research Planning Report. Taiwan: National Science Council.

Lee, K. W. (2005). *Training by small and medium scale enterprises in the knowledge economy: A case study of Korea*. Seoul: Ewha Womans Univerisity Press.

Legewie, J. (2002). Control and co-ordination of Japanese subsidiaries in China: Problems of an expatriate-based management system. *International Journal of Human Resource Management, 13*, 901–919.

Li, Y. Q., Sheldon, P., & Sun, J. M. (2011). Education, training and skills China's changing workplace. In P. Sheldon, S. H. Kim, Y. Q. Li, & M. Warner (Eds.), *China's changing workplace* (pp. 111–128). Oxon: Routledge.

Lin, S. Y. (2009). *Experiences and reflections on industrial needs orientation of vocational technical high school education in the Republic of Korea (South Korea) in linking vocational training with the enterprises—Asian perspectives*. Retrieved March 12, 2016, from http://www.unevoc.unesco.org/up/Link_Voc_End.pdf

Lin, C. Y. Y., & Wei, Y. C. (2005). An Eastern and SME version of expatriate management: An empirical study of small and medium enterprises in Taiwan. *International Journal of Human Resource Management, 16*, 1431–1453.

Littrell, L. N., & Salas, E. (2005). A review of cross-cultural training: Best practices, guidelines, and research needs. *Human Resource Development Review, 4*, 305–334.

McPherson, A. H., & Roche, W. K. (1997). Peripheral location equals localized labour? Multinationals and the internationalization of training and development in Ireland. *International Journal of Human Resource Management, 8*, 369–384.

Mehegan, P. (2003). *Cross-cultural awareness training in Australian organizations*. IDP Australian International Education Conference, Melbourne.

Mendenhall, M. E., & Wiley, C. (1994). Strangers in a strange land: The relationship between expatriate adjustment and impression management. *American Behavioral Scientist, 37*(5), 605–620.

Mendenhall, M., Kuhlmann, T. M., Stahl, G. K., & Osland, J. S. (2002). *Employee development and expatriate assignments*. London: Blackwell.

Mezias, J. M., & Scandura, T. A. (2005). A needs-driven approach to expatriate adjustment and career development: A multiple mentoring perspective. *Journal of International Business Studies, 36*, 519–538.

Mitrev, S., & Culpepper, R. (2012). Expatriation in Europe: Factor and insights. *Journal of International Management Studies, 7*, 158–167.

Morris, M., & Robie, C. (2002). A meta-analysis of the effects of cross cultural training on expatriate performance and adjustment. *International Journal of Training and Development, 5*, 112–125.

Nguyen, T. N., Truong, Q., & Buyens, D. (2011). Training and firm performance in economies in transition: A comparison between Vietnam and China. *Asia Pacific Business Review, 17*(1), 103–119.

Paik, Y. S., & Sohn, J. D. (2004). Expatriate managers and MNC's ability to control international subsidiaries: The case of Japanese MNCs. *Journal of World Business, 39*, 61–71.

POSCO. (2008). *Home*. Retrieved April 12, 2016, from http://www.poscoenc.com.cn/

Qiao, J. S., & Wang, W. (2009). Managerial competencies for middle managers: Some empirical findings from China. *Journal of European Industrial Training, 33*(1), 69–81.

Rowley, C., & Yoo, K. S. (2013). Workforce development in South Korea: A driving force in the korean miracle'. In J. Benson, H. Gospel, & Y. Zhu (Eds.), *Workforce development and skill formation in China* (pp. 67–88). Routledge: London.

Sanchez, J. I., Spector, P. E., & Cooper, C. L. (2000). Adapting to a boundaryless world: A developmental expatriate model. *Academy of Management Executive, 14*, 96–106.

Santoso, J., & Loosemore, M. (2013). Expatriate management in Australian multinational enterprises. *Construction Management and Economics, 31*(11), 1098–1109.

Scullion, H., & Brewster, C. (2002). The management of expatriates: Messages from Europe. *Journal of World Business, 36*, 346–365.

Seak, N., & Enderwick, P. (2008). The management of New Zealand expatriates in China. *International Journal of Human Resource Management, 19*, 1298–1313.

Selmer, J. (1999). Career issues and international adjustment of business expatriates. *Career Development International, 4*(2), 77–87.

Selmer, J. (2002). To train or not to train? European expatriate managers in China. *International Journal of Cross Cultural Management, 2*(1), 37–51.

Selmer, J., Torbiorn, I., & de Leon, C. T. (1998). Sequential cross-cultural training for expatriate business managers: Pre-departure and post-arrival. *International Journal of Human Resource Management, 9*, 831–840.

Shen, J. (2005). International training and management development: Theory and reality. *Journal of Management Development, 24*, 656–666.

Shen, J. (2007). *Labour disputes and their resolution in China*. Oxford, UK: Chandos Publishing.

Shen, J., & Darby, R. (2006). Training and management development in Chinese multinational enterprises. *Employee Relations, 28*(4), 342–362.

Shen, J., & Lang, B. (2009). Cross-cultural training and its impact on expatriate performance in Australian MNEs. *Human Resource Development International, 12*(4), 371–386.

Suutari, V., & Brewster, C. (2001). Making their own way: International experience through self-initiated foreign assignments. *Journal of World Business, 35*, 417–436.

Suutari, V., Raharjo, K., & Riikkilä, T. (2002). The challenge of cross-cultural leadership interaction: Finnish expatriates in Indonesia. *Career Development International, 7*, 415–429.

Taylor, R., Cho, D. Y., & Hyun, J. H. (2001). Korean companies in China: Strategies in the localisation of management. In C. Rowley, T. W. Sohn, & J. Bae (Eds.), *Managing Korean business: Organisation, culture, human resources and change* (pp. 161–181). London: Frank Cass.

Tsai, C. J., & Wang, W. L. (2013). Exploring the factors associated with employees' perceived appraisal accuracy: A study of Chinese state-owned enterprises. *The International Journal of Human Resource Management, 24*(11), 2197–2220.

Tung, R. L. (1982). Selection and training procedures of US, European, and Japanese multinationals. *California Management Review, 25*, 57–71.

Tung, R. L. (1998). A contingency framework of selection and training of expatriates revisited. *Human Resource Management Review, 8*(1), 23–37.

Vance, C. M., & Paik, Y. S. (2002). One size fits all in expatriate pre-departure training? Comparing the host country voices of Mexican, Indonesian and US workers. *Journal of Management Development, 21*(7), 557–571.

Vance, C. M., & Paik, Y. S. (2005). Forms of host-country national learning for enhanced MNC absorptive capacity. *Journal of Managerial Psychology, 20*, 590–606.

Vance, C. M., & Ring, P. S. (1994). Preparing the host country workforce for expatriate managers: The neglected other side of the coin. *Human Resource Development Quarterly, 5*(4), 337–352.

Vo, A. N. (2009). Career development for host country nationals: A case of American and Japanese multinational companies in Vietnam. *The International Journal of Human Resource Management, 20*(6), 1402–1420.

Wang, Y. L., & Tran, E. (2012). Effects of cross-cultural and language training on expatriates' adjustment and job performance in Vietnam. *Asia Pacific Journal of Human Resources, 50*, 327–350.

Wang, J., & Wang, G. G. (2006). Exploring national human resource development: A case of China management development in a transitional context. *Human Resource Development Review, 5*(2), 176–201.

Wang, X., Bruning, N. S., & Peng, S. (2007). Western high-performance HR practices in China: A comparison among public-owned, private and foreign-invested enterprises. *The International Journal of Human Resource Management, 18*(4), 684–701.

Warner, M., & Goodall, K. (2009). *Management training and development in China: Educating managers in a globalized economy*. Abingdon/New York: Routledge.

Welch, D. (1994). Determinants of international human resource management approaches and activities: A suggested framework. *Journal of Management Studies, 31*(2), 139–164.

Wong, C. S., & Law, K. S. (1999). Managing localization of human resources in the PRC: A practical model. *Journal of World Business, 34*(1), 26–40.

Wood, E. D. (2011). *Post-arrival performance interventions that assist expatriates' adjustment and performance*. PhD thesis, The College of Graduate and Professional Studies, Indiana State University, Terre Haute.

Wu, W. Y., Chen, C. P., & Gan, P. S. (2000). An empirical research on the effectiveness of cross-cultural training for expatriate managers. *NTU Management Review, 10*(2), 167–203.

Yamazaki, Y., & Kayes, D. C. (2007). Expatriate learning: Exploring how Japanese managers adapt in the United States. *International Journal of Human Resource Management, 18*, 1373–1395.

Yeung, A., Xin, K., Pfoertsch, W., & Liu, S. (2011). *The globalization of Chinese companies: Strategies for conquering international markets*. Singapore: Wiley.

Zhao, W., & Zhou, X. G. (2004). Chinese organizations in transition: Changing promotion patterns in the reform source. *Organization Science, 15*(2), 186–199.

Zou, M., & Lansbury, R. D. (2009). Multinational corporations and employment relations in the People's Republic of China: The case of Beijing Hyundai Motor Company. *International Journal of Human Resource Management, 20*(11), 2349–2369.

CHAPTER 5

International Performance Appraisal Policies and Practices

Introduction

International performance management is 'a strategic human resource management process that enables the MNE to evaluate and continuously improve individual, subsidiary unit and corporate performance against clearly defined, preset objectives that are directly linked to international strategy' (Dowling et al. 1999, p. 123, also see Festing et al. 2012; Vo and Stanton 2011). It is an important measure for MNEs to control the behaviors of expatriates as well as HCNs to ensure that foreign subsidiaries perform in appropriate ways, that is, in the interests of the corporation as a whole (Dowling et al. 2013). International performance appraisal influences promotion, compensation, and reward; consequently, it will influence employees' work attitudes and behaviors as well as performance of MNEs (e.g. Festing et al. 2012; Logger and Vinke 1995). This chapter examines performance appraisal practices in South Korea and China, and international performance appraisal policies and practices of South Korean MNEs in China. The major international performance appraisal practices investigated in this chapter include performance appraisal procedures and methods, performance appraisal criteria, performance appraisal feedback, and international performance appraisal approaches.

H. Kang, J. Shen, *International Human Resource Management in South Korean Multinational Enterprises*,
DOI 10.1007/978-981-10-3093-2_5

Performance Appraisal Practices in South Korea and China

Performance Appraisal in South Korea

Traditionally, South Korean companies adopt the seniority-based performance evaluation system, and the purpose of such a system is solely for promotion (Park and Yu 2000). This system has been criticized as being not effective because the seniority-based system adds significant burdens to labor costs when tenure or seniority increases (Rowley and Bae 2004). Due to both internal and external pressures, South Korean companies shifted their management orientation to a more performance-based HRM system, especially the performance appraisal system (Rowley and Yang 2009).

South Korean companies use various evaluation methods, such as self-evaluation, supervisor evaluation, peer evaluation, and subordinate evaluation. Self-evaluation is a common method, and it affects training and career development. Assessment by superiors is the dominant form of performance appraisal in South Korean domestic firms (Yang and Rowley 2008). Employees are asked to rate their peers and superiors on criteria such as initiative, communication skills, and leadership skills. Another recent development in performance appraisal is the adoption of the Behaviorally Anchored Rating Scales (BARS), which is a method that identifies a set of behaviors considered critical to job performance and develops rating scales for such behaviors. The BARS is developed to avoid subjective judgment of the rater (Chung et al. 1997). Nevertheless, the 360-degree approach, which involves supervisors, subordinates, peers, team members, and customers, is not popularly used in the private sector in South Korea. For example, it is only used to evaluate managers' performance in LG (Jhun et al. 2012).

In general, the performance appraisal is conducted annually or biannually. For example, LG adopts a single standardized process to evaluate employee performance annually to evaluate the achievement of goals, difficulty of goals, and competitiveness (LG 2016). Management by objective (MBO) is widely implemented by South Korean firms. According to the statistics, 49% of companies adopted this evaluation system in 2000 (Park and Yu 2000). The main appraisal criteria in South Korean firms include quality of work, ability, interpersonal skills, leadership skills, work attitudes (Kim 2001), and personality (Tan and Torrington 1998). For example, SK Telecom considers factors like mid- to long-term performance, contributions to the organization, and challenges and innovations (SK 2013). Feedback is often provided, whereas managers still tend to feel uncomfortable when criticizing subordinates' performance in face-to-face performance appraisal meetings. Managers may feel that teamwork and harmonious relationships with subordinates could be damaged if they identify their problems and criticize staff based on their performance (Rowley and Yang 2009).

In the public sector, the South Korean government has adopted various performance management approaches, such as Performance Agreement System (i.e. a process of strategic planning, setting objectives, mid-year review, reward, and feedback) and Balanced Scorecard System (i.e. a system that includes vision, mission, strategic goals, and four key performance indicators—customer, finance, internal process, and learning and growth). In 2007, the Electronic-Integrated Public Service Evaluation system (i.e. a system that ensures performance evaluations are efficient and accurate) and the E-HRM system (i.e. internet-supported way of performing HR policies and/or activities) have been established to ensure the performance evaluation procedure is transparent. Different from the private sector, the 360-degree system has been widely adopted in the public sector to appraise civil servants' performance since 2000. For Grade 5–9 civil servants, performance appraisals are conducted biannually, and the two major appraisal criteria are firstly, job performance (e.g. completeness, job difficulties) and secondly, job-fulfilling abilities (e.g. communication, customer orientation) (Kong et al. 2013).

One of the problems concerning performance management is that South Korean companies put less emphasis on the rater's ability to conduct fair and accurate performance appraisals. In most cases, managers are assumed to have the ability to appraise employees' performance accurately. In addition, only a few companies (e.g. Hana Financial Group 2013) provided training to raters to improve evaluation accuracy and fairness (Rowley and Yang 2009). Performance evaluation often tends to be subjective and biased because of managers' unwillingness to damage harmonious relationships in the workplace (Kim and Rowley 2001). Raters tend to rate leniently so that a positive culture or harmonious relationships can be maintained (Rowley and Yang 2009). Consequently, the lenient or ineffective performance appraisal fails to differentiate employees' performance and managers only consider performance appraisal as a procedure (Chung et al. 1997).

Performance Appraisal in China

The performance appraisal system was virtually non-existent during the decades of the Chinese planned economy (Warner 1995). Individual performance appraisal was rarely conducted, and in fact, performance appraisal was not linked to individual and organizational performance. Rather, the organization typically provided individuals' performance reports for promotion or transfer purposes. The major performance appraisal criteria for cadres included party loyalty, seniority, and the ability to maintain harmonious relationships with colleagues. Peer appraisals were mainly conducted to appraise performance and in the form of group discussions; hence, the appraisal results were largely based on the relationship with peers and supervisors (Shen 2007).

Since the 1980s, performance appraisal has been rigorously adopted by enterprises regardless of ownership to determine promotion and pay (Cooke 2012; Qiao et al. 2009). Performance appraisal procedures mainly include self-assessment, peer group discussion, and the superior's final comments (Shen 2008). Management by objective, which sets a series of factors such as quality of products and working hours, at the beginning of a certain period, has become very popular in Chinese enterprises. Manufacturing industries normally set goals more frequently than other industries (Shen 2007). SOEs assess both qualitative (e.g. work attitudes) and quantitative (e.g. productivity, outcome) performance appraisal criteria. In particular, quantitative criteria like quality and quantity of products are critical for production workers. Performance appraisals for workers are evaluated by direct supervisors, who would then send a copy of assessment results to the line manager for recording purposes (Zhu and Dowling 2000). Meanwhile, POEs tend to emphasize less on the 'qualitative' criteria such as party loyalty and work attitudes (Shen 2007). The common performance appraisal procedure starts from self-evaluation, and then peer group discussion, and finally, the supervisor's appraisal report (Zhu and Dowling 1998). Performance appraisal is normally held biannually or annually in enterprises (Poon et al. 2010), but sometimes, it is also conducted monthly to determine monthly bonus (Zhu and Dowling 2000). In SOEs, performance appraisal results remain confidential because managers are not willing to pass any negative comments to subordinates so that the harmonious relationship could be maintained. They usually provide limited feedback, especially negative feedback, to employees (for the sake of 'saving face' and not affecting one's bonus) (Chen and Eldridge

2010; Shen 2008). This kind of performance appraisal has been criticized as lacking transparency, fairness, and openness (Shen 2007).

In POEs, performance appraisals are used to determine pay and promotion. Appraisals are often conducted between individuals and their direct supervisors. Instead of peer appraisals, the direct supervisor usually conducts a performance appraisal meeting with the subordinate. However, effective and meaningful feedback is seldom provided to employees. In small- and medium-sized POEs, the production unit-based appraisal system is utilized for production workers. For managers and office workers, appraisals are conducted by comparing the work plan and level of work completion. Performance appraisal criteria are different for production and non-production workers. Specifically, quality and quantity of products and working hours are critical to production workers, while task completion and customers' complaints (including internal customers, i.e. workers) are important criteria for non-production workers (Shen 2007). In JVs, individuals' attitudes toward the Communist Party and interpersonal relations are not used as performance appraisal criteria. There is instead a strong focus on quantitative criteria when evaluating employee performance. Supervisors conduct formal discussions with their subordinates annually. Appraisers are normally trained and experienced in giving feedback to save employees' face and maintain interpersonal harmony (Björkman and Lu 2000).

In the public sector, civil servants' performance appraisals are normally conducted annually (Cooke 2005). The appraisal procedure includes self-evaluation and supervisor review (Ye and Ni 2013). The Key Performance Indicator approach is adopted for evaluating individual tasks, which include virtue (*de*), ability (*neng*), diligence (*qin*), achievement (*ji*), and freedom from corruption (*lian*). Qualitative questionnaires are used to evaluate virtue and freedom from corruption, while quantitative measures are designed to measure the remaining indicators. For example, ability, diligence, and achievement are given values of 20%, 30%, and 50% out of a total score of 100. Diligence is measured by checking the individual's attendance record; ability is measured on employees' performance and attendance at training to assess the professional skills being developed (Ye and Ni 2013).

There are significant problems in Chinese workplace performance management systems. For example, many companies are unable to align performance indicators with their strategic objectives (Chen 2011). Employees' feedback is normally not sought and performance appraisal results are not used to identify performance areas for improvement. As such, employees consider performance appraisals as merely an organizational procedure (Shen 2004). Secondly, *guanxi* plays an important role in performance appraisals. Raters often give biased ratings when they evaluate their favored subordinates. In addition, there is also a lack of communication between managers and employees, thereby causing misunderstandings of appraisees' performance (Chow 1995). Employees do not actively ask for help from their superiors, and on the other hand, superiors do not show support in terms of making improvement to their subordinates (Chen 2011). Furthermore, the appraisers normally do not have adequate and proper skills to evaluate employees' performance. Most companies do not provide systematic training to the managers, and companies do not pay enough attention to performance appraisal results in order to improve their job performance (Chen 2011). It is suggested that to address the abovementioned problems, Chinese enterprises should develop clear formal policies and procedures for performance appraisals. Supervisors should be provided with more training on how to fairly evaluate employee performance and provide feedback to employees, especially for those workers who are not performing well. Finally, an effective audit system needs to be established to prevent management bias (Solutions Consultant 2014).

International Performance Appraisal of South Korean MNEs

Interestingly enough, while the focus of the general international performance appraisal literature has been put on expatriates' performance appraisals (e.g. Gregersen et al. 1996; Woods 2003), past research on international performance appraisal of South Korean MNEs mainly investigated performance appraisal practices of HCNs (Taylor et al. 2001; Lansbury et al. 2006; Zou and Lansbury 2009). Taylor et al. (2001) revealed that performance appraisals of HCNs in South Korean MNEs are conducted by line managers and HR officers in subsidiaries. Appraisal criteria mainly include work attitudes, work behavior, work results, and work hours. The appraisal results are translated into 'points' which determine employees' level of pay. Similarly, Lansbury et al. (2006) also examined performance appraisal criteria for HCNs. According to the authors, discipline, cooperation, punctuality, and attendance are the important appraisal criteria. Zou and Lansbury (2009) reported that BHMC changed from a seniority-based to a more performance-based appraisal system in the late 2000s. In addition to objective performance appraisal criteria, BHMC considers work ethic and the ability to minimize mistakes at work to be important. However, a number of important issues such as international performance appraisal approaches and expatriates' performance appraisals, including performance appraisal criteria, appraisal procedure, frequency of appraisals, and provision of feedback, have been largely unexplored.

The Importance of International Performance Appraisal

International performance appraisal is critical to MNEs for a number of reasons. First, effective international performance appraisal ensures a subsidiary to implement the corporate strategy effectively (Sparrow et al. 1994). Secondly, effective international performance appraisal ensures international managers do their job in an appropriate way. It is in fact an essential tool for controlling expatriates' behavior and international operations in general. Thirdly, international performance appraisal affects employees' career development, promotion, and compensation (Logger and Vinke 1995). Fourthly, international performance appraisal influences employees' job satisfaction motivation and work in-role and extra-role behavior and thus, the MNE's performance (Shen 2005a). Research in the US indicates that organizations with strong performance management systems are 51% more likely to outperform their competitors on financial measures (Bernthal et al. 2003).

International performance appraisal is also viewed as one of the most difficult management practices to implement (Chiang and Birtch 2010; Fletcher and Perry 2002; Huo and Von Glinow 1995; Suutari and Tahvanainen 2002). When conducting performance appraisals in a different country, factors such as language barriers, different values, and different cultures all come into play. These factors all help to make international performance appraisal more complex (Appelbaum et al. 2011; Brewster 1988). Managers at headquarters often do not know exactly what their employees accomplish in their company's subsidiaries due to the geographical distance (Shen 2004). Appelbaum et al. (2011) and Brewster (1988) argued that complexity in the system has resulted from the lack of knowledge of what is the correct way to assess the performance of employees. The problem lies in different norms and policies, legal systems, and economic environments between home and host countries.

International Performance Appraisal Practices

To be effective in international performance appraisals, MNEs should use appropriate raters, performance appraisal criteria, and appraisal frequency to ensure performance appraisals are effective (Shay and Baack 2006). Accurate performance appraisal depends largely on whether raters are knowledgeable of appraisees' performance (Blau 1999; Gabris and Ihrke 2001; Martin and Bartol 2003). Particularly, in the expatriate setting, the extent of this knowledge is often affected by the rater's location, that is, whether he or she is in the home or host country. Ideally, the 360-degree (multi-rater) appraisal method which involves multiple raters could ensure an accurate and fair appraisal outcome (Appelbaum et al. 2011). However, the 360-degree appraisal method has also been criticized because it is based on observers' memory, which is often an incomplete appraisal of past performance. In addition, the observer may also be unable to evaluate performance objectively (Garavan et al. 1997).

Given the complexity in conducting international performance appraisals, it has been suggested that raters of expatriate performance appraisals include direct supervisors and peers in both the foreign subsidiaries and home country (Gregersen et al. 1996). Immediate supervisors are usually considered well qualified to evaluate overall performance due to their close observation of expatriates' work behavior (Cleveland et al. 1989; Harris and Schaubroeck 1988; Murphy and Cleveland 1991). For example, in American and Finnish MNEs, expatriates' immediate supervisors (either HCNs or senior expatriates) in foreign subsidiaries rate expatriates' performance (Gregersen et al. 1996; Suutari and Tahvanainen 2002). HCNs in general are appropriate expatriate performance appraisal raters due to the fact they are familiar with the soft criteria and contextual factors. Subsequently, they have greater knowledge concerning expatriates' performance (Briscoe and Claus 2008; Mendenhall and Oddou 1991). However, the drawback of using HCN managers as raters is that they evaluate expatriates' performance within their own cultural contexts and, thus, do not necessarily focus on issues important to the MNE as a whole (Briscoe and Claus 2008). As a result, it is important for MNEs to specify in advance the most important performance areas for the term of the assignment and indicate who will appraise each area (Logger and Vinke 1995).

It is suggested that allowing appraisees to challenge performance ratings is critical to fair appraisals. Hence, self-assessment is also important

(Furnham and Stringfield 1998). Self-assessment provides employees with an opportunity to: firstly, be more involved and committed to their personal goals (Jackson and Schuler 2003); and secondly, have a level of control over the strength and direction of their evaluations (Jawahar 2006). Most studies on self-evaluation indicate self-evaluation results in positive outcomes for employees. For example, Farh et al. (1991) stated that self-evaluations could improve the effectiveness of performance appraisal and result in more positive employees' satisfaction with the evaluation and their perceptions of justice and fairness.

Research shows formal international performance appraisals are normally conducted on an annual basis, for example, in the Chinese and Finnish MNEs (Shen 2004; Suutari and Tahvanainen 2002). Sometimes, organizations require appraisals be done more frequently (Martin and Bartol 2003). Frequent performance appraisals can result in employees having a greater understanding of their jobs, with subsequent improvement in job performance (Cascio 1998; Nathan et al. 1991). Infrequent appraisal may hinder the timeliness of corrective actions and delay continuous improvement initiatives (Chiang and Birtch 2010). Gregersen et al. (1996) reported that both biannual and annual expatriate performance appraisals are regarded as appropriate and relate positively to perceived expatriate performance appraisal accuracy.

All interviewees reported performance appraisal to be one of the most important HRM functions in their companies due to its role in employee compensation, promotion, and career development. All case companies were clearly serious about performance appraisals and had formulated formal appraisal policies in relation to procedures, methods, and criteria. Appraisal procedures and methods differed for expatriates and HCNs in the case companies. In all the companies studied, performance appraisals for expatriates were evaluated by managers in both subsidiaries and headquarters, regardless of appraisees' hierarchal positions. Expatriates who were junior managers reported to superiors in both local subsidiaries and headquarters. Raters included immediate supervisors in local subsidiaries and in headquarters, and departmental managers in headquarters. Generally, the procedures and methods of expatriate appraisals were as follows:

- Step 1. Expatriates conducted self-evaluation periodically (mostly monthly) and uploaded their reports to the company's online evaluation systems.

- Step 2. Direct supervisors (either HCN managers or senior expatriate managers) in local subsidiaries then provided comments on expatriates' performance. It should be noted that, although onsite managers' comments on performance of expatriates are extremely important in ensuring expatriates will be accurately and fairly evaluated (HR Manager in Electronics A), they did not usually have control over the final appraisal results.
- Step 3. Immediate supervisors in headquarters appraised expatriates' performance based on expatriates' self-evaluations and comments provided by supervisors in foreign subsidiaries, and their interviews with expatriates. During these interviews, immediate supervisors in headquarters and appraisees discussed and mutually agreed on final grades.
- Step 4. Subsequently, supervisors passed on their evaluation results to departmental managers for their final approval.

Although expatriates conducted self-evaluations and their immediate supervisors provided comments on expatriates' performance frequently, that is, normally monthly (in order to monitor expatriates' performance, a common interviewees' statement says), immediate supervisors and departmental managers in headquarters conducted formal performance appraisals for expatriates only biannually (Telecom B, Electronics A, and Electronics B) or annually (Chemical A, Telecom A, Advertising A, Telecom C, Auto A, Finance A, and Telecom D). Interviewees were also asked why performance appraisals for expatriates needed to be conducted at the headquarters rather than in Chinese subsidiaries. The following remark is a typical answer to this question:

> The headquarters is responsible for compensation, training, promotion, expatriation, and manager transfer for expatriates. It therefore needs to know how well expatriates perform in subsidiaries and how competent they are in their respective roles in order to make well-informed decisions about the abovementioned issues that will have a significant effect on expatriates. (Finance Manager, Electronics B)

Performance appraisals for HCNs were conducted in Chinese subsidiaries. Headquarters did not play any direct role in assessing HCNs' performance. Seven companies, specifically Telecom A, Chemical A, Telecom B, Telecom C, Electronics A, Electronics B, and Auto A, used multiple raters in appraising HCNs' performance. Raters included immediate supervisors, co-workers, peers, and departmental managers. A common reason for the use of multiple raters was: 'We use multiple raters to ensure we do not miss anything in employee performance so that we conduct appraisals fairly and accurately.' The performance appraisal procedures for HCNs in these seven firms included the following:

- Step 1. HCNs completed self-evaluation reports using standard forms and submitted their reports to immediate supervisors.
- Step 2. Once immediate supervisors received the reports, they sought comments from employees' co-workers and peers.
- Step 3. Next, immediate supervisors had meetings with employees to discuss their performance and to determine mutually agreed appraisal results, which were recorded using grade systems.
- Step 4. The appraisal results were then forwarded to departmental managers for their final approval. The approved results were then archived in the employees' personnel files, for use in determining compensation, employees' attendance at training, and possibilities of promotion.

In the remaining three South Korean MNEs, only immediate supervisors and departmental managers served as raters. The appraisal procedures in these three firms differed from those in the other seven MNEs in two important ways. Firstly, there was no consultation with peers or co-workers; and secondly, there were two rounds of interviews with supervisors, with one focusing on performance and the other on capability.

Overall, performance appraisals were conducted more frequently for HCN production workers than for office workers. There were also different frequencies for HCN office workers and for production workers across the case companies. For office workers in Chemical A, Advertising A, Telecom C, Electronics A Office, Electronics B Office, Auto A Office, Finance A, and Telecom B, performance appraisals were conducted annually, usually at the end of the year. For the other two firms, performance appraisals for office workers were conducted biannually. For production workers in Electronics A, Electronics B, and Auto A, performance appraisals were undertaken twice a year, at the end of June and December.

In Telecom A, Chemical A, Electronics A, Electronics B, and Auto A, employees' social performance was considered as one of the performance appraisal criteria. In addition, all interviewees agreed that the performance appraisals in their companies were just and fair. There was one comment: 'Based on my observations, both expatriates and HCNs are content with how their performance is appraised. I think the key contributors to such a high level of employee satisfaction are fairness and recognition' (HR Manager in Advertising A). Another common statement was, 'I feel that my company tries its best to make every appraisal fair and accurate. Using different criteria for office workers and for production workers, for example, improves appraisal accuracy' (HR Manager in Auto A).

Performance Appraisal Criteria

Clearly defined performance appraisal criteria help to increase accuracy in performance rating and create organizational climates of fairness and trust (Cleveland et al. 2007; Maley 2009; Tziner et al. 2001). Performance appraisal criteria include hard goals, soft goals, and contextual goals (Gregersen et al. 1996; Woods 2003). Hard goals are objective and quantifiable which measure performance such as production, return on investment, sales, and profits (Whitford and Coetsee 2007). Since it is necessary to recruit CSR-relevant staff, individuals' social performance should be assessed in their performance appraisals (Shen 2011). It has been suggested that using hard goals was associated with many problems because results-oriented measures only considered a small proportion of job performance (McGovern 1999; Muchinsky 2002).

Soft goals take into account factors that are difficult to quantify, such as work attitudes and behavior, leadership skills, interpersonal skills, and customer service quality (Janssens 1994). Assessing soft goals is important in the international setting because it is the key to expatriate success (Gregersen et al. 1996; Maley and Kramar 2007). However, the use of soft goals is also not without limitations. For example, the focus on effort and behavior instead of on outcomes encourages some employees to pretend to be busy and to cultivate their relationships with their superiors in order to obtain a promotion (Cooke 2008).

Contextual goals consider environmental factors that impact on employees' performance (Dowling et al. 2013; Gregersen et al. 1996). Environmental factors represent external factors, which may affect both hard and soft goals when the performance occurs. The use of comprehensive criteria improves the accuracy of expatriate performance appraisals (Gregersen et al. 1996). In Western economies, performance appraisals focus more on job competence, abilities, and achievements. Less emphasis is put on personality, attitudes, and interpersonal relationships (Siders et al. 2001). On the other hand, in the East, for example, China, interpersonal relationships are considered to be important in performance appraisal. Other main criteria include employee's political attitudes, competence, skill level, work attitude, and work performance (Cooke 2008; Shen 2004).

According to the interviewees, all case companies had formal and written performance appraisal criteria, broadly including work performance, work attitudes, and competence. The three major components underpinned key performance indicators (KPI) for evaluating both expatriates' and HCNs' work. All case companies adopted a grade system to classify employees' performance. As a General Manager in Telecom C explained:

> Once an employee's performance is assessed, a grade (A to E) will be assigned. A represents outstanding, B good, C satisfactory, D poor, and E unacceptable. Each grade was associated with a certain level of bonus, ranging from 5% to 10% of employees' compensation.

There were similarities in appraisal criteria for expatriates in all case companies. Headquarters set KPIs for expatriates at the beginning of each year. Work performance was linked to the standards of job task completion. Work attitudes emphasized loyalty to the company, teamwork, supervisor–subordinate relationship, and moral standards. Work competence focused on knowledge of work and skills and ability required to do particular jobs. The difficulty in assessing expatriates' relationships with HCNs was often mentioned in interviews. A typical response was given by Operation Manager (expatriate) in Telecom C:

> A good relationship with HCNs may not be an effective relationship. Managers in the headquarters often do not understand this difference. For example, if an expatriate strictly implements the company's disciplinary policies, this expatriate may not be popular among HCNs. For this reason, this expatriate's relationships with some HCNs may not sound good. Therefore, it is important to investigate the nature and causes of the problems rather than just giving the expatriate a poor appraisal if there is a relationship problem.

Consequently, 'The fulfillment of job responsibilities is regarded as the most important criterion for expatriates and it weighs at least 50% of the overall performance score in my company's grading system' (Operation

Manager in Telecom C). Party loyalty in China means all citizens are required to support the Communist Party (Bian et al. 2001). However, no South Korean MNEs included party loyalty in appraisal criteria when operating in Communist-ruled China.

Composition and weighting of subcomponents of appraisal criteria for HCNs were also similar across the case companies. For example, in Telecom A, 50% of assessment weight was given to employees' performance (task completion), 30% to competence (work ability and leadership), and 20% to work attitudes (e.g. cooperation and absenteeism). In Telecom B, completion of task accounted for 50%, work attitude 30% (effort 15% and team spirit 15%), and competence 20% (knowledge 10% and responsibility 10%). Peer (or co-worker) evaluation (also called horizontal evaluation) accounted for 10% of the overall score in Telecom A and supervisor evaluation (also called vertical evaluation) accounted for 90%. Similar weightings were implemented in other South Korean MNEs. Again, the work performance of office workers when compared to production workers was evaluated differently in all case companies. As the HR Manager in Electronics A stated: 'Production workers are assessed against product quantity and quality while office workers are assessed against general tasks.' Appraisal criteria for expatriates and HCNs are summarized in Table 5.1.

Performance Appraisal Feedback

Identifying employees' strengths and weaknesses, assessing training needs, and creating targeted skill supply strategies have become modern business imperatives (Chiang and Birtch 2010; Pfeffer 2005). Providing appropriate feedback to employees can communicate deficiencies in performance and guide training and development plans which aim to increase the skills and abilities of human capital (Cardy and Dobbins 1994; De Luque and Sommer 2000; Fenwick 2004; Milliman et al. 2000; Williams 2002). According to the main theories of work motivation, such as goal-setting theory (Locke and Latham 1990) and control theory (Carver and Scheier 1982), effective self-regulation toward goals consistently requires the types of performance feedback inherent in high-quality international performance appraisal. Research shows that providing feedback in international performance appraisal produces positive results as far as job satisfaction, work attitudes, and behaviors of international assignees are concerned (Jawahar 2006; Lindholm 1999).

Table 5.1 Performance appraisal criteria in sample MNEs

Company	*Work performance*	*Work attitude*	*Competence*	*Party/Company loyalty*
Telecom A	Task completion: Exp/HCN (+*)	Teamwork: Exp/HCN (+), attendance: Exp/HCN (+*), interpersonal relationship: HCN (+)	Knowledge: Exp (+); work skills/ability: Exp/HCN (+), language ability: HCN (−)	Company loyalty: Exp/HCN(+), Party loyalty: Exp/HCN (n/a)
Chemical A	Task completion: Exp/HCN (+*)	Relationship with HCNs: Exp (+), responsibility: Exp (−), HCN(+), teamwork: HCN (+), interpersonal relationship: HCN (+)	Knowledge: Exp/HCN (+), leadership/coaching skills: Exp (−), work ability: Exp/HCN (+)	Company loyalty: Exp/HCN(+), Party loyalty: Exp/HCN (n/a)
Telecom B	Task completion: Exp/HCN (+*)	Work effort: Exp/HCN (+), teamwork: Exp/HCN (−), moral standard: Exp (−), responsibility: Exp/HCN (+), attendance: HCN (+)	Knowledge: Exp/HCN (+), work ability: Exp/HCN (+), language ability: Exp/HCN (−)	Company loyalty: Exp/HCN(+), Party loyalty: Exp/HCN (n/a)
Advertising A	Task completion: Exp/HCN (+*)	Teamwork: Exp/HCN (+), compliance with company rules: Exp/HCN (+), interpersonal relationship: HCN (+), customer service: HCN (+)	Professional/work skills: Exp/HCN (+), creativity: Exp (+), HCN(−)	Company loyalty: Exp/HCN(+), Party loyalty: Exp/HCN (n/a)
Telecom C	Task completion: Exp/HCN (+*)	Supervisor–subordinate relationship: Exp (−), relationship with HCNs: Exp (+), teamwork: HCN (−), compliance with company rules: HCN (+), interpersonal relationship: HCN (+), attendance: HCN (+)	Professional/work skills: Exp/HCN (+), leadership: Exp (+), knowledge: HCN (+)	Company loyalty: Exp/HCN(+), Party loyalty: Exp/HCN (n/a)

(*continued*)

Table 5.1 (continued)

Company	*Work performance*	*Work attitude*	*Competence*	*Party/Company loyalty*
Electronics A	Task completion: Exp/HCN (+*), productivity: HCN (+)	Responsibility: Exp/HCN (+), teamwork: Exp/HCN (−), interpersonal relationship: HCN (+)	Professional/work skills: Exp/HCN (+), language ability: Exp (−), leadership: Exp (+), creativity: Exp/HCN (+)	Company loyalty: Exp/HCN(+), Party loyalty: Exp/HCN (n/a)
Electronics B	Task completion: Exp/HCN (+*), productivity: HCN (+)	Relationship with HCNs: Exp (+), supervisor–subordinate relationship: Exp/HCN (+), attendance: HCN (+), compliance with company rules: HCN (+), creativity: Exp/HCN (−)	Leadership: Exp (−); professional knowledge/skills: Exp/HCN (+)	Company loyalty: Exp/HCN(+), Party loyalty: Exp/HCN (n/a)
Auto A	Task completion: Exp/HCN (+*), productivity: HCN (+)	Teamwork: Exp/HCN (+), responsibility: Exp/HCN(+), attendance: HCN (+), interpersonal relationship: HCN (+)	Leadership: Exp (+), work skills/ability: Exp/HCN (+)	Company loyalty: Exp/HCN(+), Party loyalty: Exp/HCN (n/a)
Finance A	Task completion: Exp/HCN (+*), productivity: HCN (+)	Responsibility: Exp/HCN (+), compliance with company rules: Exp/HCN (−), interpersonal relationship: HCN (+), attendance: HCN (+), customer service: HCN (+)	Professional/work knowledge and skills: Exp/HCN (+), leadership: Exp (−); communication skills: Exp (−)	Company loyalty: Exp/HCN(+), Party loyalty: Exp/HCN (n/a)
Telecom D	Task completion: Exp/HCN (+*), productivity: HCN (+)	Responsibility: Exp/HCN (+), relationship with peers/supervisors: Exp/HCN (−), attendance: HCN (+)	Leadership: Exp (−); interpersonal skills: Exp (−), professional/work knowledge: Exp/HCN (+)	Company loyalty: Exp/HCN(+), Party loyalty: Exp/HCN (n/a)

Notes: Exp, expatriate; HCN, host country national; +*, very strong; +, strong; −, weak; and n/a, not applicable

Due to the long distance existing between supervisors and subordinates, providing frequent, timely, and accurate feedback can be problematic for international managers (Maley and Kramar 2007). Some scholars suggest that feedback should be provided by multi-evaluators who are knowledgeable about a given subordinate's performance and workplace environment (Suutari and Tahvanainen 2002). How and what feedback is given is strongly influenced by national cultures, traditions, and customs (Briscoe and Claus 2008; Cascio 2006). For example, in some Asian cultures, indirect feedback or feedback provided to employees via a mutually respected third party is often considered to be more appropriate than Western-style direct feedback (Stone 2008).

When face-to-face interviews were conducted, oral feedback was provided to appraisees (both expatriates and HCNs) during the interview process in every company. Written feedback was only provided to HCNs whose performance was classified as Grade E. A typical statement was:

> Employees who receive E grade normally request feedback. Direct supervisors are on the frontline to provide feedback that recognizes and congratulates achievement and identifies the improvement areas and training needs. Departmental managers provide feedback as well if there are requests from employees. Of course, underperformers also be given written warnings as well.

In addition to oral feedback, Telecom A, Chemical A, Telecom B, Telecom C, Electronics A, Electronics B, and Auto A provided written feedback online to expatriates regardless of performance standards. Some expatriates from Advertising A, Finance A, and Telecom D who had not been provided with written feedback expressed their dissatisfaction with this state of affairs. One statement that typified people's attitude to this issue was made by the Marketing Manager (expatriate) in Advertising A: 'I would rather receive negative feedback from my superior than be removed from the position without knowing what I have done wrong.'

International Performance Appraisal Approaches

While there is a consensus on the importance of international performance appraisals, agreement is lacking with reference to what the best international appraisal practices are (Appelbaum et al. 2011). According to Shen (2004), MNEs can implement three alternative approaches—standardized, localized, and integrative—for managing international performance appraisals. With the standardized approach, which is also known as the home-based approach, the MNE transfers the performance appraisal practices from the home company to its foreign subsidiaries (Shen 2004). This approach results from the country-of-origin effect, whereby the appraisal practices in foreign subsidiaries resemble those of the parent company. According to Schuler et al. (1993), there are two major reasons for MNEs transferring home appraisal practices abroad: firstly, MNEs might believe their home practices are superior to the practices of companies in host countries; and secondly, MNEs might be new to the international market or a particular host country and thus be inexperienced in localizing. This requires the home company to make significant changes to its management style in a host country.

The localized approach is also known as the adaptation approach, which specifically is the adaptation to local performance appraisal practices in response to the host nation's institutional influences. Using the integrative approach, the MNE integrates the home performance appraisal practices and those of the host as well as good appraisal practices implemented by other MNEs (Shen 2005b). This approach can potentially achieve local responsiveness, coordination, and internal consistency simultaneously. It is important for MNEs to take into account a range of contextual and firm-specific factors to achieve the best organization–environment fit in order to manage international performance appraisals (Dowling et al. 2013; Schuler et al. 1993; Shen 2005b). The best-fit IHRM practices for a MNE are not necessarily those copied from the well-known role models of the US, Japanese, and German enterprises (Smith and Meiksins 1995).

The major advantage in adopting the standardized approach is the equitability for expatriates assigned to different host countries. The main disadvantage of this approach is a lack of local responsiveness, which often results in resistance from HCNs. Conversely, for the localized approach, the main advantage is responsiveness to host environments, while the disadvantages are inequity between subsidiaries and the possible loss of control by headquarters. The integrative approach has the advantages of both standardized and localized approaches. It is, however, hard to operate (Shen 2005a).

To assist in analyzing the extent of localization or standardization (Table 5.2), a five-point Likert scale was developed, in which 1 represented completely localized, 2 mostly localized, 3 integration, 4 mostly standardized, and 5 completely standardized. Each component of the

Table 5.2 Extent of localization and standardization of the international performance appraisals of South Korean MNEs in China

	Procedures and methods		*Criteria*		*Feedback*		*Overall*		
	HCN	*Expat*	*HCN*	*Expat*	*HCN*	*Expat*	*HCN*	*Expat*	*Overall*
Telecom A	3	5	4	5	5	5	4	5	4.5
Chemical A	3	5	4	5	5	5	4	5	4.5
Telecom B	3	5	4	5	5	5	4	5	4.5
Advertising A	5	5	4	5	5	4	4.7	4.7	4.7
Telecom C	3	5	4	5	5	5	4	5	4.5
Electronics A	3	5	4	5	5	5	4	5	4.5
Electronics B	3	5	4	5	5	5	4	5	4.5
Auto A	3	5	4	5	5	5	4	5	4.5
Finance A	5	5	4	5	5	4	4.7	4.7	4.7
Telecom D	5	5	4	5	5	4	4.7	4.7	4.7

international performance appraisal practices was scored and overall those of South Korean MNEs are standardized.

According to the analysis above, the case study MNEs tended to standardize performance appraisal procedures and methods for expatriates. In seven out of ten case study South Korean MNEs, performance appraisals for HCNs integrated the localization and standardization approaches, but with a strong tendency toward standardization. The other three firms (Advertising A, Finance A, and Telecom D) standardized appraisals for HCNs. The results also showed that appraisal criteria in the MNEs were standardized for expatriate appraisals but integrative for HCN appraisals. In addition, South Korean MNEs were localizing in giving feedback.

When explaining why the MNEs standardized their appraisal practices, it becomes obvious that the relative economic strength between host and home economies determined whether they localized or standardized their performance appraisal practices. This is consistent with the 'relative strength theory' (Myloni 2002; Pudelko and Harzing 2007). The strength or otherwise of South Korea's economy played a certain role in determining the approaches to international performance appraisal adopted in MNEs. As Smith and Meiksins (1995) suggested, MNEs originating from advanced economies where the best management practices are supposed to exist are more likely to believe their home appraisal practices are superior to those of foreign local firms. These MNEs tend to transfer their home appraisal practices to foreign subsidiaries. Normally, HCNs in underdeveloped or developing countries are more likely to expect MNEs originating from advanced economies to manage people differently from local companies by bringing in the best practices. As shown in this study, HCNs were more satisfied when MNEs did so. It therefore can be reasoned from this that HCNs may be more likely to require MNEs originating from less-developed economies to localize, although this was not tested in this research.

Discussion

This chapter explored how performance appraisals for expatriates and HCNs are conducted and the approaches to international performance appraisal in South Korean MNEs operating in China. Our results show expatriates' performance was evaluated through self-evaluations and interviews with direct supervisors and relevant departmental managers in headquarters. Direct supervisors in the Chinese subsidiaries assisted in appraisals by providing comments on subordinating expatriates, but they did not determine appraisal results. Department (or co-worker group) discussions, which are commonly used for appraisals in Chinese companies, were not used in performance appraisals for expatriates in sample MNEs. Similar to the findings of the current study, Taylor et al. (2001) found that South Korean MNEs in India involved line managers (supervisors) and HR officers in appraisals. Clearly, the case study South Korean MNEs tended to adopt standardized (i.e. home-based) performance appraisal procedures and methods for expatriates.

Seven out of ten case companies evaluated HCNs' performance through self-evaluations, supervisors' consultations with peers and co-workers, and interviews with direct supervisors. While consultations with peers or co-workers represent a modified form of group discussion, conducting interviews with supervisors is not a conventional Chinese way of appraising performance. This indicates that performance appraisals for HCNs in these seven MNEs integrated the localization and ethnocentric approaches, but with a strong tendency toward the ethnocentric approach. This provides some support to Zou and Lansbury (2009), who reported Hyundai also gradually adopted an integrative approach for some of its HRM practices, for example, a combination of the seniority-based and performance-based appraisal systems, in its Beijing subsidiary. In the other three remaining firms (Advertising A, Finance A, and Telecom D), consultation with co-workers was not conducted, and self-evaluations and interviews with supervisors were the major appraisal methods. Therefore, appraisals for HCNs in these three firms were ethnocentric in character. This finding provides some support for the literature that Western MNEs (i.e. US, Canada) tend to adopt an ethnocentric approach to manage performance appraisal when operating overseas (Chen and Eldridge 2010; Gregersen et al. 1996; Vo and Stanton 2011). Similar to the case study MNEs, Chinese MNEs often adopt different performance appraisal approaches for different nationals and managerial levels (Shen 2004).

Work performance, work attitudes, and competence were the three major performance appraisal criteria for both expatriates and HCNs. Unlike local Chinese firms, South Korean MNEs did not consider party loyalty as an appraisal criterion. Local Chinese firms generally emphasize work attitudes and moral standards/work ethics. Differently, South Korean MNEs put more weight on work performance, while still taking into account work attitudes and moral standards/work ethics. South Korean MNEs also emphasized the importance of interpersonal relationships in HCNs' appraisals than in expatriates' appraisals. These results show that South Korean MNEs' appraisal criteria tended to be ethnocentric for expatriates' appraisals but integrative for HCNs' appraisals. These findings generally agree with the studies by Lansbury et al. (2006) and Taylor et al. (2001), which revealed South Korean MNEs' appraisal criteria include work performance, behavior, attitudes, teamwork, and attendance. Industry-wise, the firms in service sectors including Advertising A, Finance A, and four telecom firms put more weight on work attitudes, such as attendance and customer service.

In local Chinese firms or Chinese overseas MNEs, Chinese appraisers normally do not communicate feedback, especially negative feedback, to appraisees (Cooke 2008; Shen 2004). Different from their Chinese counterparts, South Korean MNEs provided feedback to all appraisees during face-to-face interviews, and provided additional written feedback to underperformers. The case study South Korean MNEs were therefore ethnocentric when they gave feedback. As shown in Table 5.2, overall, the international performance appraisal practices of the case study South Korean MNEs tended to be ethnocentric. These findings are consistent with the study by Zou and Lansbury (2009), which reported the Hyundai Motor Company tended to transfer its core HRM practices that are beyond appraisal practices from its headquarters to the Beijing joint venture in order to maintain control over employment relations.

This research contributes to the international performance appraisal literature in several ways. Firstly, the knowledge about how South Korean

MNEs manage performance appraisals in their overseas MNEs is rather limited. This study enriches the existing international performance appraisal literature. Secondly, there is very limited research exploring performance appraisal practices for both expatriates and HCNs. By examining performance appraisals of both expatriates and HCNs, this research adds to the knowledge base of international performance appraisal literature significantly. Thirdly, this research is one of the few to investigate the international performance appraisal approaches and underlying factors associated with the approach. In doing so, this research provides a better understanding of the factors that affect MNEs' decisions on international performance appraisal practices.

Conclusion

How MNEs conduct international performance appraisals and adopt appraisal approaches has to date received little research attention, despite the importance of performance appraisals having been widely recognized. This research provides important insights into how South Korean MNEs manage and what approaches they adopt to managing performance appraisals in their Chinese subsidiaries. It reveals that South Korean MNEs tend to adopt the ethnocentric approach to managing performance appraisal practices for expatriates and an integrative approach for HCNs in their Chinese subsidiaries due to the relative strength effect and contextual differences between China and South Korea. Based on the findings, it can be argued that MNEs originating from advanced economies and operating in less-developed countries tend to adopt an ethnocentric approach to international performance appraisals. Conversely, MNEs from less-developed economies operating in developed countries are more likely to adopt a multi-domestic (localized) approach to international performance appraisals. However, such an assumption needs testing using larger data involving MNEs from many countries and operating in many host countries. We will focus on international reward and compensation in the next chapter.

Bibliography

Appelbaum, S. H., Roy, M., & Gilliland, T. (2011). Globalization of performance appraisals: Theory and applications. *Management Decision, 49*, 570–585.

Bernthal, P., Rogers, R., & Smith, A. (2003). *Managing performance: Building accountability for organizational success.* Pittsburgh: Development Dimensions International, Inc..

Bian, Y., Shu, X., & Logan, J. R. (2001). Communist Party membership and regime dynamics in China. *Social Forces, 79*(3), 805–841.

Björkman, I., & Lu, Y. (2000). Local or global? Human resource management in international joint ventures in China. In M. Warner (Ed.), *Changing workplace relations in the Chinese economy* (pp. 117–138). London: Palgrave Macmillan.

Blau, G. (1999). Testing the longitudinal impact of work variables and performance appraisal satisfaction on subsequent overall job satisfaction. *Human Relations, 52*, 1099–1113.

Brewster, C. (1988). *The management of expatriates* (Human Resource Research Centre monograph, No. 2). Bedford: Cranfield School of Management.

Briscoe, D. R., & Claus, L. (2008). Employee performance management: Policies and practices in multinational enterprises. In A. Varma, P. S. Budhwar, & A. DeNisi (Eds.), *Performance management systems: A global perspective* (pp. 15–39). New York: Routledge.

Cardy, R. L., & Dobbins, G. H. (1994). *Performance appraisal: Alternative perspectives.* Cincinnati: South-Western Publishing.

Carver, C. S., & Scheier, M. F. (1982). Control theory: A useful conceptual framework for personality–social, clinical, and health psychology. *Psychological Bulletin, 92*, 111–135.

Cascio, W. F. (1998). *Managing human resources.* Boston: McGraw-Hill.

Cascio, W. F. (2006). Global performance management systems. In G. K. Stahl & I. Bjorkman (Eds.), *Handbook of research in international human resource management* (pp. 187–188). Cheltenham: Edward Elgar.

Chen, D. (2011). Research on performance management of Chinese SME. *International Journal of Business and Management, 6*(4), 263–265.

Chen, J., & Eldridge, D. (2010). Are "standardized performance appraisal practices" really preferred? A case study in China. *Chinese Management Studies, 4*(3), 244–257.

Chiang, F. F. T., & Birtch, T. A. (2010). Appraising performance across borders: An empirical examination of the purposes and practices of performance appraisal in a multi-country context. *Journal of Management Studies, 47*, 1365–1393.

Chow, H. S. (1995). An opinion survey of performance appraisal practices in Hong Kong and the People's Republic of China. *Asia Pacific Journal of Human Resources, 32*(3), 67–79.

Chung, K. H., Lee, H. C., & Jung, K. H. (1997). *Korea management: Global strategy and cultural transformation.* Berlin/New York: Walter de Gruyter.

Cleveland, J. N., Murphy, K. R., & Williams, R. (1989). Multiple uses of performance appraisal: Prevalence and correlates. *Journal of Applied Psychology, 74*, 130–135.

Cleveland, J. N., Lim, A. S., & Murphy, K. R. (2007). Feedback phobia? Why employees do not want to give or receive performance feedback. In J. Langan-Fox, C. L. Cooper, & R. J. Klimoski (Eds.), *Research companion to the dysfunc-*

tional workplace: Management challenges and symptoms (pp. 172–176). Cheltenham: Edward Elgar.

Cooke, F. L. (2008). The changing dynamics of employment relations in China: An evaluation of theorising level of labour disputes. *Journal of Industrial Relations, 50*, 111–138.

Cooke, F. L. (2012). *Human resource management in China: New trends and practices*. New York: Routledge.

De Luque, M. F. S., & Sommer, S. M. (2000). The impact of culture on feedback-seeking behavior: An integrated model and propositions. *Academy of Management Review, 25*(4), 829–849.

Dowling, P. J., Welch, D. E., & Schuler, R. S. (1999). *International human resource management*. Cincinnati: South-Western.

Dowling, P. J., Festing, M., & Engle, A. D. (2013). *International human resource management*. London: Cengage Learning.

Farh, J., Dobbins, G. H., & Cheng, B. (1991). Cultural relativity in action: A comparison of self-ratings made by Chinese and US workers. *Personnel psychology, 44*(1), 129–147.

Fenwick, M. (2004). International compensation and performance management. In A. W. K. Harzing & J. Van Ruysseveldt (Eds.), *International HRM: Managing people across borders* (pp. 307–332). Newbury Park: Sage.

Festing, M., Knappert, L., Dowling, P. J., & Engle, A. D. (2012). Global performance management in MNEs: Conceptualization and profiles of country-specific characteristics in China, Germany, and the United States. *Thunderbird International Business Review, 54*, 825–843.

Fletcher, C., & Perry, P. (2002). Performance appraisal and feedback: A consideration of national culture and a review of contemporary and future trends. In N. Anderson, D. Ones, H. Sinangil, & C. Viswesvaran (Eds.), *International handbook of industrial, work and organizational psychology* (pp. 127–144). Beverly Hills: Sage.

Furnham, A., & Stringfield, P. (1998). Congruence in job-performance ratings: A study of 360 feedback examining self, manager, peers, and consultant ratings. *Human Relations, 51*(4), 517–530.

Gabris, G. T., & Ihrke, D. M. (2001). Does performance appraisal contribute to heightened levels of employee burnout? The results of one study. *Public Personnel Management, 30*, 157–172.

Garavan, T. N., Morley, M., & Flynn, M. (1997). 360 degree feedback: Its role in employee development. *Journal of Management Development, 16*(2), 134–147.

Gregersen, H. B., Hite, J. M., & Black, J. S. (1996). Expatriate performance appraisal in US multinational firms. *Journal of International Business Studies, 27*, 711–738.

Hana Financial Group. (2013). *2013 Hana Financial Group sustainability report*. Retrieved April 11, 2016, from, http://www.hanafn.com/eng/csr/sustainability/sustainabilityFileDown.do?fileName=report_2013_english.pdf

Harris, M. M., & Schaubroeck, J. (1988). A meta-analysis of self-supervisor, self-peer, and peer-supervisor ratings. *Personnel Psychology, 41*, 43–62.
Huo, Y. P., & Von Glinow, M. A. (1995). On transplanting human resource practices to China: A culture-driven approach. *International Journal of Manpower, 16*(9), 3–15.
Jackson, S., & Schuler, R. S. (2003). *Managing human resources through strategic partnerships*. Cincinnati: South-Western.
Janssens, M. (1994). Evaluating international managers' performance: Parent company standards as control mechanism. *The International Journal of Human Resource Management, 5*, 853–873.
Jawahar, I. M. (2006). An investigation of potential consequences of satisfaction with appraisal feedback. *Journal of Leadership & Organizational Studies, 13*, 14–28.
Jhun, S., Bae, Z. T., & Rhee, S. Y. (2012). Performance change of managers in two different uses of upward feedback: A longitudinal study in Korea. *The International Journal of Human Resource Management, 23*, 4246–4264.
Kim, P. S. (2001). Utilising 360-degree feedback in the public sector: A case study of the Korean central government. *Asian Journal of Political Science, 9*, 95–108.
Kim, J. W., & Rowley, C. (2001). Managerial problems in Korea-Evidence from the nationalized industries. *International Journal of Public Sector Management, 14*(2), 129–149.
Kong, D., Kim, S., & Yang, S. B. (2013). *Individual performance appraisal in the government of Korea, Knowledge Sharing Program: KSP Modularization*. Seoul: KDI School of Public Policy and Management.
Lansbury, D. R., Kwon, S. H., & Suh, C. S. (2006). Globalization and employment relations in the Korean auto industry: The case of the Hyundai Motor Company in Korea, Canada and India. *Asia Pacific Business Review, 12*(2), 131–147.
LG. (2016). *Fair evaluation*. Retrieved March 15, 2016, from http://www.lg.com/global/sustainability/employee/fair-evaluation
Lindholm, N. (1999). Performance management in MNC subsidiaries in China: A study of host country managers and professionals. *Asia Pacific Journal of Human Resources, 37*, 18–35.
Locke, E. A., & Latham, G. P. (1990). *A theory of goal setting & task performance*. Eaglewood Cliffs: Prentice- Hall.
Logger, E., & Vinke, R. (1995). Compensation and appraisal of international staff. In A. Harzing & J. Ruysseveldt (Eds.), *International human resource management* (pp. 252–269). London: Sage.
Maley, J. F. (2009). The influence of performance appraisal on the psychological contract of the inpatriate manager. *SA Journal of Human Resource Management, 7*(1), 100–109.
Maley, J. F., & Kramar, R. (2007). International performance appraisal: Policies, practices and processes in Australian subsidiaries of healthcare MNCs. *Research and Practice in Human Resource Management, 15*, 21–40.

Martin, D. C., & Bartol, K. M. (2003). Factors influencing expatriate performance appraisal system success: An organizational perspective. *Journal of International Management, 9*, 115–132.

McGovern, P. (1999). HRM policies and management practices. In L. Govern, V. Hope Hailey, P. Stiles, & C. Truss (Eds.), *Strategic human resource management*. Oxford: Oxford University Press.

Mendenhall, M., & Oddou, G. (1991). Expatriate performance appraisal: Problems and solutions. In M. Mendenhall & G. Oddou (Eds.), *Readings and cases in international human resource management*. Boston: PWS-Kent.

Milliman, J., Taylor, S., & Czaplewski, A. (2000). Performance feedback in MNC: Opportunities for organizational learning. *Human Resource Planning, 25*, 29–44.

Muchinsky, P. M. (2002). *Psychology applied to work* (6th ed.). Wadsworth: Belmont.

Murphy, K. R., & Cleveland, J. N. (1991). *Performance appraisal: An organizational perspective*. Needham Heights: Allyn & Bacon.

Myloni, B. (2002). *The transfer of human resource management practices within multinational companies in Greece—A comparative analysis of human resource management practices in subsidiaries of European and US multinationals and Greek companies*. Unpublished doctoral dissertation, University of Bradford, Bradford.

Nathan, B. R., Mohrman Jr., A. M., & Milliman, J. (1991). Interpersonal relations as a context for the effects of appraisal interviews on performance and satisfaction: A longitudinal study. *Academy of Management Journal, 34*, 352–369.

Park, W. S., & Yu, G. C. (2000). *Transformation and new patterns of HRM in Korea*. Michigan: Citeseer.

Pfeffer, J. (2005). Changing mental models: HR's most important task. *Human Resource Management, 44*(2), 123–128.

Poon, H. F., Wei, Q., & Rowley, C. (2010). The changing face of performance management in China. In C. Rowley & F. L. Cooke (Eds.), *The changing face of management in China* (pp. 149–169). Oxon: Routledge.

Pudelko, M., & Harzing, A. (2007). Country of origin, localization, or dominance effects? An empirical investigation of HRM practices in foreign subsidiaries. *Human Resource Management, 46*(4), 535–559.

Qiao, K., Khilji, S., & Wang, X. Y. (2009). High-performance work systems, organizational commitment, and the role of demographic features in the People's Republic of China. *The International Journal of Human Resource Management, 20*(11), 2311–2330.

Rowley, C., & Bae, J. S. (2004). Human resource management in South Korea after the Asian financial crisis: Emerging patterns from the labyrinth. *International Studies of Management & Organization, 34*(1), 52–82.

Rowley, C., & Yang, H. S. (2009). The development of Asian performance management systems: The example of South Korea. Performance management in South Korea. In A. Varma et al. (Eds.), *Performance management systems: A global perspective*. Abingdon: Routledge.

Schuler, R. S., Dowling, P. J., & De Cieri, H. (1993). An integrative framework of strategic international human resource management. *Journal of Management, 19*(2), 419–459.

Shay, J. P., & Baack, S. (2006). An empirical investigation of the relationships between modes and degree of expatriate adjustment and multiple measures of performance. *International Journal of Cross Cultural Management, 6*(3), 275–294.

Shen, J. (2004). International performance appraisals. *International Journal of Manpower, 25*, 547–563.

Shen, J. (2005a). Effective international performance appraisals: Easily said, hard to do. *Compensation & Benefits Review, 37*, 70–79.

Shen, J. (2005b). Towards a generic IHRM model. *Journal of Organisational Transformation & Social Change, 2*(2), 83–102.

Shen, J. (2007). *Labour disputes and their resolution in China*. Oxford: Chandos Publishing.

Shen, J. (2008). HRM in Chinese privatised enterprises. *Thunderbird International Business Review, 50*(2), 91–104.

Shen, J. (2011). Developing the concept of socially responsible international human resource management. *The International Journal of Human Resource Management, 22*(6), 1351–1363.

Siders, M. A., George, G., & Dharwadkar, R. (2001). The relationship of internal and external commitment foci to objective job performance measures. *Academy of Management Journal, 44*, 570–579.

SK. (2013). *SK Telecom annual report*. Retrieved April 15, 2016, from http://www.sktelecom.com/img/kor/persist_report/20140806/SUSTAIN_REPORT_2013_ENG.pdf

Smith, C., & Meiksins, P. (1995). System, society and dominance effects in cross-national organisational analysis. *Work, Employment & Society, 9*(2), 241–267.

Solutions Consultant. (2014). *Tips for performance appraisal*. Retried March 12, 2016, from http://china.smetoolkit.org/china/zh/content/en/376/Tips-for-Performance-Appraisal

Sparrow, P. R., Schuler, R. S., & Jackson, S. E. (1994). Convergence of divergence: Human resource practices and policies for competitive advantage worldwide. *The International Journal of Human Resource Management, 5*(2), 267–300.

Stone, J. R. (2008). *Managing human resource*. Milton: Wiley.

Suutari, V., & Tahvanainen, M. (2002). The antecedents of performance management among Finnish expatriates. *The International Journal of Human Resource Management, 13*, 55–75.

Tan, C. H., & Torrington, D. (1998). *Human resource management for Southeast Asia and Hong Kong*. Singapore: Prentice Hall.

Taylor, R., Cho, D. Y., & Hyun, J. H. (2001). Korean companies in China: Strategies in the localisation of management. In C. Rowley, T. W. Sohn, & J. Bae (Eds.), *Managing Korean business: Organisation, culture, human resources and change* (pp. 161–181). London: Frank Cass.

Tziner, A., Murphy, K. R., Cleveland, J. N., & Roberts-Thompson, G. P. (2001). Relationships between attitudes toward organizations and performance appraisal systems and rating behavior. *International Journal of Selection and Assessment, 9*, 226–239.

Vo, A., & Stanton, P. (2011). The transfer of HRM policies and practices to a transnational system: The case of performance management practices of the US and Japanese MNEs operating in Vietnam. *International Journal of Human Resource Management, 22*(17), 3513–3527.

Warner, M. (1995). *The management of human resources in Chinese industry*. New York: St. Martin's Press.

Whitford, C. M., & Coetsee, W. J. (2007). A model of the underlying philosophy and criteria for effective implementation of performance management. *SA Journal of Human Resource Management, 4*(1), 63–73.

Williams, R. S. (2002). *Managing employee performance: Design and implementation in organizations*. London: Thompson Learning.

Woods, P. (2003). Performance management of Australian and Singaporean expatriates. *International Journal of Manpower, 24*(5), 517–534.

Yang, H. S., & Rowley, C. (2008). Performance management in South Korea. In A. Varma, P. S. Budhwar, & A. DeNisi (Eds.), *Performance management systems: A global perspective* (pp. 211–270). New York: Routledge.

Ye, L., & Ni, X. (2013). *Performance management in China: In pursuit of accountability and legitimacy*. Retrieved April 10, 2016, from http://www.umdcipe.org/conferences/GovernmentCollaborationShanghai/Submitted%20Papers/Ye_Ni_Paper.pdf

Zhu, C. J., & Dowling, P. J. (1998). Performance appraisal in China. In J. Selmer (Ed.), *International management in China: Cross-cultural issues* (p. 115). London: Routledge.

Zhu, C. J., & Dowling, P. J. (2000). Managing people during economic transition: The development of HR practices in China. *Asia Pacific Journal of Human Resources, 38*(2), 84–106.

Zou, M., & Lansbury, R. D. (2009). Multinational corporations and employment relations in the People's Republic of China: The case of Beijing Hyundai Motor Company. *International Journal of Human Resource Management, 20*(11), 2349–2369.

CHAPTER 6

International Reward and Compensation Policies and Practices

Introduction

International reward and compensation influences the work attitudes and behaviors of both expatriates and HCNs, which in turn affect MNEs' business performance (Bonache 2006; Dowling et al. 2013; Lowe et al. 2002). Effective international reward and compensation motivates employees and helps improve their productivity (Suutari and Tornikoski 2001). In contrast, badly designed international reward and compensation policies and practices are likely to result in expatriate failure, that is, premature return and poor work performance (Shen and Darby 2006). For example, Hamill (1989) found a high expatriate failure rate in US MNEs and this was largely due to poorly designed reward and compensation systems. This chapter addresses international reward and compensation in South Korean MNEs. It is structured as follows: firstly, we will review the literature on the reward and compensation policies and practices in South Korea and China, respectively; secondly, we will outline the key findings of the past research on international reward and compensation systems of South Korean MNEs; and thirdly, empirical findings of the current research on a range of international reward and compensation issues will be reported. These include the components of an international compensation package, and the international reward and compensation approaches adopted by South Korea MNEs operating in China and their associated factors.

H. Kang, J. Shen, *International Human Resource Management in South Korean Multinational Enterprises*,
DOI 10.1007/978-981-10-3093-2_6

Reward and Compensation in South Korea

The compensation system in South Korea has historically been largely based on seniority and group orientation, which reflects the traditional and collective-minded cultural values in South Korea. In addition, an individual's education and length of service are key determining factors. Under the traditional pay system, employees receive pay rises every year. The advantage of this seniority system is that a person's wage is clearly defined and predictable. This system has been continually used for a long period of time, and it is one that fully reflects South Korean firms' lifetime employment practices (Chung 2008). The traditional wage structure in South Korean firms includes base pay, allowances or benefits, and bonuses. Base pay is the largest component and is primarily based on one's education and experience. Allowances are predicated on one's special skills, responsibilities, tasks, and job hardship (Chung et al. 1997).

South Korean companies provide a range of benefits to their employees, which actually manifest their paternalistic, group-oriented, and harmony-oriented culture. Benefit packages include retirement contributions, medical insurance, and paid vacation. In addition to these benefits, large South Korean firms also provide other fringe benefits, for example, child support, free lunch, commuting buses, holiday expenses, dormitory and housing, college tuition support for children, support for various entertainment activities, and gifts/donations for special events (e.g. marriage, birthday) (Chung et al. 1997). Most of these benefits are based on seniority, which complicates the overall wage structure. The seniority-based compensation system has been criticized as being ineffective because it is unable to improve workers' productivity (Lee and Kim 2006). This changed after 1993 when many companies began to adopt the Japanese ability-based pay system, one that rewarded employees based on their ability to perform the task. Nevertheless, a large number of workers still persisted in preferring the traditional seniority-based compensation system which provides employees with job and pay security (Chung 2008).

By 1997, most South Korean enterprises had changed the seniority-based compensation system to performance-based compensation, or pay for performance. The so-called '*Yonbongje*' system has become the norm in South Korea's corporate world (Chung 2008). The '*Yonbongje*' system sets employee wages on the basis of job-related skills and performance. This wage system intends to simplify the existing wage structure, improve employee productivity, and to attract talent (Chung et al. 1997; Chung 2008).

According to the national survey results, the percentage of South Korean firms adopting *Yonbongje* rose from 20% in 2000 to 66.6% in 2012 (Tung et al. 2013). With the *Yonbongje* system, the portion of variable pay is increased and is based on both performance and individual ability (Kim et al. 2013). Merit-based increment is often added to the following year's base pay. This system has resulted in stronger competition among employees due to the increased pay differentials (Yang and Rowley 2008). For example, in LG, all employees are evaluated based on what they have achieved measured against the pre-set company goals. Outstanding performance will be rewarded so that employees are motivated to strive for better performance (LG 2016). South Korean companies do not make a distinction between resignation and retirement when calculating retirement pay (Chen 2004).

There are three kinds of individual performance-based pay in South Korea, and specifically these are: merit pay, lump-sum bonus, and mixed plan. Firstly, merit pay links annual increases in an individual's base pay to an objective evaluation of his or her previous year's performance. Secondly, lump-sum bonus is one in which individual performance is rewarded by a onetime bonus. Thirdly, the mixed plan is a combination of merit pay and lump-sum bonus. It was found that 46% of South Korean companies adopted mixed plans by 2007 (Chung 2008). South Korea began implementing the Minimum Wage Act in 1988 in order to ensure workers enjoyed the minimum standard of living (Liu and Wu 1999). In 2013, the minimum wage for shop-floor workers was around Won 1,015,740 (RMB 5500) per month (GMA News 2013), and it increased over time. As a point of comparison, in the same year, the average salary for executive managers was around Won 169,782,945 per year (RMB 926,335) (Average Salary Survey 2013).

Reward and Compensation in China

During 1953–1956, the grading system in China was firstly used to differentiate employee pay levels. Workers were classified into different grades based on their education and experience. The wage system was fixed, which was called the 'iron wage system' (*tie gong zi*), and employees were provided with lifetime secured employment. In this situation, individuals were paid according to a uniform grade wage system, which was adopted from the Soviet model. The system had 8 levels for factory workers and 25–28 levels for cadres. The wage grade was mainly based on the level of education and work experience. Pay increases were allocated depending on government regulations, and wages remained unchanged for a very long period. According to Meng and Kidd (1997) '[t]he centrally determined employment quota combined with the wage system implied that enterprises faced an annual quota for their total wage bill' (p. 405). Under the 'iron wage system', workers and managers received a very low and egalitarian wage; regardless of the SOEs' profitability, all front-line employees received similar rewards and benefits. Most SOEs did not provide financial rewards; instead, they gave awards and honors to outstanding workers, such as being awarded the title 'labor model' (Gong and Yang 2012). The major weakness of this wage system was the lack or complete non-existence of a link between the grade system and performance. Not surprisingly, this system hugely impeded organizational productivity (Meng and Kidd 1997).

During the past six decades, the compensation system in China has experienced three major reforms. The first wage reform began in the late 1970s when enterprises were made responsible for production and profits, which resulted in linking reward to individual and organizational performance (Warner 1995). The wage-setting policies in SOEs became more decentralized, and companies were allowed to retain part of their profits so that bonuses could be allocated to workers (Ding et al. 2010). The concept of 'pay for labor' was taken up at the State Council in 1978 at the beginning of the economic reform. The purpose of the 'pay for labor' scheme was to motivate and increase workers' productivity. Contribution made by shop-floor workers 'may generally refer to the skill required of and responsibility vested in a job, as may be manifested in the form of position and skill-based pay (*gangwei jineng gongzi*)' (Sun 2000, p. 205). For professional and managerial employees, pay-for-labor schemes might involve incentive pay and performance bonuses (Sun 2000). The centrally fixed total wage quota has been replaced by a floating total wage system, which allowed enterprises to link their total wage to profitability. Two levels of floating wages were practiced. At the enterprise level, total pay was assigned based on the firm's completion of predetermined performance targets; at the individual level, an individual's wage was divided again into a fixed part and a variable or 'floating' part. The variable component was linked to either individual or divisional performance (Jackson and Littler 1991). According to Zhu et al. (1998), in 1979, the average annual take-home pay (i.e. base wage plus bonus) was RMB 717, while subsidies paid by the enterprises and the government were RMB 269.54 and RMB 610.11, respectively.

Since the 1980s, SOEs have been given the freedom to decide the level of remuneration as stipulated by the state wage regulations. By the mid-1980s, enterprises began adopting various wage systems, such as floating wages, structural wages, efficiency wages, and elastic wages (Korzec 1992). The floating wage system was the core system, which directly related employees' performance to rewards (Yao 1999). In the late 1980s, more than 1500 factories and about 15% of employees were paid under the floating wage system (Jackson and Littler 1991). Domestic enterprises were allowed to distribute bonuses to employees. However, the bonuses were restricted to a maximum 5% of their total compensation during the 1980s and 1990s (Meng and Kidd 1997). In JVs, nevertheless, bonuses could reach as much as 75% of total compensation. The wage package included basic wage, bonus, and subsidies. The base wage and subsidies varied, including insurance, welfare, and housing funds (Tsang 1994).

The second major pay system reform was implemented in 1985, which 'linked the total wage bill of a given state-owned or collectively-owned enterprise with the enterprise's economic performance, instead of solely linking the floating portion of the wage with actual output' (Wang et al. 2009, p. 331). A worker's wage normally included basic wage, positional wage, longevity pay, and bonus. Basic wage was the same for everyone regardless of their positions. Positional wage depended on one's managerial or technical position and responsibility. Longevity pay was a subsidy which accrued each year to a maximum of 40 years, while bonus was designed to reward workers who were outstanding in their work (Cooke 2005). Such a wage system 'represented a marked shift from the earlier egalitarian wage principle by placing far greater emphasis on one's position which should reflect competence and responsibility' (Cooke 2005, p. 66).

In 1990, the Chinese government issued further guidelines to enhance wage distribution. In particular, the third pay reform was pursued in 1993. The Labor Law of the People's Republic of China issued in 1994 replaced all previous regulations. Since then, all firms regardless of ownership are free to set their wages (Wang et al. 2009). Since the beginning of 1994–1995, publicly listed enterprises have been permitted to set their own wages; however, unlisted/non-stock firms are still subject to the strictures of the prior system (Yueh 2004). This reform has allowed the Chinese reward and compensation to enter a new phase, that is, enterprises can now design their own reward systems to meet the requirements of the market economy (Zhang et al. 2010). The Chinese government has ceded its control over the wage system except for setting up minimum wages. In SOEs, the State only controls, to some extent, the total sum of wages and the general level of wages. SOEs have been given more power to decide how and in what forms wages are to be allocated. They can freely determine the wage scales and bonuses according to each employee's work skill, work intensity, responsibility, working conditions, and actual contribution (Chen 2004) and organizational financial performance (Ding and Warner 2001). In the new system, the wage is divided into two parts: fixed wage (weighting around 70%) and flexible wage (weighting around 30%) (Cooke 2005). The weight of flexible wages has increased in the last two decades. The reward practices in public and private sectors tend to converge in a way that performance becomes a key factor in the determination of the level of pay. Firms in both sectors adopt similar wage structures, which include basic wage, bonus, and a range of allowances or subsidies, despite the fact that details may vary from firm to firm. Meanwhile, more varieties of pay schemes have emerged, for example, variable pay schemes, which offer stock options to key employees (Cooke 2005).

From 1996 to 2000, general pay structure was also modified to various degrees to incorporate reforms that were underway in other areas of Chinese social life. For example, enterprises ceased to allocate enterprise-owned housing to their employees in 1998 and replaced the direct benefit with a housing fund (*zhu fang gong ji jin*), in which half of the estimated cost of housing was deducted directly from employees' paychecks. Employers now had to provide the other half via matching payments. All employers have to make contributions to five publicly managed funds including pension, medical, accident and disability, maternity, and unemployment insurance (Ding et al. 1997). In JVs, salaries are generally higher compared to domestic firms. They provide competitive benefits packages ranging from housing, pensions, insurance to overseas training. They also implement the performance-based bonus system by linking employees' rewards to their performance (Björkman and Lu 2000). Wage dispersion has increased sharply between managers and line workers. An annual salary system to managerial staff was introduced in recent years, the purpose of which is to increase the difference in earnings between managers and workers. This has been implemented so that managers are financially motivated to improve the company's overall business performance (Ding et al. 2010).

Performance-related pay (PRP) combined with fixed pay has been the dominant remuneration system in China since the 1990s (Xiu and Gunderson 2013). Fixed pay mainly includes basic wage, annual increment, insurance (medical, unemployment, and pensions), and housing subsidies (Cooke 2012). PRP is determined by both individual performance and firm performance (Wei and Rowley 2009). According to Chiu et al. (2002), the ratio of PRP for urban Chinese employees is approximately 40% of their total compensation. In small POEs, they use at least one type of bonus or incentive scheme to motivate employees so that the desired work behaviors are encouraged. Performance-related schemes are widely utilized, for instance, giving employees 1% of the gross profits as a bonus. Performance-related pay can constitute as much as 30–50% of a worker's total income. Offering a monthly bonus (about 10% of base pay) is also a common practice and is given to employees as a reward for displaying full attendance and good workplace behaviors. Moreover, companies also give an end-year bonus to employees, which is a typical practice in China for rewarding employees (Cooke 2005). Currently, many indigenous Chinese companies (e.g. Huawei, Haier, and TCL) are attractive to talented people because they are more flexible than FOEs in structuring compensation with a variety of allowances and benefits. Some private companies may offer stock options to senior management, while SOEs (e.g. Wuhan Iron and Steel Corporation) provide housing subsidies (Tian et al. 2014).

The government first launched the minimum wage regulation in the 1990s. According to the new regulation in 2004, there are two types of minimum wage: monthly and hourly. There are a number of factors determining the monthly minimum wage, such as the average salary, urban resident consumption price index, and employment rate. Factors like local monthly minimum wage and working conditions could influence setting the hourly minimum wage (Shen 2007). Salary standards for Chinese shop-floor workers vary between cities and regions. According to the Chinese official statistics, the average monthly salary for workers was around RMB 3055 in 2011. The highest monthly salary in Shanghai was around RMB 5100 compared to the lowest in Tibet and Shanxi, RMB 2500 (China Statistical Yearbook 2012). At the executive level, the average salary in China was around RMB 355,150 per year. Some executive managers in large SOEs earned up to RMB 700,000 in 2011 (China Labour Bulletin 2013).

The Existing Literature with Respect to International Reward and Compensation of South Korean MNEs

Taylor et al.'s (2001) study investigated South Korean MNEs' reward and compensation policies and practices for local Chinese employees. This study revealed that the HCNs' remuneration package in general included base salary, bonus, and PRP, and sometimes also included welfare and various allowances. Bonuses were considered to be a key incentive to improve employee performance. According to Lansbury et al. (2006), the wage policy in Hyundai Motor Company aimed to minimize labor costs and linked the allowances to workers' improved efficiency. The wage standard for trainees and junior technicians at Hyundai India was slightly higher than those of other multinational automobile companies, and much higher than India's domestic automobile companies.

Lee's (2003) study also examined the reward and compensation system for local Chinese workers in South Korean MNEs. It revealed that clerical workers normally received RMB 1900 per month, while production workers were only paid RMB 700 per month as their starting salaries in Tianjin in 2002. The wage for production workers was quite low and only slightly higher than the minimum wage, RMB 600, in Tianjin in 2002. Workers also received a 3% wage increase each year and overtime pay. Performance-based merit pay has been in operation since 2001. High performers can receive up to 300% of their annual base salaries as an incentive. Seniority as a criterion that determined pay was no longer considered. Lee's study reported that the sample Chinese workers in general were dissatisfied with their wages because their base salaries were too low and they had to work overtime to earn enough to meet their living needs.

Paik et al. (2007) examined people's perceptions of compensation inequalities between HCNs and expatriates and their impact on organizational commitment in South Korean MNEs. They found that local employees received significantly less compensation than expatriates did. Consequently, they were not inclined to display a high level of commitment to their workplace. Zou and Lansbury's study (2009) reported that the average monthly wage for Chinese production workers in BHMC was around RMB 2000 in 2007, which was only one-seventh of South Korean expatriates'. Chinese workers received bonuses, which were distributed equally among workers and based on the company's overall performance. Performance-based pay constituted 10% of wages. In addition, workers received overtime pay and allowances. It is apparent that past studies on international reward and compensation of South Korean MNEs mainly examined HCNs' compensation, which indicates an urgent need to explore both expatriates' and HCNs' reward and compensation in South Korean MNEs.

Components of an International Compensation Package

Reward and Compensation for Expatriates

Generally, there are four key components in an expatriate's compensation package: base salary, inducement, allowance, and benefit. Base salary is a major component and its level is influenced by the compensation approach adopted by the MNE. Foreign service inducements may include foreign service premiums, mobility premiums, hardship premiums, and danger pay. They often make up 5–40% of the base salary (Dowling et al. 2013). Allowances are additional payments which are typically used to bridge the gap between expenditure in the home and the host country (Torrington 1994). MNEs are willing to pay allowances to encourage employees to accept international assignments in order to maintain their home country's living standard (Schell and Solomon 1997). Thus, allowances play a more critical role in expatriate compensation when the home-based approach is adopted. On the other hand, when the host-based approach is employed, some additional allowances such as relocation costs are included. Finally, benefits may include social security benefits, paid time-off, medical care, and pension plans (Bonache 2006; Burnett and Von Glinow 2011). It is noted that the provision of benefits varies widely between MNEs (Dowling et al. 2013). Socially responsible MNEs also provide incentives for CSR-related achievements by rewarding employees' outstanding social performance (Maon et al. 2009; Shen 2011).

Relating to our sample, expatriates' salary package includes base pay, performance-based pay, allowances, and benefits. In three firms, namely Advertising A (3 expatriates), Finance A (6 expatriates), and Telecom D (6 expatriates), expatriates' salaries were paid in headquarters according to South Korean salary standards. In the words of the HR manager in Advertising A, 'Expatriates are on the headquarters' pay system.'

In Telecom A (3 expatriates), Chemical A (14 expatriates), Telecom B (2 expatriates), Telecom C (2 expatriates), Electronics A (17 expatriates), Electronics B (2 expatriates), and Auto A (4 expatriates), expatriates' salaries were paid by the Chinese subsidiaries, also according to South Korean salary standards, although converted into Chinese currency, RMB. The reason for adopting this policy, according to General Manager in Telecom A, is: 'Korean companies want to be consistent with their wage standards to encourage employees to take up international assignments in lower wage countries. Wages in South Korea are currently higher than in China. We do not want expatriates to be financially disadvantaged when working overseas.' All the interviewed expatriate managers reported that South Korean employees who were assigned to other countries also received base salaries at South Korean standards, although allowances and benefits might be different. For example, Operation Manager in Telecom A remarked that he was paid the same salary when he was on an international assignment in the US before being assigned to China.

Base salary was related to expatriates' positions and job grades. Overall, the percentage of base pay was 30–35% of the total compensation package. For example, Marketing Manager in Chemical A remarked, 'At the level of *Bujang* (Department head), the base pay is around Won 25,000,000 per year (RMB 138,000) which constitutes around 35% of the total salary.' Six companies (Chemical A, Electronics A, Electronics B, Auto A, Advertising A, and Finance A) adopted both individual performance-based pay and collective performance-based pay in their Chinese operations. Expatriates' individual performance was appraised by supervisors in subsidiaries and managers (including their immediate supervisors and Head of Overseas Department) at headquarters. Individual performance-based pay that was given according to appraisal grades was classified into 8%, 5%, 3%, and 0% of base salary's four categories. Company-based incentive pay depended on subsidiary performance. The company performance-based pay could be as much as seven months of expatriates' base salaries. The standard of performance-based pay was decided by headquarters. It ranged from 20% to 35% out of total compensation in the ten sample companies. For example, in Electronics B, performance-based pay was around 35% of the total compensation.

The other four sample companies distributed company performance bonuses annually, but did not adopt the individual performance-based pay policy for expatriates. A typical reason for this policy was: 'We believe individual performance-related pay does not really motivate people. In fact it makes things more complicated and causes conflict among employees' (Chief Operating Officer, Telecom C). Normally, bonuses were paid as a lump sum at the end of the year. For instance, in 2010, expatriates in Telecom A received 6.5 months of base salaries as year-end bonus. HCN managerial employees and non-managerial employees received around 4.5 months and two months of base salaries, respectively (General Manager). Hence, it becomes obvious that the standards and structures of base pay and performance-based pay for expatriates were consistent with the South Korean system.

A range of allowances and benefits were provided to expatriates, including safety insurance, housing allowance, children's education allowance, living allowance, and transport allowance in the ten sample companies. The amount of allowances depended on expatriates' positions and varied between companies. Generally, allowances and benefits amounted to about 27–35% of the total compensation for expatriates; however, they varied due to positions. For example, Auto A provided a housing allowance worth RMB 20,000 to rent an apartment for '*Bujang*', that is, middle-level managers who are equivalent to department heads. In Electronics B, directors of departments received a travel allowance of approximately RMB 15, 000–16,000, while lower-level managers received RMB 12,000 per trip when traveling between China and South Korea. According to Marketing Manager in Auto A, the company (the subsidiary) rented a 200m^2 apartment for him and paid his children's tuition fees for their international school in China. The living allowance varied between RMB 3000 and RMB 5000 per month in the sample companies. For instance, in Electronics A, it was around RMB 3000 for non-executive managers and RMB 4000 for executive-level managers (HR Manager, Electronics A). Other benefits for expatriates included company cars, drivers paid by companies, and recreational leave. One common statement made by expatriate managers was: 'The Korean MNEs take into account the host country's costs of living and locations as well as the home standards when distributing allowances and benefits to expatriates.'

Reward and Compensation for HCNs

Similarly, the compensation package for HCNs in the sample companies regardless of positions included base salary, performance-based pay, allowances, and benefits. Base salary, allowances, and benefits were determined depending on positions, qualifications, and years of employment, while performance-based pay was determined by individual and organizational performance. Reward and compensation for HCN executive-level managers in the ten South Korean MNEs were decided by headquarters, while other employees' salaries were determined by subsidiaries. In order to attract high-caliber local talent, the sample South Korean MNEs paid HCN executive managers seven to eight times more than non-managerial employees. Salaries for executive managers were around RMB 40,000, including allowances and benefits, for deputy executive-level managers around RMB 30,000, and for non-executive managers between RMB 5000–20,000, respectively. For instance, in Telecom A, HCN executive-level managers received around RMB 45,000 per month compared to RMB 7000 for non-managerial employees.

There was obvious salary inequality between HCN managers and expatriates. For example, in Chemical A, a non-executive manager received RMB 15,000 per month compared to RMB 35,000 for the same level of expatriate managers. Many HCN managers complained about this salary inequality during their interviews. Typically, the HR Manager in Auto A commented:

> As a senior manager one thing I feel unfair is that my salary is much less than those of my Korean colleagues even they are in lower positions and I overall do much more than they do.

In theory, HCNs could negotiate their compensation packages with senior managers. However, in practice, there was not much room for negotiation. When asked why HCN managers still worked there given they complained about pay inequality, a common answer was that their salaries were higher than those of working in local companies. At other levels, for example, office workers, the starting salary package was around RMB 3500–5000 per month, and for production workers, RMB 2500–3000 per month, which was also relatively higher than local standards. HCNs also received annual increments that were linked to employment years.

Most of the sample companies (Chemical A, Telecom A, Electronics A, Electronics B, Auto A, Advertising A, Finance A, and Telecom B) provided performance-based pay to HCN employees to reward excellent performance. Production workers' performance bonuses were based on the quantity and quality of products. Non-production workers' performance bonuses were based on work attitudes and behaviors, such as attendance, cooperation, and task completion. A typical statement was, 'If production workers perform well, they can earn more than white collar employees' (HR Manager, Auto A). In addition, the sample companies gave all HCN employees, except for those who made serious mistakes, such as violating company regulations or breached laws, year-end bonuses (normally one-month salary) as a 'thank you' for employees' hard work during the year. This practice complies with the Chinese tradition of giving festival presents (usually at the Chinese Spring Festival). Moreover, HCN employees also received firm performance-based bonuses; the amount of bonuses, however, varied between positions. General Manager in Telecom A explained:

> The amount of bonus depends on company's profit over the year. Last year, executive level managers in my company received bonuses of six months of base salaries, middle managers received two months of base salaries and 1 month base salary for non-managerial employees.

Normally, such bonuses were paid biannually. The extent of performance-based pay was similar to those in local firms. However, base salaries were higher than local standards and, therefore, the amount of performance-based pay was superior. There is evidence that the sample companies took into account both home and host standards and structures when formulating and implementing base pay and performance-based pay policies and practices for HCNs.

Allowances and benefits for HCN employees in the ten sample companies were referred to the practices of local firms. Although varying between companies and positions, they normally included transport allowance, telecommunication allowance, lunch allowance, housing allowance, unemployment insurance, pension insurance, health insurance, housing fund, and festival gifts. For example, in Telecom D, 'The housing allowance for managers is around RMB 600 per month and non-managerial employees around RMB 200 per month' (HR Manager, Telecom D). It is evident that the sample MNEs localized allowances and benefits practices for HCNs by considering local traditions and living standards.

The following two tables summarize the differences between the various compensation components for expatriates and HCNs in the ten sample companies (Tables 6.1 and 6.2).

Table 6.1 Expatriates' compensation

Company	*Base pay*	*Performance-based pay*	*Allowances and benefits*
Telecom A	HQ standard	No	1, 2, 3, 4, 5, 7, 8, 9, 12, 13, 14
Chemical A	HQ standard	30%	1, 2, 3, 4, 5, 8, 9, 10, 11, 12, 13
Telecom B	HQ standard	No	1, 2, 3, 4, 7, 8, 9, 10, 11, 12, 13
Advertising A	HQ standard	30%	1, 2, 3, 4, 5, 8, 9, 11, 12, 13, 14
Telecom C	HQ standard	No	1, 2, 3, 4, 5, 7, 8, 9, 10, 11
Electronics A	HQ standard	35%	1, 2, 3, 4, 5, 6, 8, 9, 10, 11, 12, 13
Electronics B	HQ standard	30%	1, 2, 3, 4, 5, 6, 8, 9, 10, 11, 12, 13, 14
Auto A	HQ standard	28%	1, 2, 3, 4, 8, 9, 10, 11, 12, 13
Finance A	HQ standard	20%	1, 2, 3, 4, 5, 6, 8, 9, 11, 12, 13
Telecom D	HQ standard	No	1, 2, 3, 4, 7, 8, 9, 11, 12, 13, 14

Note: 1, safety insurance; 2, housing allowance; 3, education allowance; 4, living allowance; 5, transport allowance; 6, lunch allowance; 7, mobile allowance; 8, paid annual leave; 9, paid family visit; 10, free car; 11, gym/golf membership; 12, holiday gifts; 13, monthly/annual dinner; 14, laptop; 15, unemployment insurance; 16, pension insurance; 17, medical insurance; 18, housing fund; 19, medical check; 20, company-organized trip; 21, production worker accommodation; 22, bus service; 23, birthday party

Table 6.2 HCNs' compensation

Company	*Base pay*	*Performance-based pay*	*Allowances and benefits*
Telecom A	Local standard	Yes	5,6,7,8,15,16,17,18,19
Chemical A	Local standard	Yes	5,6,8,10,11,12,13,15,16,17,18,19,20,23
Telecom B	Local standard	Yes	6,7,8,12,13,15,16,17,18,19
Advertising A	Local standard	Yes	6,8,12,13,15,16,17,18,23
Telecom C	Local standard	No	6,7,8,12,13,15,16,17,18,19,23
Electronics A	Local standard	Yes	6,8,11,12,13,15,16,17,18,19,20,21,22
Electronics B	Local standard	Yes	6,8,11,12,13,14,15,16,17,18,19,20,21
Auto A	Local standard	Yes	5,6,8,11,12,13,15,16,17,18,20,21,22
Finance A	Local standard	Yes	6,8,10,11,12,13,15,16,17,18,23
Telecom D	Local standard	No	6,7,8,11,12,13,15,16,17,18,19,23

Note: 1, safety insurance; 2, housing allowance; 3, education allowance; 4, living allowance; 5, transport allowance; 6, lunch allowance; 7, mobile allowance; 8, paid annual leave; 9, paid family visit; 10, free car; 11, gym/golf membership; 12, holiday gifts; 13, monthly/annual dinner; 14, laptop; 15, unemployment insurance; 16, pension insurance; 17, medical insurance; 18, housing fund; 19, medical check; 20, company-organized trip; 21, production worker accommodation; 22, bus service; 23, birthday party

International Reward and Compensation Approaches and Associated Factors

Theoretically, MNEs implement two major strategies when managing international reward and compensation: the 'home-based approach (also called the balance sheet approach)' and 'host-based approach (also called the local going rate)' (Anderson 1990; Reynolds 1986). The 'home-based approach' is based on typical market values in the home country (Dowling et al. 2013; Wentland 2003). The principle is to keep expatriates as 'economically whole' in order to minimize any disadvantage expatriates may experience when they relocate in another country (Mahajan 2011). This approach has several variations such as a split-pay approach, which allows expatriates to choose what currency they want to be paid in, and a flexible pay approach, where expatriates are paid a lump-sum amount and can choose to allocate this amount between the expense accounts (Burns 2003; Shelton 2008). This approach makes sure that expatriates can maintain their standard of living and prevents them from experiencing financial losses due to the expenses involved with foreign assignments (Burnett and Von Glinow 2011). It therefore facilitates repatriation on the completion of international assignments. Furthermore, this approach is particularly useful for expatriates who are at senior or middle managerial levels, and the assignment is for no more than five years (Reynolds 1997). The major disadvantages of this approach are great disparities between expatriates of different nationalities and between expatriates and HCNs, and administrative difficulties. HCNs might perceive compensation inequality particularly when there is no reasonable justification for giving higher compensation to expatriates (Mahajan 2011).

The 'host-based' approach, on the other hand, aligns expatriates' compensation with the host country salary standard and structure (Anderson 1990; Reynolds 1986). This approach creates a sense of equity between local employees and expatriates from different countries. It, however, may cause significant income discrepancies between expatriates and those working at home. This approach is sometimes used by MNEs to reduce high expatriate costs. Another advantage is that it is relatively easier to administer. However, due to the variation between the home and host salary standards and structures, this approach results in potential re-entry problems and high turnover among expatriates (Dowling et al. 2013). The advantages and disadvantages of both approaches are summarized in Table 6.3.

Table 6.3 Advantages and disadvantages of the international reward and compensation approaches

Approach	*Advantages*	*Disadvantages*
Balance sheet approach	Equity between assignments	Results in great disparities between expatriates of different nationalities; between expatriates and local nationals
	Equity between expatriates of the same nationality	Difficult to administer
	Facilitates expatriate re-entry	
	Easy to communicate	
Going rate approach	Equality with local nationals	Variation between assignments for the same employee
	Simplicity	Variation between expatriates of the same nationality in different countries
	Identification with host country	Potential re-entry problems
	Equity among different nationalities	

Source: Dowling et al. (2013)

Because both the home-based and host-based approaches have disadvantages, many MNEs tend to use hybrid systems by mixing appropriate home and host policies and practices (Schell and Solomon 1997). A hybrid system involves both policy transfer and localization in order to achieve the best fit with external and internal environments (Shen 2004).

The adoption of integrative international reward and compensation systems can be rationalized by institutional theory, which posits that national institutional environments, such as 'regulative, normative, and cognitive structures and activities', influence organizational behaviors (Scott 1995, p. 33, also see DiMaggio and Powell 1983). To achieve the best fit with external environments and to earn organizational legitimacy, MNEs must conform to the social norms in multicultural environments (Rosenzweig and Singh 1991; Sayim 2010). Therefore, MNEs are under diverse institutional pressures from home and various host countries. These pressures can be typically reflected in international reward and compensation practices. Understandably, the host-contextual factors tend to exert a pull effect, while the home-contextual factors are likely to have a push effect on reward and compensation practices in MNEs. That is to say, to varying degrees, all MNEs transfer their home reward and compensation practices to international subsidiaries and simultaneously to a certain extent localize in host countries. Nevertheless, it is worth noting that national institutions are not static, but change over the time because of the interactive influences of local actors, such as trade unions, and external factors, such as the World Trade Organization.

We now know MNEs will simultaneously transfer and localize reward and compensation in their international operations. Hence, the key question here is what factors influence the extent of transfer and localization of reward and compensation practices? Two emerging models, namely the national culture model (Bloom et al. 2003; Vo and Stanton 2011) and the dominance effect model (Pudelko and Harzing 2007; Smith and Meiksins 1995), have been increasingly used to explain the determinants of IHRM approaches. According to Bloom et al. (2003, p. 1351), 'the national cultural model asserts the pre-eminence of local host contexts.' Host-contextual factors extend beyond sociocultural aspects and include host country legal and economic factors (Schuler et al. 1993; Welch 1994). Vo and Stanton (2011) argued that contextual differences between host and home countries are a major reason for policy localization in MNEs.

From a different perspective, Pudelko and Harzing (2007) and Smith and Meiksins (1995) argued that international transfer and localization is due to the dominance effect, that is, the relative strength of the home economy and host economy in terms of economic and technological advancement. HRM practices of MNEs originating from dominant economies are more likely to be regarded as the 'best practice' and as transferable. When the host country is a dominant economy, the reverse occurs (Smith and Meiksins 1995). There is empirical evidence that because the US is a dominant economy, US MNEs tend to transfer HRM practices to their international subsidiaries in Germany and Japan (Pudelko and Harzing 2007), Greece (Myloni 2002), and Turkey (Sayim 2010). Dominance effects are especially logical when receiver countries depend economically or politically on sender countries. When there is no dominant economy, for example, between Japan and Germany, Japanese MNEs in Germany or German MNEs in Japan are more likely to adopt more balanced, integrated HRM systems that combine both host and home HRM practices.

These discussions indicate that, due to multiple institutional pressures when operating in various locations, MNEs tend to transfer the home reward and compensation practices to foreign operations and localize in host countries simultaneously. The extent of transfer and localization is influenced by the interactive effect of cultural (contextual) differences and economic dominance. To date, research into IHRM practices transfer has focused on the MNEs from 'central countries' such as the US, European

Union nations, and Japan to other countries (Sayim 2010). More research into other economies is needed to test the applicability and generalizability of the extant literature. Although the dominance of the South Korean economy over China's economy has been weakening over the past decade or so, due to the rapid development of the Chinese economy, South Korea's economy is still relatively dominant in terms of economic and technological advances. Hence, we expect that South Korean MNEs will tend to transfer home reward and compensation practices to China. Moreover, although both China and South Korea are East Asian countries and South Korean culture was heavily influenced by Chinese culture historically (e.g. Confucianism) for millennia, there are nonetheless significant cultural and institutional differences between these two nations (Kim et al. 1998).

These differences are reflected in different compensation structures and standards in the home and host countries, and we therefore expect this will result in some degree of localization. Therefore, we hypothesize that South Korean MNEs will adopt integrative international reward and compensation policies and practices in their Chinese subsidiaries by taking into account both home and host compensation systems. More specifically, South Korean MNEs would tend to transfer the core reward and compensation practices (i.e. pay standards and structures) to China for expatriates due to the economic dominance effect. Consequently, they would localize reward and compensation practices for HCNs due to cultural differences.

The findings show that the sample South Korean MNEs adopted a home-based approach to the focal components (i.e. base pay and performance-based pay) of reward and compensation for expatriates in order for expatriates not to be financially disadvantaged on international assignments. This practice can be understood due to the influence of the relative dominance of the Korean economy. The sample MNEs adopted an integrative approach to peripheral components, such as allowances and benefits for expatriates, and to focal components of reward and compensation for HCNs due to the interactive effect of economic dominance of the Korean economy and cultural differences between China and South Korea. Moreover, the sample MNEs adopted a host-based approach to peripheral components of compensation practices for HCNs. This practice can be interpreted as being due to the cultural difference effect. These results therefore support our hypotheses that the relative dominance of the Korean economy and cultural differences between China and South Korea interactively influence international reward and compensation practices in

South Korean MNEs when operating in China. However, the results also indicate that MNEs tend to adopt different approaches to different components of international reward and compensation practices and directed to different nationalities.

Discussion

This chapter set out to explore the approaches to, and the factors influencing the approaches to international reward and compensation adopted by South Korean MNEs operating in China. The results show that a salary package for both expatriates and HCNs consists of base pay, performance-based pay, allowances, and benefits. The base salary for expatriates is based on headquarters' standards, indicating that the sample South Korean MNEs adopt the home-oriented base salary policy. The performance-based pay for expatriates considers both individual performance and subsidiary performance. The percentage of performance-based pay ranged from 20% to 35% of total salaries, which is less than that of most Chinese enterprises (50–80%) (Shen 2008). Performance-based pay was distributed according to South Korean standards. The evidence therefore points to the sample MNEs transferring performance-based pay practices from business headquarters to their Chinese subsidiaries for expatriates, and providing a range of allowances and benefits to expatriates. Fundamentally, the components of allowances and benefits meet home standards, and are also simultaneously influenced by the host country context, including living costs and traditions.

The results also reveal that HCN executive management salaries are determined by headquarters, while those of other employees are decided by local subsidiaries. Base salaries are lower than home standards, but higher than local standards, and vary between positions. Performance-based pay for HCNs is related to both individual performance and firm performance. Although individual performance-based pay is dependent on individual's performance, firm performance-based pay is distributed according to firms' profits and individual positions. The amount of overall performance-based pay is up to six months of a base salary, which is higher than home standards. There are considerable salary discrepancies between South Korean expatriates and HCN employees, and between organizational hierarchal levels. Comprehensive allowances and benefits are provided to HCNs, and the components and standards are consistent with those of local firms. This indicates that the sample South Korean

MNEs adopt an integrative approach to managing HCN base salaries and performance-based pay and a localized approach to allowances and benefits.

A major purpose of this research is to explore factors influencing MNEs' approaches to international reward and compensation. The findings of the study are in alignment with institutional theory positing national institutions influence organizational behaviors. The results also suggest that the relative strength between the host and home economies has the dominant effect on the focal components of reward and compensation for expatriates. In other words, when the home economy has relative strength over the host economy, MNEs are likely to adopt the home-based approach to determine the focal components of reward and compensation, including base salaries and performance-based pay, for expatriates. Logically, the reverse should occur when the host economy has relative strength over the home economy. Both the relative strengths between the host and home economies and the cultural differences between the host and home countries influence peripheral components of international reward and compensation for expatriates, and focal components for HCNs. This results in an integrative approach to those particular international reward and compensation practices. The national cultural differences wield the biggest impact on peripheral components of reward and compensation for HCNs, leading to localization. As the limited research has been conducted to investigate reward and compensation in non-Western MNEs, this study extends institutional theory and adds to the knowledge base of IHRM literature with regard to international reward and compensations approaches and associated factors in MNEs.

Conclusion

This chapter investigates how expatriates and HCNs are remunerated in South Korean MNEs operating in China. It reveals that the sample companies adopt: firstly, the home-oriented approach to the focal reward and compensation policies and practices (including base pay and performance-based pay); and secondly, an integrative approach to peripheral components (including allowances and benefits) for expatriates. Conversely, the companies adopt an integrative approach to focal components of reward and compensation and a localized approach to peripheral components for HCNs. These findings indicate that South Korean MNEs initiate different approaches to reward and compensation for expatriates and HCNs, as well as to focal and peripheral components of reward and compensation practices. The transfer of reward and compensation is due to the dominance effect resulting from the fact that the home economy is relatively more advanced than the host economy. On the one hand, the tendency to localize reward and compensation results from contextual differences between host and home nations, such as economic development, living costs, and compensation traditions. The next chapter will examine the use and management of non-traditional expatriates of South Korean MNEs in China.

Bibliography

Anderson, J. B. (1990). Compensating your overseas executives, part 2: Europe in 1992. *Compensation & Benefits Review, 22*(4), 25–35.

Average Salary Survey. (2013). *Average salary in South Korea*. Retrieved July 20, 2013, from http://www.averagesalarysurvey.com/article/average-salary-in-southkorea/12190513.aspx

Björkman, I., & Lu, Y. (2000). Local or global? Human resource management in international joint ventures in China. In M. Warner (Ed.), *Changing workplace relations in the Chinese economy* (pp. 117–138). London: Palgrave Macmillan.

Bloom, M., Milkovich, G. T., & Mitra, A. (2003). International compensation: Learning from how managers respond to variations in local host contexts. *International Journal of Human Resource Management, 14*(8), 1350–1367.

Bonache, J. (2006). The compensation of expatriates: A review and future research agenda. In G. Stahl & I. Bjo rkman (Eds.), *Handbook of research in international human resource management* (pp. 158–175). Cheltenham: Edward Elgar.

Burnett, M., & Von Glinow, M. A. (2011). Total rewards in the international context. In A. W. Harzing & A. H. Pinnington (Eds.), *International human resource management* (pp. 468–496). London: Sage.

Burns, S. M. (2003). Flexible international assignee compensation plans. *Compensation & Benefits Review, 35*(3), 35–42.

Chen, M. (2004). *Asian management systems*. Hampshire: Cengage Learning EMEA.

China Labour Bulletin. (2013). *Wages in China*. Retrieved July 20, 2013, from http://www.clb.org.hk/en/content/wages-china

China Statistical Yearbook. (2012). *Average wage of employed persons in urban units by sector*. Retrieved August 15, 2013, from http://www.stats.gov.cn/tjsj/ndsj/2012/indexeh.htm

Chiu, R. K., Luk, V. W. M., & Tang, T. L. P. (2002). Retaining and motivating employees: Compensation preferences in Hong Kong and China. *Personnel Review, 31*(4), 402–431.

Chung, K. T. (2008). Korea's shift to pay-for-performance. *SERI Quarterly, 1*(2), 9–17.

Chung, K. H., Lee, H. C., & Jung, K. H. (1997). *Korea management: Global strategy and cultural transformation.* Berlin/New York: Walter de Gruyter.

Cooke, F. L. (2012). *Human resource management in China: New trends and practices.* New York: Routledge.

DiMaggio, P. J., & Powell, W. W. (1983). The iron cage revisited: Institutional isomorphism and collective rationality in organizational fields. *American Sociological Review, 48*, 147–160.

Ding, D., & Warner, M. (2001). China's labour–management system reforms: Breaking the 'three old irons' (1978–1999). *Asia Pacific Journal of Management, 18*(3), 315–334.

Ding, D. Z., Akhtar, S., & Ge, G. L. (2010). Effects of inter- and intra-hierarchy wage dispersions on firm performance in Chinese enterprises. In M. Warner (Ed.), *Making sense of human resource management in China* (pp. 202–213). Oxon: Routledge.

Ding, D., Fields, D., & Akhtar, S. (1997). An empirical study of human resource management policies and practices in foreign-invested enterprises in China: The case of Shenzen Special Economic Zone. *International Journal of Human Resource Management, 8*(5), 595–613.

Dowling, P. J., Festing, M., & Engle, A. D. (2013). *International human resource management.* London: Cengage Learning.

GMA News. (2013). *Korea hikes minimum wage for workers—DOLE.* Retrieved July 20, 2013, from http://www.gmanetwork.com/news/story/292870/economy/companies/korea-hikesminimumwage-for-workers-dole

Gong, Y., & Yang, W. G. (2012). Performance management at Shenhua Guohua Electric Power. In J. C. Hayton, M. Byron, L. C. Christiansen, & B. Kuvaas (Eds.), *Global HRM case book* (pp. 253–265). New York: Routledge.

Hamill, J. (1989). Expatriate policies in British multinationals. *Journal of General Management, 14*(4), 18–33.

Jackson, S., & Littler, C. R. (1991). Wage trends and policies in China: Dynamics and contradictions. *Industrial Relations Journal, 22*(1), 5–19.

Kim, D. H., Pan, Y. G., & Park, H. S. (1998). High- versus low-context culture: A comparison of Chinese, Korean, and American cultures. *Psychology & Marketing, 15*(6), 507–521.

Kim, H. D., Sutton, K. L., & Gong, Y. P. (2013). Group-based pay-for-performance plans and firm performance: The moderating role of empowerment practices. *Asia Pacific Journal of Management, 30*(1), 31–52.

Korzec, M. (1992). *Labour and the failure of reform in China.* London/New York: Macmillan/St. Martin's Press.

Lansbury, D. R., Kwon, S. H., & Suh, C. S. (2006). Globalization and employment relations in the Korean auto industry: The case of the Hyundai Motor

Company in Korea, Canada and India. *Asia Pacific Business Review, 12*(2), 131–147.

Lee, C. W. (2003). Changing labor relations and human resources management of Korean Businesses in China and future challenges. *e-Labor News*, 21. Retrieved August 21, 2013, from http://unpan1.un.org/intradoc/groups/public/documents/APCITY/UNPAN020894.pdf

Lee, E., & Kim, S. (2006). Best practices and performance-based HR system in Korea. *Seoul Journal of Business, 12*(1), 3–17.

LG. (2016). *Fair evaluation*. Retrieved March 15, 2016, from http://www.lg.com/global/sustainability/employee/fair-evaluation

Liu, E., & Wu, J. (1999). *Minimun wage systems*. Retrieved April 15, 2016, from http://www.legco.gov.hk/yr98-99/english/sec/library/989rp08.pdf

Lowe, K. B., Milliman, J., De Cieri, H., & Dowling, P. J. (2002). International compensation practices: A ten-country comparative analysis. *Human Resource Management, 41*(1), 45–66.

Mahajan, A. (2011). Host country national's reactions to expatriate pay policies: Making a case for a cultural alignment pay model. *International Journal of Human Resource Management, 22*(1), 121–137.

Maon, F., Lindgreen, A., & Swaen, V. (2009). Designing and implementing corporate social responsibility: An integrative framework grounded in theory and practice. *Journal of Business Ethics, 87*(1), 71–89.

Meng, X., & Kidd, M. P. (1997). Labor market reform and the changing structure of wage determination in China's state sector during the 1980s. *Journal of Comparative Economics, 25*(3), 403–421.

Myloni, B. (2002). *The transfer of human resource management practices within multinational companies in Greece—A comparative analysis of human resource management practices in subsidiaries of European and US multinationals and Greek companies*. Unpublished doctoral dissertation, University of Bradford, Bradford.

Paik, Y. S., Parboteeah, P. K., & Shim, W. S. (2007). The relationship between perceived compensation, organizational commitment and job satisfaction: The case of Mexican workers in the Korean Maquiladoras. *International Journal of Human Resource Management, 18*(10), 1768–1781.

Pudelko, M., & Harzing, A. (2007). Country of origin, localization, or dominance effects? An empirical investigation of HRM practices in foreign subsidiaries. *Human Resource Management, 46*(4), 535–559.

Reynolds, C. (1986). Compensation of overseas personnel. In J. J. Famularo (Ed.), *Handbook of human resources administration* (pp. 47–61). New York: McGraw-Hill.

Reynolds, C. (1997). Expatriate compensation in historical perspective. *Journal of World Business, 32*(2), 118–132.

Rosenzweig, P. M., & Singh, J. V. (1991). Organizational environments and the multinational enterprises. *The Academy of Management Review, 16*(2), 340–361.
Sayim, K. Z. (2010). Pushed or pulled? Transfer of reward management policies in MNCs. *International Journal of Human Resource Management, 21*(14), 2631–2658.
Schell, M. S., & Solomon, C. M. (1997). *Capitalizing on the global workforce: A strategic guide to expatriate management.* New York: McGraw Hill.
Schuler, R. S., Dowling, P. J., & De Cieri, H. (1993). An integrative framework of strategic international human resource management. *Journal of Management, 19*(2), 419–459.
Scott, W. R. (1995). *Institutions and organizations.* Thousand Oaks: Sage.
Shelton, T. (2008). Global compensation strategies: Managing and administering split pay for an expatriate workforce. *Compensation & Benefits Review, 40*(1), 56–60.
Shen, J. (2004). Compensation in Chinese multinationals. *Compensation & Benefits Review, 36*(1), 15–25.
Shen, J. (2007). *Labour disputes and their resolution in China.* Oxford: Chandos Publishing.
Shen, J. (2008). HRM in Chinese privatised enterprises. *Thunderbird International Business Review, 50*(2), 91–104.
Shen, J. (2011). Developing the concept of socially responsible international human resource management. *The International Journal of Human Resource Management, 22*(6), 1351–1363.
Shen, J., & Darby, R. (2006). Training and management development in Chinese multinational enterprises. *Employee Relations, 28*(4), 342–362.
Smith, C., & Meiksins, P. (1995). System, society and dominance effects in cross-national organisational analysis. *Work, Employment & Society, 9*(2), 241–267.
Sun, B. (2000). Pay and motivation in Chinese enterprises. In M. Warner (Ed.), *Changing workplace relations in the Chinese economy* (pp. 205–223). London: Palgrave Macmillan.
Suutari, V., & Tornikoski, C. (2001). The challenge of expatriate compensation: The sources of satisfaction and dissatisfaction among expatriates. *International Journal of Human Resource Management, 12*(3), 389–404.
Taylor, R., Cho, D. Y., & Hyun, J. H. (2001). Korean companies in China: Strategies in the localisation of management. In C. Rowley, T. W. Sohn, & J. Bae (Eds.), *Managing Korean business: Organisation, culture, human resources and change* (pp. 161–181). London: Frank Cass.
Tian, X., Harvey, M., & Slocum, J. W. (2014). The retention of Chinese managers: The Chinese puzzle box. *Organizational Dynamics, 43*(1), 44–52.
Torrington, D. (1994). *International human resource management: Think globally, act locally.* London: Prentice-Hall.

Tsang, E. W. K. (1994). Human resource management problems in Sino-foreign joint ventures. *International Journal of Manpower, 15*(9), 4–21.

Tung, R. L., Paik, Y. S., & Bae, J. S. (2013). Korean human resource management in the global context. *International Journal of Human Resource Management, 24*(5), 905–921.

Vo, A., & Stanton, P. (2011). The transfer of HRM policies and practices to a transnational system: The case of performance management practices of the US and Japanese MNEs operating in Vietnam. *International Journal of Human Resource Management, 22*(17), 3513–3527.

Wang, L. H., Nicholson, J., & Zhu, J. (2009). Pay systems in Chinese state-owned enterprises: A review. *Chinese Management Studies, 3*(4), 328–355.

Warner, M. (1995). *The management of human resources in Chinese industry.* New York: St. Martin's Press.

Wei, Q., & Rowley, C. (2009). Pay for performance in China's non-public sector enterprises. *Asia-Pacific Journal of Business Administration, 1*(2), 119–143.

Welch, D. (1994). Determinants of international human resource management approaches and activities: A suggested framework. *Journal of Management Studies, 31*(2), 139–164.

Wentland, D. M. (2003). A new practical guide for determining expatriate compensation: The comprehensive model. *Compensation & Benefits Review, 35*(3), 45–50.

Xiu, L., & Gunderson, M. (2013). Gender earnings differences in china: Base pay, performance pay, and total pay. *Contemporary Economic Policy, 31*(1), 235–254.

Yang, H. S., & Rowley, C. (2008). Performance management in South Korea. In A. Varma, P. S. Budhwar, & A. DeNisi (Eds.), *Performance management systems: A global perspective* (pp. 211–270). New York: Routledge.

Yao, S. (1999). Economic growth, income inequality and poverty in China under economic reforms. *The Journal of Development Studies, 35*(6), 104–130.

Yueh, L. Y. (2004). Wage reforms in China during the 1990s. *Asian Economic Journal, 18*(2), 149–164.

Zhang, M., Nyland, C., & Zhu, C. J. (2010). Hukou-based HRM in contemporary China: The case of Jiangsu and Shanghai. *Asia Pacific Business Review, 16*(3), 377–393.

Zhu, C. J., De Cieri, H., & Dowling, P. J. (1998). The reform of employee compensation in China's industrial enterprises. In *Management and international review* (pp. 65–87). Wiesbaden: Gabler Verlag.

Zou, M., & Lansbury, R. D. (2009). Multinational corporations and employment relations in the People's Republic of China: The case of Beijing Hyundai Motor Company. *International Journal of Human Resource Management, 20*(11), 2349–2369.

CHAPTER 7

The Use and Management of Non-traditional Expatriates Working for South Korean MNEs in China

Introduction

International assignees have dominated the agenda of IHRM research over the last few decades (Collings et al. 2007). Such assignees, commonly referred to as 'expatriates', are employees assigned to work and live in other countries for a stipulated period of time. Expatriates play a critical role in subsidiary leadership, filling the gaps in skills, management, and organizational development and, ultimately, helping ensure that international business ventures are successful (Dowling et al. 2013). Much of the previous IHRM research focused on what could be termed 'traditional' expatriates (Bonache and Noethen 2014), those employees who are taking up international assignments and who relocate to a host country for a year or more (Bonache et al. 2001).

Increasingly, we are witnessing a variety of international assignees who differ from traditional expatriates. Assignments for these expatriates tend to be shorter and often do not involve family relocation. In part, this is a result of technological advances where MNEs are able to manage international business differently from how it was done in the past. As the growing use of non-traditional expatriates is a more recent phenomenon, these various types of expatriates have not been the focus of sustained research and the complexities involved in managing them have often been underestimated in IHRM research (Collings et al. 2007). This deficiency has been compounded by the fact that the research on non-traditional

H. Kang, J. Shen, *International Human Resource Management in South Korean Multinational Enterprises*,
DOI 10.1007/978-981-10-3093-2_7

expatriates has been largely conducted in Western MNEs (Demel and Mayrhofer 2010; Tharenou and Harvey 2006; Welch et al. 2003). As a result, knowledge about non-traditional expatriates in non-Western MNEs, where organizational structures and management may be different (Whitley 1992), is rather limited.

This chapter bridges the literature gap by exploring the use and management of non-traditional expatriates of South Korean MNEs in China. South Korea is Asia's fourth-largest economy. South Korean MNEs such as Samsung and Hyundai have grown rapidly and have become major players in international business (Yoon 2007). Unlike their Western counterparts where the senior management team is normally involved in the decision-making process, South Korean MNEs, known as *chaebols*, have conglomerate structures (Whitley 1992). These companies are normally based on a strong vertical hierarchy, with much authority resting in the office of the chairman (Rowley and Bae 2004). However, it remains unknown how these unique organizational characteristics influence expatriation practices. In this chapter, we will firstly review the literature on the definition of non-traditional expatriates, the trend of using non-traditional expatriates, the reasons for using these expatriates, and the management (including recruitment and selection, training, performance appraisal and reward) of non-traditional expatriates. Secondly, we present the empirical findings.

Non-traditional Expatriates

Dowling and Welch (1988) wrote one of the earliest studies on recognizing various types of expatriates. These ranged from foreign travelers (trouble shooters) with an average posting that lasted up to six months, foreign service specialists working on special projects for up to 12 months, and long-term foreign service providers on assignment for 3–4 years. The last description most closely resembles what is referred to as an expatriate, and the earlier two descriptions would fall under the label of a non-traditional expatriate. Specifically, non-traditional expatriates include short-term assignees, flexpatriates, and international business travelers (Shaffer et al. 2012; Suutari et al. 2013; Welch et al. 2003). Short-term assignees are Parent country nationals (PCNs) assigned overseas for up to 12 months, although normally shorter than 6 months, and are the most popular form of non-traditional expatriates (Collings et al. 2007; Shaffer et al. 2012; Tahvanainen et al. 2005). In these cases, the short-term expatriate's family usually remains in the home country, although exceptions do occur. For example, in Tahvanainen et al.'s (2005) study, 4 out of the 11 case study companies relocated the families of their short-term expatriates, a process that meant incurring extra expenses and disruption in family life. Flexpatriates are PCNs taking up short-term assignments on a regular basis (Mayerhofer et al. 2004). They are often appointed on a commuter, rotational, or contractual assignment basis (Welch et al. 2003). International business travelers, also known as frequent flyers, are PCNs who occasionally make extended international business trips for up to three weeks (Welch and Worm 2006). Some non-traditional expatriates, especially international business travelers, are relatively difficult to identify and less visible compared to traditional expatriates (Welch et al. 2007).

The Use of Non-traditional Expatriates

Advances in modern computer-related technologies, such as the internet, make it possible to limit and reduce the use of traditional expatriates (Suutari et al. 2013). Mayerhofer et al. (2004) revealed that one third of the staff in the Exploration and Production Division of an Austrian natural resource MNE (250–300) were short-term expatriates whose assignments lasted from a few days to several weeks. Tharenou and Harvey (2006) found that 74% of the top 50 Australian MNEs used short-term assignees who relocated abroad for less than a year. According to Schaaper et al. (2013), French MNEs used short-term expatriates in production, engineering, commercial activities, and training of local employees.

The findings of a number of industry surveys are consistent with these empirical studies. General Motors Acceptance Corporation (GMAC) 2004 conducted a survey involving 134 sinor human resource (HR) managers or international relocation managers from 125 MNEs of varying sizes. The survey revealed that 70% of international assignments were for one year or less in duration, and only 19% lasted three years or more; 56% of the companies were seeking alternatives to long-term assignments. PricewaterhouseCoopers' (2005) International Assignment Global Policy and Practice Survey found that 80% of MNEs from North America, Europe, and the Asia-Pacific region used short-term international assignees and that more than half of the 203 participating MNEs intended to increase the use of these types of expatriates. The Global Relocation Trends Survey, conducted by Brookfield Global Relocation Services (2012) and involving 123 MNEs worldwide, revealed that senior HR managers/international relocation managers are more likely to deploy short-term assignees than long-term expatriates. According to the Worldwide International Assignments Policies and Practices Survey (Mercer 2013), more than 70% of the 750 participating MNEs increased the use of short-term expatriates in 2013.

Both the empirical research and industry surveys revealed that the use of non-traditional expatriates has risen, that the number of non-traditional expatriates exceeded those of traditional expatriates, and that utilizing these types of expatriates is likely to increase in the future. Theoretically, the use of non-traditional expatriates is underpinned by resource-based theory, which posits that a firm's resources affect its economic performance and behavior (Barney 1991). Managerial resources are scarce and hence need to be deployed effectively (Tan and Mahoney 2006). With the advances in communication and transportation, more of the tasks of long-term expatriates, such as implementing corporate strategies, control, and problem-solving, can now be completed by non-traditional expatriates. The deployment of non-traditional expatriates increases organizational flexibility, allowing MNEs to utilize their managers' talents more effectively and economically.

The use of non-traditional expatriates in our case study MNEs has generally increased steadily during the last decade, while that of traditional expatriates has declined. In most companies (except Chemical A, Telecom C, and Electronics A), the number of non-traditional expatriates has exceeded traditional expatriates since 2009. Some companies (e.g. Telecom A, Finance A, and Telecom D) reduced the use of non-traditional expatriates slightly in 2010 and 2012 for two major reasons. Firstly, during that period, South Korean direct investment in China decreased slightly (Korea Eximbank 2013); and secondly, at the same time, according to the interviewees, South Korean MNEs shifted their staffing approach from an ethnocentric to a polycentric one by reducing expatriates and appointing more HCN managers in the Chinese operations. Generally, the telecommunications and electronics companies used more non-traditional expatriates than companies in other industries due to the large number of project workers involved. In most companies, the use of non-traditional expatriates increased by around 20–25% during 2009–2013, with the exception of Telecom D which reduced its employment of non-traditional expatriates by 10%. Table 7.1 details the number of traditional and non-traditional expatriates used by all case study companies from 2004 to 2013.

Table 7.1 Number of traditional and non-traditional expatriates used in the Chinese subsidiaries from 2004 to 2013

Company		*2004*	*2005*	*2006*	*2007*	*2008*	*2009*	*2010*	*2011*	*2012*	*2013*
Telecom A	T	8	8	10	12	8	6	6	5	5	5
	N	5	5	5	8	8	10	12	12	10	12
Chemical A	T	23	18	18	16	15	16	15	8	6	6
	N	5	7	7	6	7	8	8	10	13	13
Telecom B	T	10	8	10	8	6	6	6	4	4	4
	N	4	4	6	6	8	8	6	6	8	10
Advertising A	T	6	6	5	5	4	3	4	2	2	2
	N	2	2	2	3	3	5	5	5	6	6
Telecom C	T	8	8	7	8	6	6	4	4	2	2
	N	3	4	4	4	5	8	6	8	8	10
Electronics A	T	19	23	25	23	25	20	20	20	10	10
	N	8	8	10	10	13	14	13	15	15	18
Electronics B	T	10	10	8	8	8	10	6	6	8	13
	N	5	6	8	8	10	12	12	14	14	15
Auto A	T	15	10	10	12	8	8	6	6	6	5
	N	5	8	8	8	10	12	11	14	15	14
Finance A	T	N/A	5	4	4	5	3	3	3	2	2
	N		2	2	3	3	5	6	6	5	6
Telecom D	T	10	8	8	8	7	5	6	6	5	3
	N	3	4	5	5	7	10	8	10	9	9

Note: T, traditional expatriates; N, non-traditional expatriates

Reasons for Using Non-traditional Expatriates

The literature has identified a range of reasons for using non-traditional expatriates. Mayerhofer et al. (2004) found that an Austrian MNE used flexpatriates for skill transfer and management development, while Tahvanainen et al. (2005) discovered Finnish MNEs used short-term assignees mainly for skill transfer and problem-solving, managerial control, and management development (e.g. obtaining international experience through frequent business traveling or working in global teams). These studies received support from the PricewaterhouseCoopers (2000) Survey of MNEs having three main reasons for using short-term assignments: technology transfer or consulting, career development, and training of local personnel. The research shows that there are a range of benefits in using non-traditional expatriates. Minbaeva and Michailova (2004), for example, found that the use of non-traditional assignments increases the ability to share knowledge, while Collings et al. (2007) argued that using international business travelers proved to be very effective in face-to-face interactions with clients and employees in host countries. Welch et al. (2007) suggested that international business travelers are also used for knowledge transfer, performance monitoring, and control in Australian and Danish MNEs. In addition, short-term assignments appear to be increasingly regarded by MNEs as a form of rigorous, cross-cultural training (Shen and Lang 2009).

MNEs also prefer non-traditional expatriates because they have several advantages over traditional expatriates. Utilizing non-traditional expatriates reduces the difficulties involved in traditional expatriation, such as unwillingness of staff to relocate overseas due to family and career development issues (Mayerhofer et al. 2004; Welch and Worm 2006). Goals for short-term assignments are also easier to set and evaluate than for long-term assignments (Tahvanainen et al. 2005). The use of flexpatriates provides organizations with flexibilities (e.g. a flexpatriate can work concurrently in multiple countries on several tasks), help develop global networks, and facilitate informal knowledge sharing (Mayerhofer et al. 2004; Tahvanainen et al. 2005). In a dynamic business environment, MNEs often need to adjust their international business strategies and plans, and different tasks require different expertise for international assignments. The utilization of non-traditional expatriates can contribute significantly to this type of flexibility (Wittig-Berman and Beutell 2009).

Deployment of traditional expatriates is a costly exercise because an expatriate compensation package typically includes family relocation and support, such as accommodation and children's schooling, social security, and a variety of allowances (Collings et al. 2007; Petrovic et al. 2000; Wittig-Berman and Beutell 2009). The use of non-traditional expatriates is less expensive since they generally do not involve family relocation (Tahvanainen et al. 2005). Tharenou and Harvey (2006) reported that one of the reasons for Australian MNEs' use of short-term expatriates is to reduce high expatriation costs. In addition, Mayerhofer et al. (2004) found that using non-traditional expatriates can reduce expatriates' failure rates. According to Tung (1987), the major reasons that cause expatriates' failure in US MNEs are family issues, for instance, families' inability to adjust to the new environment, which can be substantially avoided if non-traditional expatriates are deployed. Expatriates' failure can cause financial and non-financial damage (e.g. relationships with customers, the company's reputation) to MNEs. The risk of such damage can be minimized if non-traditional expatriates are used (Toh and DeNisi 2005). Furthermore, it is evident that non-traditional expatriates provide HCNs with increased management development and career opportunities (Wong and Law 1999), as traditional expatriates normally occupy senior positions for considerable periods of time which can seriously limit HCNs' opportunities. The use of non-traditional expatriates will therefore in all likelihood increase HCNs' morale and organizational commitment significantly (Toh and DeNisi 2005).

Employing non-traditional expatriates will also be beneficial to their career development because: firstly, they are significantly less likely to be disrupted; and secondly, expatriates' failure rates are normally low. Non-traditional expatriates are able to maintain relationships with colleagues at home and hence receive career support from them (Mayerhofer et al. 2004). Traditional expatriates normally expect promotion or at least to resume the same levels within the organization they held prior to departure (Stahl et al. 2002). However, research shows that it is often difficult for MNEs to meet these expectations (Bolino 2007; Lazarova and Cerdin 2007). Traditional expatriation may not necessarily result in career advancement but consequently may result in high turnover among repatriates. One study, for example, concluded that between 20% and 50% of repatriates leave their companies within two years of returning home (Bossard and Peterson 2005).

The research reviewed above suggests that non-traditional expatriates are utilized for the transfer of technology, consulting, training, performance monitoring, and control. Moreover, this research asserted that non-traditional expatriates helped to overcome a number of problems typically associated with traditional expatriates, for example, costs, family issues, and high rates of expatriates' failure as well as being more beneficial to the career paths of expatriates.

The major reasons given for the use of non-traditional expatriates in the case study companies were knowledge transfer, technical support, and management control. The comment made by the Technical Support Team Manager in Electronics B was typical of responses given:

> Knowledge transfer was relatively intensive at the beginning and became intermittent once operations were stabilized. In the later stage, knowledge transfer can be achieved through training conducted by short-term expatriates.

The above comment reinforced the importance of knowledge transfer, which has been considered an important aspect of non-traditional expatriates' jobs, especially in the telecommunications and electronics industries. According to the Operating Team Manager at Telecom B:

> In our company, knowledge and techniques relating to IT are updated frequently. Therefore, we need someone from headquarters to provide the most updated knowledge to subsidiaries. This happens periodically or on a project-basis.

This statement was also supported by other expatriate managers in Advertising A, Finance A, and Auto A. The Finance Director at Finance A added: 'We need to know information like the most recent marketing strategy being promoted by the headquarters. The headquarters will send people to convey this kind of information periodically'. Technical support was another important role of short-term expatriates in the case study companies:

> When employees face technical difficulties which cannot be solved within subsidiaries, short-term expatriates will be sent here to assist. Their responsibilities are to provide local employees with technical support, solve problems, and supervise projects. They normally stay around one month. (Operation Manager, Telecom D)

Another commonly mentioned role of non-traditional expatriates is management control. Four companies, Chemical A, Telecom A, Telecom C, and Finance A, used short-term expatriates to supervise or control subsidiaries' operations. All of them mentioned that the level of trust between expatriates and HCNs has improved markedly with the introduction of non-traditional expatriates. This is illustrated at Telecom A where the Operation Manager commented: 'We rely heavily on our local employees to implement strategies. They have enough skills and knowledge to handle their tasks. However, proper instructions from supervisors (headquarters) ensure the subsidiary is on the right track'.

One of the most commonly cited reasons for reducing the use of traditional long-term expatriates involved advances in IT systems. As the Finance Director in Finance A stated:

> Thanks to IT advancements it is possible to use short-term expatriates. Headquarters can monitor and control subsidiaries' operations remotely. I have to give briefings to my direct supervisor in headquarters on a weekly basis by using tele-conferences. Important documentations are also sent electronically to make sure work is done efficiently.

This statement was also supported by the Operations Manager in Telecom C who remarked: 'We have a monthly video-conference with other department heads at headquarters, which can cover much broader issues in the whole company. Whenever we have problems, we can have discussions through Skype or video calls immediately'.

Eight of the ten case study companies have been operating in China for over ten years. The interviewees in those companies felt that their operations in China were going well, and as a consequence, fewer traditional expatriates were needed. In the words of the General Manager in Telecom C:

> Our company has been doing business in China for more than 10 years. Now, the operation here is smooth. We don't need the same number of long-term expatriates as we did at the start-up stage. Our company has shifted the staffing approach from ethnocentric to polycentric. Some issues still need to be dealt with by managers from the headquarters. However, they only need to stay here for a short period.

Some companies also mentioned that more non-traditional expatriates were being used to address the limitations concerning long-term expatriates, such as family issues and the high turnover rate. In the words of the Marketing Manager in Advertising A:

> South Koreans regard their families as very important. When long-term expatriates accept their assignments, both parties need to consider lots of issues, such as the children's education and spouse's career; all these issues are complex and not easy to deal with. Using fewer long-term expatriates can help to avoid these problems.

Furthermore, the Research and Development Team Manager in Chemical A commented that:

> One of the problems of using long-term expatriates is probably the high repatriate turnover rate, given that most Korean companies do not guarantee a promotion after assignments are completed. There is no career planning for expatriates. It will be a great loss for companies if repatriates leave after having gained a lot of international experience. For companies, using short-term expatriates is a smart move in this regard.

Some interviewees suggested that using non-traditional expatriates could provide companies with organizational flexibility. For example, the Operations Manager in Telecom D mentioned that:

> The project managers including senior managers and engineers carry out different projects in different subsidiaries in various countries. Compared to traditional long-term expatriates, using short-term expatriates allow companies to more effectively utilize managerial resources.

Several companies' representatives explained that using short-term expatriates was done in order to reduce costs. The Human Resources Manager in Chemical A, for example, commented 'We need to minimize operational costs. Using long-term expatriates is very expensive as the company needs to bear many costs such as relocation, family housing and children's education. Using short-term expatriates can avoid such costs'.

It is evident that the case study interviewees' comments on the reasons for South Korean MNEs using non-traditional expatriates are much the same as that outlined in the literature reviewed earlier in this chapter. The results suggest that South Korean MNEs encounter many of the same cost and market pressures as their Western counterparts, as well as experiencing many of the downsides when employing traditional expatriates. Clearly, the use of non-traditional expatriates represents an effective solution to an important human resource issue facing contemporary MNEs. It does not appear to be limited to companies structured along Western lines.

Managing Non-traditional Expatriates

Despite non-traditional expatriates having some clear advantages over traditional expatriates, they also face a number of expatriate-related problems if not properly managed. Several studies suggest that non-traditional expatriates may experience high levels of stress during assignments caused by their separation from families, failure to fulfill family responsibilities, and the difficulties in adjusting to local environments due to short assignment periods (Dowling and Welch 2004; Mayerhofer et al. 2004; Suutari et al. 2013; Tahvanainen et al. 2005). It is also harder for flexpatriates to develop good relationships with HCNs as their short expatriation periods mean they are unable to develop the level of understanding and communication that traditional expatriates achieve. As a consequence, conflicts between flexpatriates and HCNs are more likely to occur, particularly if flexpatriates ignore or are unaware of local customs and practices (Tahvanainen et al. 2005).

Research shows that organizational support reduces flexpatriates' stress and influences their job performance and job satisfaction (Demel and Mayrhofer 2010; Mayerhofer et al. 2011; Welch et al. 2007). It has also been suggested that the significant differences between traditional and non-traditional expatriates mean that different ways to manage them would be appropriate (Collings et al. 2007; Welch et al. 2003). As such, it is important for MNEs to formulate and implement appropriate HRM policies and practices in order to effectively support and manage non-traditional expatriates. Yet, only a small number of studies have explored HRM policies and practices for non-traditional expatriates, and this limited research shows that MNEs normally do not develop formal HRM policies and practices for this group of expatriates (Suutari et al. 2013). For example, Mayerhofer et al. (2004) found that flexpatriates in Austrian MNEs lacked formal employment contracts, did not undergo appropriate preparation prior to departure, and received minimal organizational support while on assignment. This finding supported an earlier survey conducted by PricewaterhouseCoopers (2000) that more than 50% of MNEs did not have formal HRM policies for non-traditional expatriates.

Specifically, formal selection processes were typically lacking for non-traditional assignees (Collings et al. 2007; Suutari et al. 2013). For example, in Finnish MNEs, short-term assignments were used for specific international projects or solving major problems. The pool of available and capable employees able to undertake such assignments was limited and normally well known to recruiters. Consequently, senior managers typically undertook the critical role of selection, and no formal selection procedures and written criteria had been developed for short-term assignees (Tahvanainen et al. 2005). Despite this lack of formal, written selection criteria, it was evident that MNEs placed considerable emphasis on skills, knowledge, and experience when selecting short-term assignees for specific projects and problem-solving and on self-nomination for management development (Collings et al. 2007; Tahvanainen et al. 2005). Yet, expatriate success in international assignments also depends on family/spouse issues, and thus these matters should be considered in expatriate selection (Starr and Currie 2009). Notwithstanding such matters, family/spouse issues have been largely ignored by MNEs in the recruitment and selection of non-traditional expatriates (Tahvanainen et al. 2005).

MNEs generally do not provide appropriate pre-departure training for non-traditional expatriates mainly because of short notice periods given or the need for more technical training. For example, Tahvanainen et al. (2005) found that Finnish MNEs normally did not provide cross-cultural training to short-term assignees unless the cultural distance between the home and the host country was high (e.g. Finland and China) (Hofstede 1980). In rare cases, information sessions were conducted (normally by repatriates) and in-house training was provided although on a voluntary basis. Pre-departure visits were found to be offered only when the expatriates' families accompanied the employee (Tahvanainen et al. 2005). Similarly, Mayerhofer et al. (2004) noted that language and cross-cultural training were only provided in an Austrian MNE when it was deemed absolutely necessary or requested by the expatriates.

Generally, performance appraisals for non-traditional expatriates are dealt with in a similar fashion to home country employees. In Finnish MNEs, goal setting and performance evaluations are carried out once or twice a year; however, the timing of the evaluations was more flexible for short-term expatriates. The raters are usually the immediate home-based supervisors in both Finnish and Austrian MNEs (Mayerhofer et al. 2004; Suutari et al. 2013; Tahvanainen et al. 2005). This led to problems as expatriates often complain about the problematic appraisal system, such as using single raters at home that do not have adequate knowledge about the working situation in subsidiaries and are not able to provide feedback on performance (Suutari et al. 2013).

Non-traditional expatriates are usually paid in the home country (Suutari et al. 2013; Tahvanainen et al. 2005). According to Tahvanainen et al. (2005), in Finnish MNEs, in addition to normal salary, short-term assignees receive a tax-free daily allowance (*per diem*), a cost of living allowance (when assigned to host countries where salary levels are higher than in Finland), and a hardship allowance (depending on host country's 'toughness', stressful nature of project work, and frequency of travel). According to Suutari et al. (2013) these financial benefits can be the major motivators for non-traditional expatriates. The compensation can also vary in terms of assignment duration. Suutari et al. (2013) and Tahvanainen et al. (2005) found that if the duration of an assignment lasted between 6 and 12 months, non-traditional expatriates were paid the same as traditional expatriates. The limited number of studies that have empirically examined the HRM practices referred to non-traditional expatriates, which means there is little definitive knowledge of how this group of employees is managed.

Recruitment and Selection

The interview results indicated that no case study companies developed formal recruitment and selection policies for non-traditional expatriates. Although the use of non-traditional expatriates was on the rise in most companies, interviewees generally did not consider it was necessary to establish a separate policy for this group of expatriates. Short-term assignments were normally regarded as extended business trips. In most cases, the selection of non-traditional expatriates was on a task basis; whenever there was a need in a subsidiary, these types of expatriates were sent to solve the problem. There was no open recruitment and selection; rather, employees were appointed for assignments. Due to the lack of a formal selection procedure, many interviewees, especially the HR managers, expressed a concern as to whether appointees were able to manage their assignments. The selection decision was often made quite quickly and the supervisors may not have clearly known whether the appointees were competent enough to take on the assignments. The outcome of such an approach was that the pool of available candidates was quite limited which led to case study companies tending to rely on employees who had been selected previously. This places a stronger emphasis on the evaluation of employees on assignment and the communication of that result to other relevant managers.

The selection criteria used by the case study companies tended to focus on technical skills, expertise, problem-solving skills, and international work experience. As the Research and Development Team Manager in Chemical A commented:

> The most important factor influencing the appointment of short-term assignees is expertise in different areas, such as technology, leadership and communication skills. These skills would enable assignees to complete their task, such as solving problems, transferring knowledge and coordination. International experience is also important to some assignments.

Several interviewees also commented that employees who were qualified for such assignments and subsequently selected experienced good relationships with senior managers. For example, the Operation Manager in Telecom A mentioned that 'People who have close relationships with senior managers are more likely to be selected for short-term assignments. Taking this kind of overseas trips is beneficial to employees' career development'.

As family relocation was not required, family issues were normally not considered as an appointment criterion in most case study companies. However, if a family issue arose that prevented an employee from taking a short-term assignment, they would normally be excused. According to the Marketing Manager in Advertising A, most employees were happy to take up short-term assignments because 'they can temporarily walk away from their work routines and no family relocation is required'. He further added that 'employees can decline assignments if the timing is not suitable or for other reasons, such as family issues or personal issues (e.g. health problems) that mean that they are unwilling to make international trips'.

Training

The training provided to non-traditional expatriates included some limited pre-departure and post-arrival training. Formal pre-departure training was generally not provided although all case study companies encouraged assignees to study the Chinese language and Chinese culture. One of the reasons for not offering such training was a general perception, clearly expressed by the Research and Development Team Manager in Chemical A that:

> People who are chosen should have adequate knowledge and expertise to perform the task in subsidiaries; also, the language and cultural issues are not big deals because of the short-term nature. We have translators and ethnic Chinese-Korean employees who can help with the language problem.

It was also reported that the short notice given for assignments made it difficult for companies to arrange training for short-term assignees. Information sessions on Chinese culture were generally provided, however, only on the request of assignees. Three companies—Electronics A, Auto A, and Telecom B—provided resources, such as DVDs and books, to help non-traditional expatriates familiarize themselves with the language and culture. As the Research and Development Team Manager in Electronics A stated:

> Our company did not provide formal pre-departure training to short-term expatriates. However, the company provided time and financial support to employees who wanted to take some Chinese language lessons.

Formal post-arrival training was typically not afforded to non-traditional expatriates. However, all the case study companies provided post-arrival language and cross-cultural training to traditional, long-term expatriates. Such training was open to short-term assignees if the timing was right. However, 'attending such training is purely on a voluntary basis and the record shows that no short-term assignee has attended such training due to time constraint' (Technical Support Team Manager, Electronics B).

Performance Appraisal

Six out of ten case study companies (Telecom A, Chemical A, Telecom B, Electronics A, Electronics B, and Auto A) conducted short-term expatriates' performance appraisals on a project basis. In these companies, performance was evaluated by both subsidiaries and headquarters. Raters included immediate supervisors in headquarters and managers responsible for projects in local subsidiaries. Evaluations of raters in subsidiaries were considered most important because they knew how short-term expatriates performed and the working conditions in local subsidiaries. As suggested by the Operation Team Manager at Auto A, 'local supervisors' evaluations are normally perceived as accurate and objective because they are the closer observers of assignees' performance'. In general, the performance appraisal procedures in the case study companies consisted of four steps:

- *Step 1*: Non-traditional expatriates submitted self-evaluations to their immediate supervisors (South Korean managers) in subsidiaries.
- *Step 2*: Raters in local subsidiaries reviewed self-evaluations and provided comments.
- *Step 3*: Upon returning home, immediate supervisors at headquarters would arrange performance review meetings to finalize mutually agreed grades for assignments.
- *Step 4*: Evaluation results were sent to HR departments and became a key part of annual performance appraisals.

Four companies (Advertising A, Telecom C, Finance A, and Telecom D) conducted performance appraisals for flexpatriates in the same way as they did for other home-based employees. Their performance appraisals were usually conducted at the end of the year at the head office. All case study companies adopted a grade system for evaluating non-traditional short-term expatriates. Generally speaking, there were five grades—A (outstanding), B (good), C (satisfactory), D (poor), and E (unacceptable). For example, the Operation Manager in Telecom C explained that:

> The final performance result is composed of three parts including performance (50%), competence (30%), and attitude (e.g. attendance) (20%). Each grade has different weights, say Grade A weighs 15 points, Grade B for 13 points, Grade C for 11 points, and so on. The final grade is the composite of all appraisal criteria.

Some companies (Telecom A, Electronics A, Auto A) also required appraisers to provide written comments with the grading results. Typical comments addressed whether the appraisee was competent for the job, whether any mistakes were made during the assignment, as well as providing some overall comments and suggestions for the assignee.

Work performance was considered to be the most important criterion. 'In particular, completion of core tasks is especially important, which has the highest weighting' (Operation Manager, Telecom A). Competence broadly included knowledge, expertise, and leadership. 'In particular, for project-based assignees, problem solving skills, communication abilities, self-discipline, and the ability to conduct workshops and meetings are key components' (Operation Manager, Telecom D). Workplace attitudes included attendance, responsibility, and interactions with supervisors and peers. For flexpatriates, who were used commonly for chairing meetings and administration purposes, coordinating ability and leadership skills were highly valued. These criteria were applicable to both project-based appraisals and annual appraisals. Feedback was provided by immediate supervisors at headquarters, normally in a written form. 'Face-to-face discussions were only conducted for poor performances, for example, if the short-term assignee did not complete his task successfully' (Operation Manager, Telecom A).

Compensation

Non-traditional assignees did not have separate contracts and their compensation was based on their company's respective travel policy. Generally, expatriates received different levels of allowances according to their positions and length of assignment. In all case study companies, expatriates received their salaries in the home country and in home country currency. 'Short-term assignments are normally considered as extended business trips; of course their pay is managed in the home country' (General Manager, Electronics B). The only difference was the amount and categories of allowances and benefits. For short-term expatriates who only stayed for less than one week, the allowances and benefits were normally a travel allowance, meal allowances, and a free company car during their stay. In the words of the HR Manager in Auto A: 'For expatriates who only stay a few days, their salaries will be paid at the headquarter standard. Air tickets and accommodation (hotel standards depend on positions) were paid by the company. During their stay they are also provided with a company car'. This statement was supported by other interviewees. The HR Manager in Telecom D also added that 'short-term expatriates were also paid to have some day-tours during their visit. Meals were also arranged and paid by us'.

For expatriates who stayed between two and four weeks, they normally received a daily living allowance. The General Manager in Electronics B explained that:

> Expatriates who stay a few weeks are normally provided with employee accommodation. Instead of being provided with meals they are given a liv-

> ing allowance based on their positions; normally 1000 RMB per week for middle-management, 600 RMB for non-managerial staff.

Most interviewees reported that the maximum stay for short-term assignment was three months. For expatriates who stayed more than one month, they had more allowances and benefits such as paid family visits, gym/golf membership, and company-organized trips. In the words of the Operation Manager in Telecom A:

> My assignment was for three months. My accommodation was paid by the company—it is a nice apartment close to the company. My family was also paid to visit me once during my stay. I have enjoyed most benefits like long-term expatriates had here, such as golf club membership.

It is clear based on the above analysis that non-traditional expatriates are treated quite differently compared to their traditional counterparts. Most companies did not have a formal recruitment and selection policy pertaining to this group of employees, nor did they receive any significant level of pre- or post-departure training. Performance appraisal was often conducted locally, although final grades were determined at headquarters, and compensation was more aligned with the head office travel policy.

Discussion

This study explored the use and management of non-traditional expatriates in South Korean MNEs operating in China. This is an important area of investigation as the research to date has mainly focused on traditional expatriates and almost exclusively on Western MNEs. Three key findings emerged from this study. Firstly, the results demonstrated that there was an increase in the use of non-traditional expatriates and a decrease in the use of traditional expatriates in the case study MNEs. Most interviewees indicated that their companies intended to replace the traditional long-term expatriates with the use of more talented local employees and short-term assignees wherever possible. These findings are consistent with recent industry surveys, such as those conducted by KPMG (2010) and Brookfield Global Relocation Services (2012).

Secondly, the study provided support for the arguments of Collings et al. (2007), Mayerhofer et al. (2004), and Shen and Lang (2009), who suggested that the trend for MNEs to use more short-term assignees or flexpatriates was due to them being more cost-effective and easier to manage. The major reasons for using non-traditional expatriates in the case study companies included less need for long-term expatriates, flexibility, and addressing the long-term expatriate-related problems (i.e. family and repatriation issues). These results are consistent with findings from studies conducted on Western MNEs (Tharenou and Harvey 2006) and highlight the strong pressures for convergence despite the significant differences in South Korean MNEs' structure and strategies.

Thirdly, most case study companies managed their non-traditional expatriates quite differently from the way long-term expatriates are managed. Positions are normally assigned rather than openly recruited, and the main selection criteria are technical skills/expertise, problem-solving skills, and work performance. Such an approach is quite different from the selection of traditional, long-term expatriates in South Korean MNEs (Kang and Shen 2013). However, the results are quite consistent with Tahvanainen et al. (2005) who maintain there is a lack of formal selection policy for non-traditional expatriates. The case study companies provided limited pre-departure training and post-arrival training to non-traditional expatriates due to the short-term nature of the assignment. Two possible reasons may explain this situation. Firstly, the cultural similarity between South Korea and China may make cross-cultural training less necessary, which is consistent with Finnish MNEs' practices (Tahvanainen et al. 2005). Secondly, there is often not enough time between selection and departure for non-traditional assignees to attend pre-departure training (Tahvanainen et al. 2005). Due to time constraints, no non-traditional expatriate in the case study MNEs attended post-arrival training such as language instruction and cross-cultural training, which—while they had been designed for long-term expatriates—were also open to them. We believe that this is a significant weakness because cross-cultural training is also critical to non-traditional expatriates, such as business travelers and those involved in virtual assignments (Collings et al. 2007).

Most companies conducted performance appraisals for non-traditional expatriates on a project basis, usually by their immediate supervisor in both subsidiaries and headquarters. This is in contrast to the findings of Suutari et al. (2013) who found that short-term assignees' evaluations were conducted annually, and the findings of Mayerhofer et al. (2004) who found that non-traditional expatriates' performances were only assessed by immediate supervisors in the local subsidiary. Finally, the compensation for non-traditional expatriates depended on the duration of the assignments and the level of the position. Non-traditional expatriates did not have separate contracts, and as the assignment duration was generally less than three months, their compensation was aligned with the company's travel policy. This is consistent with the findings of Suutari et al. (2013). Moreover, a number of other allowances and benefits were available to non-traditional expatriates who stayed longer. The results of this study appear to be consistent with the practices in Finnish MNEs, suggesting that compensation is based on the length of assignments (Tahvanainen et al. 2005).

Conclusion

There is limited research on the use and management of non-traditional expatriates in MNEs, especially non-Western ones. The current study explores the trend of using and managing non-traditional expatriates of South Korean MNEs operating in China. This chapter firstly reviews the literature on non-traditional expatriates, the trend and reasons for employing non-traditional expatriates, and the management practices of this type of expatriate. Consequently, it reports the empirical findings in relation to South Korean MNEs. This study reveals that the utilization of non-traditional expatriates has increased in the sample MNEs. Non-traditional expatriates undertake similar roles to those of long-term expatriates including control, problem-solving, management development, and knowledge transfer. This shift toward the use of more non-traditional expatriation has been brought about by the decreased need for long-term assignments and the desire to develop more organizational flexibility. This shift represents a strategic response to the issues surrounding the deployment of traditional expatriates such as family, career, and high expatriate failure. The use of non-expatriates is, however, not without problems as the research found that there was a lack of formal recruitment and selection processes, and that training for non-traditional expatriates was limited. These problems will need to be effectively solved given that more and more non-traditional expatriates are deployed in MNEs. The next chapter will examine the effect of IHRM practices on the willingness of HCNs to do extra for MNEs, that is, to help expatriates at work and beyond.

Bibliography

Barney, J. B. (1991). Firm resources and sustained competitive advantage. *Journal of Management, 17*(1), 99–120.

Bolino, M. C. (2007). Expatriate assignments and intra-organizational career success: Implications for individuals and organizations. *Journal of International Business Studies, 38*(5), 819–835.

Bonache, J., & Noethen, D. (2014). The impact of individual performance on organizational success and its implications for the management of expatriates. *The International Journal of Human Resource Management, 25*(14), 1960–1977.

Bonache, J., Brewster, C., & Suutari, V. (2001). Expatriation: A developing research agenda. *Thunderbird International Business Review, 43*(1), 3–20.

Bossard, A. B., & Peterson, R. B. (2005). The repatriate experience as seen by American expatriates. *Journal of World Business, 40*(1), 9–28.

Brookfield Global Relocation Services. (2012). *Global relocation trends 2012 survey report.* Retrieved March 10, 2014, from http://espritgloballearning.com/wp-content/uploads/2011/03/2012-Brookfield-Global-Relocations-Trends-Survey.pdf

Collings, D. G., Scullion, H., & Morley, M. J. (2007). Changing patterns of global staffing in the multinational enterprise: Challenges to the conventional expatriate assignment and emerging alternatives. *Journal of World Business, 42*(2), 198–213.

Demel, B., & Mayrhofer, W. (2010). Frequent business travelers across Europe: Career aspirations and implications. *Thunderbird International Business Review, 52*(4), 301–311.

Dowling, P. J., & Welch, D. E. (1988). International human resource management: An Australian perspective. *Asia Pacific Journal of Management, 6*(1), 39–65.

Dowling, P. J., & Welch, D. E. (2004). *International human resource management. Managing people in a multinational context.* London: Thomson.

Dowling, P. J., Festing, M., & Engle, A. D. (2013). *International human resource management.* London: Cengage Learning.

General Motors Acceptance Corporation. (2004). *Global relocation trends 2003/2004 survey report.* Retrieved March 10, 2014, from http://www.nftc.org/default/hr/GRTS%202003-4.pdf

Hofstede, G. (1980). Culture and organizations. *International Studies of Management and Organization, 10*(4), 15–41.

Kang, H. Y., & Shen, J. (2013). International recruitment and selection practices of South Korean multinationals in China. *The International Journal of Human Resource Management, 24*(17), 3325–3342.

Korea Eximbank. (2013). *Investment statistics by country*. Retrieved April 10, 2013, from http://211.171.208.92/odisas_eng.html

KPMG. (2010). *Global assignment policies and practices survey*. Retrieved March 10, 2014, from, https://www.kpmg.com/ZA/en/IssuesAndInsights/ArticlesPublications/Tax-and-Legal-Publications/Documents/GAPP-Survey-2010.pdf

Lazarova, M. B., & Cerdin, J. L. (2007). Revisiting repatriation concerns: Organizational support versus career and contextual influences. *Journal of International Business Studies, 38*(3), 404–429.

Mayerhofer, H., Hartmann, L. C., Michelitsch-Riedl, G., & Kollinger, I. (2004). Flexpatriate assignments: A neglected issue in global staffing. *The International Journal of Human Resource Management, 15*(8), 1371–1389.

Mayerhofer, H., Schmidt, A., Hartmann, L., & Bendl, R. (2011). Recognising diversity in managing work life issues of flexpatriates. *Equality, Diversity and Inclusion: An International Journal, 30*(7), 589–609.

Mercer. (2013). *Mercer's Worldwide International Assignments Policies and Practices report*. Retrieved March 10, 2014, from http://m.mercer.com/press-releases/1521435?detail=D

Minbaeva, D. B., & Michailova, S. (2004). Knowledge transfer and expatriation in multinational corporations: The role of disseminative capacity. *Employee Relations, 26*(6), 663–679.

Petrovic, J., Harris, H., & Brewster, C. (2000). *New forms of international working CReME research report*. Retrieved October 18, 2014, from https://dspace.lib.cranfield.ac.uk/bitstream/1826/3702/3/New_forms_of_international_working-2000.pdf

PricewaterhouseCoopers. (2000). *Managing in a virtual world*. London: PricewaterhouseCoopers.

PricewaterhouseCoopers. (2005). *International assignments: Global policy and practice: Key trends 2005*. Retrived October 18, 2014, from http://www.pwc.lu/en_LU/lu/hr/docs/hrs062005.pdf?q=assignments

Rowley, C., & Bae, J. S. (2004). Human resource management in South Korea after the Asian financial crisis: Emerging patterns from the labyrinth. *International Studies of Management & Organization, 34*(1), 52–82.

Schaaper, J., Amann, B., Jaussaud, J., Nakamura, H., & Mizoguchi, S. (2013). Human resource management in Asian subsidiaries: Comparison of French and Japanese MNCs. *International Journal of Human Resource Management, 24*(7), 1454–1470.

Shaffer, M. A., Kraimer, M. L., Chen, Y. P., & Bolino, M. C. (2012). Choices, challenges, and career consequences of global work experiences: A review and future agenda. *Journal of Management, 38*(4), 1282–1327.

Shen, J., & Lang, B. (2009). Cross-cultural training and its impact on expatriate performance in Australian MNEs. *Human Resource Development International, 12*(4), 371–386.

Stahl, G. K., Miller, E. L., & Tung, R. L. (2002). Toward the boundaryless career: A closer look at the expatriate career concept and the perceived implications of an international assignment. *Journal of World Business, 37*(3), 216–227.

Starr, T. L., & Currie, G. (2009). 'Out of sight but still in the picture': Short-term international assignments and the influential role of family. *The International Journal of Human Resource Management, 20*(6), 1421–1438.

Suutari, V., Brewster, C., Riusala, K., & Syrjäkari, S. (2013). Managing non-standard international experience: Evidence from a Finnish company. *Journal of Global Mobility: The Home of Expatriate Management Research, 1*(2), 118–138.

Tahvanainen, M., Welch, D., & Worm, V. (2005). Implications of short-term international assignments. *European Management Journal, 23*(6), 663–673.

Tan, D., & Mahoney, J. T. (2006). Why a multinational firms chooses expatriates: Integrating resource-based, agency and transaction costs perspectives. *Journal of Management Studies, 43*(3), 457–484.

Tharenou, P., & Harvey, M. (2006). Examining the overseas staffing options utilized by Australian headquartered multinational corporations. *The International Journal of Human Resource Management, 17*(6), 1095–1114.

Toh, S. M., & DeNisi, A. S. (2005). A local perspective to expatriate success. *Academy of Management Executive, 19*(1), 132–146.

Tung, R. L. (1987). Expatriate assignments: Enhancing success and minimizing failure. *Academy of Management Executive, 1*(2), 117–125.

Welch, D. E., & Worm, V. (2006). International business travellers: A challenge for IHRM. In G. K. Stahl & I. Björkman (Eds.), *Handbook of research in international human resource management* (pp. 283–301). Cheltenham: Edward Elgar.

Welch, D. E., Worm, V., & Fenwick, M. (2003). Are virtual international assignments feasible? *Management International Review, 43*(1), 95–114.

Welch, D. E., Welch, L. S., & Worm, V. (2007). The international business traveller: A neglected but strategic human resource. *International Journal of Human Resource Management, 18*(2), 173–183.

Whitley, R. (1992). *Business systems in East Asia: Firms, markets and societies.* London: Sage.

Wittig-Berman, U., & Beutel, N. J. (2009). International assignments and the career management of repatriates: The boundaryless career concept. *International Journal of Management, 26*(1), 77–88.

Wong, C. S., & Law, K. S. (1999). Managing localization of human resources in the PRC: A practical model. *Journal of World Business, 34*(1), 26–40.

Yoon, D. R. (2007, April 25–26). *Korea's outward FDI in Asia: Characteristics and prospects.* ICRIER Workshop, at Casurina Hall, India Habitat Centre, Lodhi Road New Delhi.

CHAPTER 8

The Effects of IHRM on Employee Outcomes

Introduction

Only limited research has been conducted on the consequences of IHRM practices on employees. To help fill the lack of literature on the subject, this chapter explores the relationship between IHRM practices and the willingness of HCNs to help expatriates in and outside of the workplace. Research has shown that expatriates often experience difficulties in the workplace and outside of it. As such, assistance from HCNs with work and social life plays an irreplaceable role in expatriates' adjustment and ability to do their job when on international assignments (Caligiuri et al. 1999; Farh et al. 2010; Varma et al. 2011). Providing help to co-workers often goes beyond one's job duty and it may well be considered risk-taking behavior because it may affect the help provider's own work performance (Shen and Benson 2014). Expatriates have multiple identities; in addition to being co-workers, they are also seen by HCNs as representatives of MNEs (Reiche et al. 2008; Zhou and Qin 2009). Therefore, HCNs helping expatriates represent both helping behavior toward co-workers and their positive attitudes and behaviors toward the MNEs.

The past decade has witnessed increasing academic interest in exploring factors predicting the relationship between HCNs and expatriates (e.g. Arman and Aycan 2013; Toh and DeNisi 2007; Toh and Srinivas 2012; Varma et al. 2011). However, the extant literature regarding determinants of the willingness of HCNs to help expatriates has focused on personal

H. Kang, J. Shen, *International Human Resource Management in South Korean Multinational Enterprises*,
DOI 10.1007/978-981-10-3093-2_8

and intrapersonal factors such as personality (Caligiuri 2000; Johnson et al. 2003) and social categorization (Arman and Aycan 2013; Varma et al. 2011). Thus far, organizational factors predicting the willingness of HCNs to help expatriates have been largely overlooked, indicating a need for further theoretical and empirical clarification. Due to the unique identities of expatriates, HCNs helping expatriates is not only pro-social behavior that helps co-workers; it also reflects their positive attitudes and behaviors toward MNEs. Thus, exploring organizational contextual effects on HCNs' attitudes and behaviors toward expatriates requires new theoretical frameworks that differ from those presented in past studies.

This chapter seeks to fill this important knowledge gap by exploring: firstly, the effects of MNEs' IHRM policies and practices in overseas subsidiaries on the willingness of HCNs to help expatriates; and secondly, the social and psychological processes involved. This study is significant because it aims to provide a better understanding of IHRM antecedents of HCNs' attitudes and behaviors toward expatriates, an important employee outcome. Understanding IHRM antecedents may guide MNEs to formulate and implement more effective HRM policies and practices in order to facilitate expatriates' success.

This chapter is structured as follows. We will firstly outline the theoretical background with regard to expatriates' role as representatives of MNEs, high-commitment HRM, and socially responsible HRM and develop the hypotheses. Secondly, we will present the empirical findings.

Theoretical Background and Development of Hypotheses

HCNs' Willingness to Help Expatriates

HCNs' willingness to help expatriates, such as willing to provide social support and information about their workplace role and duties, and to offer cooperation, plays a positive role in expatriate work performance in international assignments (Farh et al. 2010; Toh and DeNisi 2003; Varma et al. 2009). Expatriates who are not well accepted by HCNs are less likely to work well. As a result, the MNE's performance will be compromised (Toh and Srinivas 2012). In most cases, expatriates need to have working knowledge and good cultural understanding of the organization and the national context in order to be effective in international assignments

(Toh and DeNisi 2005). HCNs' social support is also important because it affects expatriates' leadership roles and work performance during their assignments (Benson and Pattie 2009). Social support may include providing emotional support or instrumental assistance when dealing with stressful situations (Toh and DeNisi 2005). Cooperation among employees enhances morale, organizational commitment, productivity, and interpersonal relationships and reduces conflict among group members (Tjosvold and Chia 1989).

Zeira (1979) argued that HCNs have certain expectations of expatriates, and their attitudes and behaviors toward the expatriates are often guided by the extent to which they might fulfill those expectations. So far, the literature suggests that HCNs' willingness to help is affected by a number of individual-level factors, for example, expatriates' personality, that is, level of extroversion (Caligiuri 2000; Johnson et al. 2003). Toh and DeNisi (2007) found that HCNs' willingness to help is often determined by the process of HCNs' social categorization. If a HCN categorizes an expatriate as being a member of a particular social group, the HCN is more willing to provide help to that person (Varma et al. 2011). Moreover, the job level of an expatriate is also likely to influence whether HCNs are willing to offer support. HCNs are more likely to provide role information to co-workers and subordinates than to supervisors, and furthermore they are more likely to provide role information to subordinates than peers (Varma et al. 2011). Since most expatriates are managers, HCNs are normally reluctant to help them. Furthermore, Toh and Srinivas (2012) indicated trust will have an impact on HCNs' willingness to share information with expatriates.

When an expatriate is seen as a supervisor and a representative of an MNE, the factors influencing HCNs' willingness to help are different. Research suggests that factors like supervisor leadership (e.g. Ilies et al. 2007; Judge and Piccolo 2004), supervisor personality (e.g. Smith and Canger 2004) and POS (e.g. Yoon and Thye 2000) influence the supervisor–subordinate relationship. Expatriates' supervisory and managerial roles in overseas subsidiaries mean that they are inevitably identified as the representatives or ambassadors of the MNE (Ancona and Caldwell 1992; Reiche et al. 2008; Varma et al. 2009; Zhou and Qin 2009). Understandably, HCNs' attitudes to the MNE will influence their attitudes to expatriates who are sent by, and represent, the parent company.

Expatriates' Role as Representatives of MNEs

Expatriates play many important roles in international operations (Bonache and Brewster 2001; Harzing 2001; Manolopoulos et al. 2011). Expatriates can be responsible for coordination and control of overseas operations, knowledge transfer, and network building (Arman and Aycan 2013; Ghafoor et al. 2011; Harzing 2001; Manolopoulos et al. 2011). According to agency theory, expatriates are valued agents of the MNE (the principal) (Shen and Hall 2009). Because expatriates normally hold senior managerial positions in foreign subsidiaries, they are naturally seen as spokespersons and representatives of MNEs (Reiche et al. 2008; Zhou and Qin 2009). The employee–organization relationship is 'the formal and informal, the economic, social and psychological connection between an employee and his or her employer' (Tsui et al. 2002, p. 78). It reflects the social exchange between an individual employee and the organization (Wu et al. 2010). In the employee–organization relationship, individuals in reality do not enter into an exchange agreement with the organization (Coyle-Shapiro and Shore 2007). Rather, the representative of the organization is the dyadic partner with whom the employee interacts (Ferris et al. 2009). Psychological contract theory (Rousseau 1989) assumes that employees consider promises from the supervisor to be promises from their organization. In the multinational context, since expatriates are seen as representatives of MNEs, the HCN–MNE relationship is largely reflected in the relationships between HCNs and expatriates.

Moreover, employees in general tend to interact more frequently with their supervisors than with other agents of the organization. Therefore, supervisors are in the best position to serve as organizational representatives (Richard et al. 2009; Tepper and Taylor 2003). Rousseau (1989) argued that employees consider their supervisors' promises to be those of the organization. Similarly, employees pay great attention to their treatment by supervisors, in part, because they view such treatment as indicative of how well the business values them (Eisenberger et al. 1986, 2004; Shore and Shore 1995). Employees often tend to generalize their exchange relationships from their supervisors to the organization (Eisenberger et al. 2002). Due to their supervisory and managerial roles in overseas subsidiaries, expatriates are inevitably identified as the representatives of the MNE (Reiche et al. 2008; Varma et al. 2009; Zhou and Qin 2009). Hence, employees' attitudes and behaviors toward supervisors reflect their attitudes and behaviors toward the organization. With this logic, HCNs' attitudes and behaviors toward expatriate managers should be influenced by their attitudes and behaviors toward the MNE. Moreover, employees' attitudes and behaviors toward the organization are their attitudinal and behavioral responses to perceived organizational policies and practices, such as HRM (Jiang et al. 2012). As such, IHRM practices may have an impact on HCNs' willingness to help expatriates. We will discuss this linkage in more detail below.

High-Commitment HRM and Socially Responsible HRM

Organizations and businesses may adopt a range of HRM practices serving multiple purposes, and the HR attribution literature suggests that perceived HR attributions determine the impact of HRM on employees (Nishii et al. 2008). Some HRM practices may be required by law or government regulations, while others are discretionary (Nishii et al. 2008). It is argued that compulsory requirements have a less positive impact on employees' workplace attitudes and behaviors than discretionary organizational policies and practices (Eisenberger et al. 1997; Meyer and Smith 2000). A similar finding has been reported by Nishii et al. (2008), who noted that employees attributing HRM practices to development or quality rather than cost reduction or legal compliance are likely to display more positive employee behaviors such as helping behavior. This is why there is a need to examine different HRM practices separately. In this study, we focus on two bundles of discretionary HRM practices, namely, high-commitment HRM and socially responsible HRM.

High-commitment HRM focuses on personal development, for example, training, feedback, mentoring, career and managerial development, employee participation and involvement, job security, work–life balance, and health and safety, and is positively related to perceived organizational support (POS) (Chiang et al. 2011; McClean and Collins 2011). Social exchange theory (Blau 1964) better explains the social and psychological process through which high-commitment HRM influences the willingness of HCNs to help expatriates. Social exchange theory posits that employees personalize and develop exchange relationships with the organization, and these relationships are primarily influenced by POS embedded in organizational policies and practices that address the interests and needs of employees. POS is defined as employee perceptions of the degree to which the organization values their contributions and cares for their intrinsic and extrinsic needs (Eisenberger et al. 1986). When employees perceive strong organizational support, they become more willing to do extra task for the organization. Evoking social exchange theory, we argue that POS is the underlying mechanism through which high-commitment HRM influences the willingness of HCNs to help expatriates.

According to Orlitzky and Swanson (2006) and Shen (2011), socially responsible HRM practices can be defined as HRM practices that are adopted to enhance employees' awareness of and commitment to corporate social responsibility (CSR), improve employees' skills, and motivate employees to engage in CSR activities. Socially responsible HRM may include emphasizing CSR values in recruitment and selection, providing CSR training, and taking account of social performance in promotion, appraisal, and reward processes (Orlitzky and Swanson 2006; Shen 2011). The adoption of socially responsible HRM is an organizational signal of commitment to CSR that is now a social norm worldwide (Pfeffer 2010; Porter and Kramer 2011). Social identity theory (Tajfel 1978; Tajfel and Turner 1985) proposes that employees' attitudes and behaviors toward the organization depend on how they identify with the organization; organizational identification results from employee perceptions of organizational support and external prestige. Underpinned by Tajfel's social identity theory, we will explore the mediation of organizational identification in the relationship between socially responsible HRM and the willingness of HCNs to help expatriates. Organizational identification has been defined in various ways in the literature. One widely recognized definition is offered by Ashforth and Mael (1989) that emphasizes the perception of oneness with and belonging to the organization. Furthermore, past studies indicate that POS is positively associated with organizational identification (Gibney et al. 2011; Sluss et al. 2008). Thus, POS and organizational identification would sequentially mediate the relationship between high-commitment HRM and HCNs' willingness to help expatriates.

High-Commitment HRM, POS, and Willingness of HCNs to Help Expatriates

Assistance from HCNs both in the workplace and in the community is important for expatriates due to the potential stress of moving to and working in a new country (Arman and Aycan 2013; Varma et al. 2011). Generally, all employees are expected to exhibit behaviors in the workplace conforming to the organizational culture and the requirements of job roles. Because of their national working experience and background,

HCNs have the relevant role information which is necessary for expatriates to learn in order to become effective members of the organization (Varma et al. 2011). Assistance from HCNs in the workplace by sharing role information is important for expatriates if they are to succeed during their international assignments (Mahajan and Toh 2014; Toh and Srinivas 2012). Outside the workplace, in any particular culture, only certain behaviors are deemed to be appropriate. In this connection, HCNs can play two essential roles in assisting expatriates to adjust to a new living environment. Firstly, HCNs can provide valuable social information to expatriates to help them understand and conform to social norms (Arman and Aycan 2013). Secondly, 'inclusion of expatriates in the HCNs' friendship and/or interest group would provide moral and emotional help and would make expatriates feel accepted in their new environment' (Varma et al. 2011, p. 354).

HRM practices send 'strong messages to individuals regarding what the organization expects of them and what they can expect in return and are thus indicative of the organization's intentions' (Rousseau 1995, p. 162). Once the organization implements HR practices that reflect investment in and support for employees, it signals that the organization intends to seek a social exchange and long-term relationship with its employees (Allen et al. 2003; Armstrong-Stassen and Schlosser 2010; Edwards 2009). Employees may see such HRM practices as evidence of positive support from the organization. It is recognized that high-commitment HRM practices such as providing job security and opportunities for promotion and development and caring about employee development and work–life balance (Chiang et al. 2011), developmental performance appraisal and training, and competitive pay and benefits (Whitener 2001) are important antecedents of POS. High-commitment HRM adopted in subsidiaries demonstrates that the MNE is committed to HCNs in the long term and is willing to invest in them and genuinely cares about their well-being and personal or professional development (Shen 2011). In a similar vein, high-commitment HRM practices adopted in subsidiaries should result in HCN perceptions of organizational support.

Employees' attitudes and behaviors toward their organization reflect employee–organizational social exchange relationships (Purcell and Hutchinson 2007; Rhoades and Eisenberger 2002). Social exchange refers to 'voluntary actions of individuals that are motivated by the returns they are expected to bring and typically do in fact bring from others' (Blau 1964, p. 91). Social exchange relationships evolve between employees and the organization when the latter provides sufficient support to employees to develop beneficial consequences. These include positive employee attitudes and work behaviors toward their organization (Cropanzano and Mitchell 2005; Rhoades and Eisenberger 2002). In the employee–organization relationship, individuals in reality do not enter into an exchange agreement with the organization (Coyle-Shapiro and Shore 2007). Rather, the representative of the organization is the dyadic partner with whom the employee interacts (Ferris et al. 2009).

In the MNE context, the HCN–MNE relationship is, to some extent, reflected in the relationships between HCNs and expatriates. Hence, POS will result in HCNs' positive attitudes and behaviors toward the MNE, such as helping expatriates as co-workers and as representatives of the MNE. Prior studies indicate that POS mediates the relationship between HR practices and employees' positive workplace attitudes and behaviors, such as helping behavior (Mossholder et al. 2011; Snape and Redman 2010). We expect a similar research finding for high-commitment HRM in the MNE setting. Therefore, we propose the following hypothesis:

Hypothesis 1 High-commitment HRM is positively related to HCNs' willingness to help expatriates in and outside of the workplace through the mediation of POS.

Socially Responsible HRM, Organizational Identification, and HCNs' Willingness to Help Expatriates

Porter and Kramer (2011) argue that creating a shared value with the broader community by engaging in CSR has become an organizational obligation as well as an important source of business competitive advantage. As a result, in the last few decades, CSR has increasingly becoming a key priority for business leaders and a social norm around the world (Aguinis and Glavas 2012; Pfeffer 2010; Porter and Kramer 2011). In turn this has led to the performance of MNEs being more thoroughly examined against CSR-related criteria (Porter and Kramer 2011). A growing number of organizations adopt socially responsible HRM in order to effectively implement CSR initiatives (Orlitzky and Swanson 2006; Shen 2011). Through the adoption of effective socially responsible HRM, the organization signals that it is committed to addressing the needs and interests of multiple stakeholders beyond financial return (Shen and Benson 2014). The adoption of socially responsible HRM should result in positive employee perceptions of the MNE's conformity to social norms by actively engaging in CSR. Social identity theory proposes that employees tend to identify with their organization when it conforms to social norms that enhance their self-esteem (Ashforth and Mael 1989; Dutton et al. 1994). Organizational identification is enhanced feelings of belongingness and psychological attachment to the organization (Dutton et al. 1994; Wan-Huggins et al. 1998). Therefore, the adoption of socially responsible HRM should enhance HCNs' identification with their MNE.

Social identity theory also posits that organizational identification fulfills employees' needs for belonging and membership, which in turn results in positive employee attitudes and behaviors toward the organization (Dutton et al. 1994; Kreiner and Ashforth 2004; Pratt 1998; Van Dick et al. 2004). Empirical evidence suggests that organizational identification is positively linked to employees' positive attitudes and behaviors to their workplace, and positive interactions with other organization members are manifested in helping and cooperative or collaborative behaviors (Dukerich et al. 2002; Knight and Haslam 2010). Thus, when HCNs strongly identify with their MNE, they will demonstrate positive attitudes and behaviors concerning the MNE and other organization members including expatriates. Consequently, HCNs will be more willing to 'go the extra mile' for expatriates, providing support to them in and outside the workplace. Putting these aspects together, organizational identification can be described as an underlying social and psychological process linking socially responsible HRM and HCNs' willingness to help expatriates. Subsequently, we develop the following hypothesis:

Hypothesis 2 Socially responsible HRM is positively related to HCNs' willingness to help expatriates in and outside the workplace through the mediation of employee organizational identification.

Sequential Mediation of POS and Organizational Identification

Research shows that POS is an important antecedent of organizational identification (Edwards and Peccei 2010). When organizations care about employees' well-being and development, they will feel supported and valued (Eisenberger et al. 1986). Feeling supported and valued by the organization makes employees feel that they are being perceived favorably standing in the organization. In turn their improved self-esteem and self-worth stimulate organizational identification (Ashforth and Mael 1989;

Edwards and Peccei 2010). Rhoades and Eisenberger (2002) have suggested that 'the caring, approval and respect connoted by POS should fulfill socio-emotional needs, leading workers to incorporate organizational membership and role status into their social identity' (p. 699). In a similar vein, we therefore expect HCNs' POS from the MNE to be linked to their organizational identification. As indicted in Hypotheses 1 and 2, high-commitment HRM is positively related to POS, and both POS and organizational identification are positively related to HCNs' willingness to help expatriates. These relationships constitute sequential mediation of POS and organizational identification in the relationship between high-commitment HRM and HCNs' willingness to help expatriates. Therefore, we hypothesize the following:

Hypothesis 3 HCNs' POS and organizational identification will sequentially mediate the relationship between high-commitment HRM and HCNs' willingness to help expatriates in and outside of the workplace.

Data Collection and Analysis

The data for examining the relationships proposed here were collected from 485 employees in the 10 case study companies. We sent out 870 surveys and received 475 completed and usable surveys. We performed SEM to fit our proposed model in order to test the hypotheses. For the detailed methodology, please refer to Chap. 2.

Results

Descriptive Statistics

Table 8.1 shows the means, standard deviations, correlations, and reliabilities of the variables. The willingness of HCNs to help expatriates had a high–mid-range mean (5.1) and a wide spread (SD = 2.7) allowing for prediction. Socially responsible HRM, high-commitment HRM, organizational identification, and POS were significantly correlated with the criterion variable in the expected directions, thus providing preliminary support for our hypotheses.

Table 8.1 Means, standard deviations, reliabilities, and correlations between variables

	M	*SD*	*1*	*2*	*3*	*4*	*5*	*6*	*7*	*8*	*9*	*10*	*11*
1. Age	27.6	4.3	–										
2. Gender	1.5	.50	−.06	–									
3. Education	2.0	.85	−.48**	−.07	–								
4. Position	1.15	.42	.57***	−.09*	.43**	–							
5. Personality	3.9	.21	.02	.09	.07	.03	(.91)-						
6. Social categorization	3.4	.23	.13	.06	.17*	.04	.25*	(.84)					
7. Socially responsible HRM	4.4	1.3	.14	−.10*	−.26**	.36**	.15	.09	(.89)				
8. High-commitment HRM	4.9	1.1	.13	−.05	−.22**	.35**	.07	.04	.36**	(.88)			
9. Organizational identification	4.8	1.2	.26**	−.01	−.23**	.38**	.12	.19	.49**	.43***	(.85)		
10. Perceived organizational support	4.6	1.1	.22*	−.08	−.33**	.30**	.13	.28*	.08	.40**	.27**	(.89)	
11. Willingness to help	5.1	1.7	.21*	−.01	−.26**	.33**	.23*	−.31*	.44**	.36**	.38**	.39**	(.90)

Notes: $N = 475$; $*p < .05$. $**p < .01$. Two-tailed: gender was dummy coded: female = 1, male = 2. Age was measured by years. Education was coded: 1 = primary school, 2 = high school, 3 = diploma, 4 = bachelor degree, 5 = graduate. Tenure was measured by working years. Employees' position was dummy coded: 1 = non-managerial, 2 = managerial. Cronbach's alphas are reported in the parentheses on the diagonal

The Measurement Model

We assessed discriminant validity of the measurement model. As shown in Table 8.2, the five-factor model fitted better than the four-factor model by combining high-commitment HRM and socially responsible HRM ($\Delta\chi^2_{(4)}$=153.10, p < .001). The five-factor model also fitted better than the three-factor model collapsing POS and organizational identification ($\Delta\chi^2_{(7)}$=311.04, p < .001) and the one-factor model allowing all measuring items to load on a single latent variable ($\Delta\chi^2_{(10)}$=1531.06, p < .001). These results provided support for using the five constructs as distinctive independent variables, and consequently the five-factor model was retained for substantial hypothesis tests.

Common Method Variance

Next, we assessed CMV which could have resulted from the use of a single source of data (Cascio 2012). The six-factor model, which included the method factor [$\chi^2_{(308)}$ = 892.40, p < .001, CFI = .98, TLI = .97, and RMSEA = .041] had better fit indexes ($\Delta\chi^2_{(32)}$ = 69.43, p < .001) than the five-factor measurement model [$\chi^2_{(340)}$ =961.83, p<.001; CFI=.97; TLI=.96 and RMSEA=.05]. However, the method factor explained only 12.38% of the total variance, which is about half of the variance usually

Table 8.2 Comparisons of the measurement models

Model	X^2	*df*	*CFI*	*TLI*	*RMSEA*
Measurement model 1: five-factor model (the proposed conceptual model)	961.83	340	.97	.96	.05
Measurement model 2: four-factor model (high-commitment HRM and socially responsible HRM were combined, respectively)	1114.93	344	.88	.86	.09
Measure model 3: three-factor model (high-commitment HRM and socially responsible HRM, and POS and organizational identification were combined, respectively)	1272.87	347	.82	.81	.12
Measurement model 4: one-factor model (all items were loaded on a single factor)	2492.89	350	.66	.64	.14

Note: POS, perceived organizational support

observed in prior studies (Williams et al. 1989) and the change to CFI was only .01 less than the cutoff value of .05 suggested by Bagozzi and Yi (1990). Therefore, CMV is unlikely to have distorted the results of the current study.

Hypothesis Tests

In Hypothesis 1, we were interested in whether POS mediated the relationship between high-commitment HRM and HCNs' willingness to help expatriates when the effect of socially responsible HRM was accounted for. We first fitted the proposed full mediation model by adding the paths from the control variables including personality, social categorization, and demographic variables to HCNs' willingness to help expatriates. Consistent with the literature, personality was positively related (Johnson et al. 2003) and social categorization was negatively related (Toh and DeNisi 2007) to the criterion variable. With regard to demographics, position and age were positively related and education was negatively related to the criterion variable, indicating that managerial employees tended to be more willing to help expatriates. The proposed full mediation model had a reasonably good fit to the data ([$\chi^2_{(1117)} = 2152.44$, $p < .001$, CFI = .91, TLI = .91, and RMSEA = .08]. Next, we fitted a partial mediation model by adding a direct link between high-commitment HRM and HCNs' willingness to help expatriates. The partial mediation model had a better fit to the data [$\chi^2_{(1116)} = 1930.52$, $p < .001$, CFI = .97, TLI = .96, RMSEA = .06, $\Delta\chi^2_{(1)} = 221.92$, and $p < .001$]. The third model we fitted was one without the mediation of POS by removing the direct link between POS and high-commitment HRM. This model had a poor fit [$\chi^2(_{770}) = 1947.50$, $p < .001$, CFI = .85, TLI = .85, and RMSEA = .14] and was rejected. Therefore, the partial mediation model had the best fit and was retained.

High-commitment HRM had a significant direct impact on HCNs' willingness to help expatriates ($r = .23$, $p < .01$) and was significantly related to POS ($r = .41$, $p < .001$) which in turn was significantly related to the criterion variable ($r = .28$, $p < .01$). The indirect outcome of high-commitment HRM through the mediation of POS was significant ($r = .11$, SE = .03, $p < .01$). A 95% bias corrected confidence interval using coefficients estimated from 1000 bootstrap samples did not contain zero (.07> – <.17) (Shrout and Bolger 2002). Therefore, Hypothesis 1 was partially supported as POS partially mediated the relationship between high-commitment HRM and HCNs' willingness to help expatriates.

Hypothesis 2 predicted that organizational identification mediated the relationship between socially responsible HRM and HCNs' willingness to help expatriates. We first fitted the proposed full mediation model that had a good fit with the data: $\chi^2_{(892)} = 1204.20$, $p < .001$; CFI= .97, TLI = .96, and RMSEA = .05. Next, we fitted a partial mediation model by adding a direct path involving socially responsible HRM and the criterion variable. The partial mediation model had a poor fit and fitted with the data worse than the full mediation model ([$\chi^2_{(891)} = 1442.19$, $p < .001$; CFI = .88, TLI = .87, RMSEA = .11, $\Delta\chi^2_{(1)} = 237.99$, and $p < .001$)] and was rejected. We then fitted a model without the mediation of organizational identification by removing the path involving socially responsible HRM and organizational identification. This model had a poor fit [$\chi^2(_{770}) = 1927.56$, $p < .001$; CFI = .81, TLI = .80, and RMSEA = .15] and was also rejected. Therefore, the full model mediation of organizational identification was the best fit and, for this reason, was retained. SRHRM was significantly related to organizational identification ($r = .37$, $p < .001$) which was in turn positively related to HCNs' willingness to help expatriates ($r = .39$, $p < .001$). The indirect effect of socially responsible HRM was significant for organizational identification ($r = .14$, SE = .03, $p < .01$). A test with a 95% bias corrected confidence interval using coefficients estimated from 1000 bootstrap samples (Shrout and Bolger 2002) revealed that the indirect effect did not contain zero (.11> – <.20). Therefore, Hypothesis 2 received support.

Hypothesis 3 focused on whether POS and organizational identification sequentially mediated the relationship between high-commitment HRM and the willingness of HCNs to help expatriates. The results indicated that the best model is one where: firstly, high-commitment HRM is directly and indirectly related to the criterion variable through POS; and secondly, socially responsible HRM is indirectly related to the criterion variable through organizational identification while controlling for all the control variables. We first fitted a model with a link between POS and organizational identification. The model was a good fit with the data: $\chi^2(_{1263}) = 2323.92$, $p < .001$, CFI = .97, TLI = .96, and RMSEA = .07. Next, we fitted a model in which the path between POS and organizational identification was removed. Results showed that the model had a worse fit than the one with POS and organizational identification linked [$\chi^2(_{1264}) = 2415.03$, $p < .001$, CFI = .91, TLI = .89, RMSEA = .09, $\Delta\chi^2_{(1)} = 91.11$, and $p < .001$]. POS was positively related to organizational identification ($r = .30$, $p < .01$). The indirect effect of high-commitment HRM

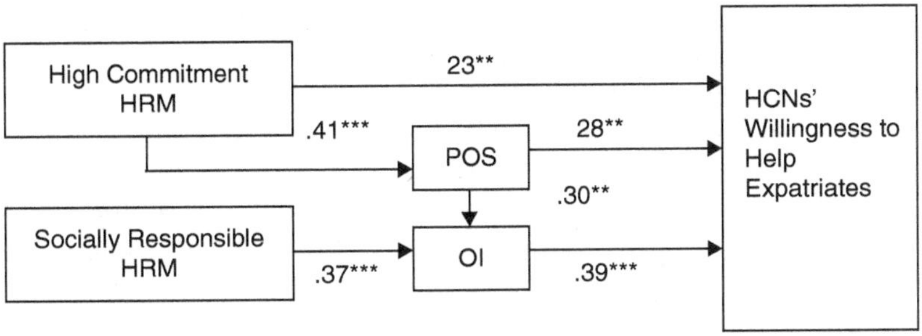

Fig. 8.1 Standardized structural coefficients (*Note*: OI, organizational identification; POS, perceived organizational support)

on organizational identification via POS was significant (r = .12, SE = .02, p < .01). The bootstrap results with a 95% bias corrected confidence interval using coefficients estimated from 1000 bootstrap samples did not contain zero (.08> – <.16). The indirect effect of POS on HCNs' willingness to help expatriates via organizational identification was significant (r = .12, SE = .02, p < .01). Bootstrap results with a 95% bias corrected confidence interval using coefficients estimated from 1000 samples did not contain zero (.06> – <.16). Therefore, Hypothesis 3 was supported. The completely standardized structural coefficients for the theoretical model are shown in Fig. 8.1.

Discussion

HCNs' assistance to expatriates in and outside of the workplace to a great extent influences expatriates' adjustment and work performance on international assignments and, consequently, contributes to the business success of MNEs (Arman and Aycan 2013; Toh and Srinivas 2012; Varma et al. 2009). This research explores the effects of two bundles of discretionary HRM practices (i.e. high-commitment HRM and socially responsible HRM) adopted by MNEs in overseas subsidiaries on HCNs' willingness to help expatriates. Results indicate that high-commitment HRM directly and indirectly influences HCNs' willingness to help expatriates through the mediation of POS. This finding is consistent with the literature which maintains that high-commitment HRM addresses the interests and needs of employees and results in employee perceptions of organizational support, which in turn leads to positive employees' workplace outcomes (Chiang et al. 2011; McClean and Collins 2011).

Socially responsible HRM adopted to implement CSR initiatives and increase employee awareness of and commitment to CSR indirectly influences HCNs' willingness to help expatriates through the mediation of organizational identification. This finding provides some support for the explanation offered by Shen and Benson (2014) regarding the mediating role of organizational identification in socially responsible HRM–employees' work attitudes and behavior relationship. Furthermore, this finding is aligned with studies such as Rupp et al. (2006) and Turban and Greening (1997), which suggest employees tend to have positive attitudes toward socially responsible organizations. It is evident that the relationship between high-commitment HRM and HCNs' willingness to help expatriates is sequentially mediated by POS and organizational identification. This lends support to the literature regarding the link between POS and organizational identification (see, for example, Edwards and Peccei 2010). Jiang et al. (2012) argue that different HRM practices influence employee outcomes through different mediating paths and with different effect strengths. This argument receives some support in this study.

This research contributes to the literature in several ways. Firstly, this study recognizes that, in addition to being co-workers, expatriates are viewed by HCNs as representatives of the MNE. As such, when HCNs help expatriates, they are not only consolidating co-worker behavior but also positive behavior toward the MNE. This finding further sheds light on organizational antecedents of HCNs' attitudes and behaviors toward expatriates that go beyond personal and intrapersonal factors. Secondly, this study builds on the IHRM literature by investigating and documenting the needs and interests of employees in the international business setting. In this way, the gap in the knowledge on this subject is filled by examining the impact of high-commitment HRM on the outcomes of HCNs in the international business scenario. Thirdly, this study adds to the knowledge base of the IHRM literature by discussing in detail the integration of IHRM and CSR. Finally, we explored the mediation of POS and organizational identification in the relationships of high-commitment HRM and socially responsible HRM with HCNs' willingness to help expatriates. These mediation relationships have not been studied previously in the IHRM literature and this study makes a contribution by developing a better understanding of social and psychological processes of HRM in the MNE context.

Conclusion

In this chapter, we propose and test a model that HCNs' willingness to help expatriates is influenced by IHRM practices in international subsidiaries of MNEs. Results of analyzing the data collected from Chinese subsidiaries of the case study South Korean MNEs showed that high-commitment HRM practices directly and indirectly influence HCNs' willingness to help expatriates through the mediation of POS. Socially responsible HRM indirectly influences the criterion variable through the mediation of organizational identification. Moreover, POS and organizational identification sequentially mediate the effect of high-commitment HRM on HCNs' willingness to help expatriates. These findings shed some light on organizational antecedents that go beyond personal and intrapersonal factors of HCNs' attitudes and behaviors toward expatriates. It can therefore be stated that this study helps us to understand the effects of IHRM on employees. The next chapter will conclude the book by discussing the theoretical contributions, the managerial implications of the research findings, limitations of this study, and future research directions.

Bibliography

Aguinis, H., & Glavas, A. (2012). What we know and don't know about corporate social responsibility: A review and research agenda. *Journal of Management, 38*(4), 932–968.

Allen, D. G., Shore, L. M., & Griffeth, R. W. (2003). The role of perceived organizational support and supportive human resource practices in the turnover process. *Journal of Management, 29*(1), 99–118.

Ancona, D. G., & Caldwell, D. F. (1992). Demography and design: Predictors of new product team performance. *Organization Science, 3*(3), 321–341.

Arman, G., & Aycan, Z. (2013). Host country nationals' attitudes toward expatriates: Development of a measure. *International Journal of Human Resource Management, 24*(15), 2927–2947.

Armstrong-Stassen, M., & Schlosser, F. (2010). When hospitals provide HR practices tailored to older nurses, will older nurses stay? It may depend on their supervisor. *Human Resource Management Journal, 20*(4), 375–390.

Ashforth, B. E., & Mael, F. (1989). Social identity theory and the organization. *Academy of Management Review, 14*(1), 20–39.

Bagozzi, R. P., & Yi, Y. (1990). Assessing method variance in multitrait-multimethod matrices: The case of self-reported affect and perceptions at work. *Journal of Applied Psychology, 75*(5), 547–560.

Benson, G. S., & Pattie, M. (2009). The comparative roles of home and host supervisors in the expatriate experience. *Human Resource Management, 48*(1), 49–68.

Blau, P. (1964). *Exchange and power in social life*. New York: Wiley.
Bonache, J., & Brewster, C. (2001). Knowledge transfer and the management of expatriation. *Thunderbird International Business Review, 43*(1), 145–168.
Caligiuri, P. M. (2000). Selecting expatriates for personality characteristics: A moderating effect of personality on the relationship between host national contact and cross-cultural adjustment. *Management International Review, 40*(1), 61–80.
Caligiuri, P. M., Joshi, A., & Lazarova, M. (1999). Factors influencing the adjustment of women on global assignments. *International Journal of Human Resource Management, 10*(2), 163–179.
Cascio, W. F. (2012). Methodological issues in international HR management research. *International Journal of Human Resource Management, 23*(12), 2532–2545.
Chiang, H. H., Han, T. S., & Chuang, J. S. (2011). The relationship between high-commitment HRM and knowledge-sharing behavior and its mediators. *International Journal of Manpower, 32*(5/6), 604–622.
Coyle-Shapiro, J. A. M., & Shore, L. M. (2007). The employee-organization relationship: Where do we go from here? *Human Resource Management Review, 17*(2), 166–179.
Cropanzano, R., & Mitchell, M. S. (2005). Social exchange theory: An interdisciplinary review. *Journal of Management, 31*(6), 874–900.
Dukerich, J. M., Golden, B. R., & Shortell, S. M. (2002). Beauty is in the eye of the beholder: The impact of organizational identification, identity, and image on the cooperative behaviors of physicians. *Administrative Science Quarterly, 47*(3), 507–533.
Dutton, E. J., Dukerich, J. M., & Harquail, V. C. (1994). Organizational images and member identification. *Administrative Science Quarterly, 39*(2), 239–263.
Edwards, M. R. (2009). HR, perceived organizational support and organizational identification: An analysis after organizational formation. *Human Resource Management Journal, 19*(1), 91–115.
Edwards, M. R., & Peccei, R. (2010). Perceived organizational support, organizational identification, and employee outcomes: Testing a simultaneous multifoci model. *Journal of Personnel Psychology, 9*(1), 17–26.
Eisenberger, R., Huntington, R., Hutchison, S., & Sowa, D. (1986). Perceived organizational support. *Journal of Applied Psychology, 71*(3), 500–507.
Eisenberger, R., Cummings, J., Armeli, S., & Lynch, P. (1997). Perceived organizational support, discretionary treatment, and job satisfaction. *Journal of Applied Psychology, 82*(5), 812–820.
Eisenberger, R., Stinglhamber, F., Vandenberghe, C., Sucharski, I. L., & Rhoades, L. (2002). Perceived supervisor support: Contributions to perceived organizational support and employee retention. *Journal of Applied Psychology, 87*(3), 565–573.
Eisenberger, R., Jones, J., Aselage, J., & Sucharski, I. (2004). Perceived organizational support. In J. Coyle-Shapiro, L. Shore, M. Taylor, & L. Tetrick (Eds.),

The employment relationship: Examining psychological and contextual perspectives (pp. 206–225). Oxford, UK: Oxford University Press.

Farh, C. I. C., Bartol, K. M., Shapiro, D. L., & Shin, J. (2010). Networking abroad: A process model of how expatriates form support ties to facilitate adjustment. *Academy of Management Review, 35*(3), 434–454.

Ferris, G. R., Liden, R. C., Munyon, T. P., Summers, J. K., Basik, K. J., & Buckley, M. R. (2009). Relationships at work: Toward a multidimensional conceptualization of dyadic work relationships. *Journal of Management, 35*(6), 1379–1403.

Ghafoor, S., Khan, U. F., Idrees, F., Javed, B., & Ahmed, F. (2011). Evaluation of expatriates performance and their training on international assignments. *Interdisciplinary Journal of Contemporary Research in Business, 3*(5), 335–351.

Gibney, R., Zagenczyk, T. J., Fuller, J. B., Hester, K., & Caner, T. (2011). Exploring organizational obstruction and the expanded model of organizational identification. *Journal of Applied Social Psychology, 41*(5), 1083–1109.

Harzing, A. W. (2001). Of bears, bumble-bees, and spiders: The role of expatriates in controlling foreign subsidiaries. *Journal of World Business, 36*(4), 366–379.

Ilies, R., Nahrgang, J. D., & Morgeson, F. P. (2007). Leader-member exchange and citizenship behaviors: A meta-analysis. *Journal of Applied Psychology, 92*(1), 269–277.

Jiang, K. F., Lepak, D., Hu, J., & Baer, J. C. (2012). How does human resource management influence organizational outcomes? A meta-analytical investigation of mediating mechanisms. *Academy of Management Journal, 55*(6), 1264–1294.

Johnson, E. C., Kristof-brown, A. L., Van Vianen, A. E. M., De Pater, I. E., & Klein, M. R. (2003). Expatriate social ties: Personality antecedents and consequences for adjustment. *International Journal of Selection and Assessment, 11*(4), 277–288.

Judge, T. A., & Piccolo, R. F. (2004). Transformational and transactional leadership: A meta-analytic test of their relative validity. *Journal of Applied Psychology, 89*(5), 755–768.

Knight, C., & Haslam, S. A. (2010). Your place or mine? Organizational identification and comfort as mediators of relationships between the managerial control of workspace and employees' satisfaction and wellbeing. *British Journal of Management, 21*(3), 717–735.

Kreiner, G. E., & Ashforth, B. E. (2004). Evidence toward an expanded model of organizational identification. *Journal of Organizational Behavior, 25*(1), 1–27.

Mahajan, A., & Toh, S. M. (2014). Facilitating expatriate adjustment: The role of advice-seeking from host country nationals. *Journal of World Business, 49*(4), 476–487.

Manolopoulos, D., Dimitratos, P., & Sapouna, P. (2011). An investigation into international assignment directions of R&D MNE employees: Evidence from Greece. *The International Journal of Human Resource Management, 22*(05), 1093–1108.

McClean, E., & Collins, C. J. (2011). High-commitment HR practices, employee effort, and firm performance: Investigating the effects of HR practices across employee groups within professional services firms. *Human Resource Management, 50*(3), 341–363.

Meyer, J. P., & Smith, C. A. (2000). HRM practices and organizational commitment: Test of a mediation model. *Canadian Journal of Administrative Sciences, 17*(4), 319–331.

Mossholder, K. W., Richardson, H. A., & Settoon, R. P. (2011). Human resource systems and helping in organizations: A relational perspective. *Academy of Management Review, 36*(1), 33–52.

Nishii, L. H., Lepak, D. P., & Schneider, B. (2008). Employee attributions of the "why" of HR practices: Their effects on employee attitudes and behaviors, and customer satisfaction. *Personnel Psychology, 61*(3), 503–545.

Orlitzky, M., & Swanson, D. L. (2006). Socially responsible human resource management. In J. R. Deckop (Ed.), *Human resource management ethics* (pp. 3–25). Charlotte: Information Age Publishing.

Pfeffer, J. (2010). Building sustainable organizations: The human factor. *Academy of Management Perspectives, 24*(1), 34–45.

Porter, M. E., & Kramer, M. R. (2011). Creating shared value. *Harvard Business Review, 89*(1/2), 62–77.

Pratt, M. G. (1998). To be or not to be: Central questions in organizational identification'. In D. Whetten & P. Godfrey (Eds.), *Identity in organizations: Developing theory through conversations* (pp. 171–207). Thousand Oaks: Sage.

Purcell, J., & Hutchinson, S. (2007). Front line managers as agents in the HRM performance causal chain: Theory, analysis and evidence. *Human Resource Management Journal, 17*(1), 3–20.

Reiche, B. S., Harzing, A. W., & Kraimer, M. L. (2008). The role of international assignees' social capital in creating inter-unit intellectual capital: A cross-level model. *Journal of International Business Studies, 40*(3), 509–526.

Rhoades, L., & Eisenberger, R. (2002). Perceived organizational support: A review of the literature. *Journal of Applied Psychology, 87*(4), 698–714.

Richard, O. C., Ismail, K. M., Bhuian, S. N., & Taylor, E. C. (2009). Mentoring in supervisor subordinate dyads: Antecedents, consequences, and test of a mediation model of mentorship. *Journal of Business Research, 62*(11), 1110–1118.

Rousseau, D. M. (1989). Psychological and implied contracts in organizations. *Employee Responsibilities and Rights Journal, 2*(2), 121–139.

Rousseau, D. M. (1995). *Psychological contracts in organizations: Understanding written and unwritten agreements.* Thousand Oaks: Sage.

Rupp, D., Ganapathi, E. J., Aguilera, R. V., & Williams, C. A. (2006). Employee reactions to corporate social responsibility: An organizational justice framework. *Journal of Organizational Behavior, 27*(4), 537–543.

Shen, J. (2011). Developing the concept of socially responsible international human resource management. *The International Journal of Human Resource Management, 22*(6), 1351–1363.

Shen, J., & Benson, J. (2014). When CSR is a social norm: How socially responsible human resource management affects employee work behavior. *Journal of Management*. p.0149206314522300.

Shen, Y., & Hall, D. T. T. (2009). When expatriates explore other options: Retaining talent through greater job embeddedness and repatriation adjustment. *Human Resource Management, 48*(5), 793–816.

Shore, L. M., & Shore, T. M. (1995). Perceived organizational support and organizational justice. In R. S. Cropanzano & K. M. Kacmar (Eds.), *Organizational politics, justice, and support: Managing the social climate of the workplace* (pp. 149–164). Westport: Quorum.

Shrout, P. E., & Bolger, N. (2002). Mediation in experimental and nonexperimental studies: New procedures and recommendations. *Psychological Methods, 7*(4), 422–445.

Sluss, D. M., Klimchak, M., & Holmes, J. J. (2008). Perceived organizational support as a mediator between relational exchange and organizational identification. *Journal of Vocational Behavior, 73*(3), 457–464.

Smith, M. A., & Canger, J. M. (2004). Effects of supervisor "big five" personality on subordinate attitudes. *Journal of Business and Psychology, 18*(4), 465–481.

Snape, E., & Redman, T. (2010). HRM practices, organizational citizenship behaviour, and performance: A multi-level analysis. *Journal of Management Studies, 47*(7), 1219–1247.

Tajfel, H. (1978). The achievement of group differentiation. In H. Tajfel (Ed.), *Differentiation between social groups: Studies in the social psychology of intergroup relations* (pp. 77–98). London: Academic Press.

Tajfel, H., & Turner, J. C. (1985). The social identity theory of intergroup behavior. In S. Worchel & W. G. Austin (Eds.), *Psychology of intergroup relations* (pp. 7–24). Chicago: Nelson-Hall.

Tepper, B. J., & Taylor, E. C. (2003). Relationships among supervisors and subordinates' procedural justice perceptions and organizational citizenship behaviors. *Academy of Management Journal, 46*(1), 97–105.

Tjosvold, D., & Chia, L. C. (1989). Conflict between managers and workers: The role of cooperation and competition. *The Journal of Social Psychology, 129*(2), 235–247.

Toh, S. M., & DeNisi, A. S. (2003). Host country national reactions to expatriate pay policies: A model and implications. *Academy of Management Review, 28*(4), 606–621.

Toh, S. M., & DeNisi, A. S. (2005). A local perspective to expatriate success. *Academy of Management Executive, 19*(1), 132–146.

Toh, S. M., & DeNisi, A. S. (2007). Host country nationals as socializing agents: A social identity approach. *Journal of Organizational Behavior, 28*(3), 281–301.

Toh, S. M., & Srinivas, E. S. (2012). Perceptions of task cohesiveness and organizational support increase trust and information sharing between host country nationals and expatriate coworkers in Oman. *Journal of World Business, 47*(4), 696–705.

Tsui, A., Wang, D., & Zhang, Y. (2002). Employment relationships with Chinese managers: Exploring differences between state-owned and non–state-owned firms. In A. Tsui & C. Lau (Eds.), *The management of enterprises in the People's Republic of China* (pp. 347–374). Boston: Kluwer Academic.

Turban, D. B., & Greening, D. W. (1997). Corporate social performance and organizational attractiveness to prospective employees. *Academy of Management Journal, 40*(3), 658–672.

Toh, S. M., & DeNisi, A. S. (2007). Host country nationals as socializing agents: A social identity approach. *Journal of Organizational Behavior, 28*(3), 281–301.

Van Dick, R., Wagner, U., Stellmacher, J., & Christ, O. (2004). The utility of a broader conceptualization of organizational identification: Which aspects really matter? *Journal of Occupational and Organizational Psychology, 77*(2), 171–191.

Varma, A., Pichler, S., Budhwar, P., & Biswas, S. (2009). Chinese host country nationals' willingness to support expatriates: The role of collectivism, interpersonal affect and guanxi. *International Journal of Cross Cultural Management, 9*(2), 199–216.

Varma, A., Budhwar, P., & Pichler, S. (2011). Chinese host country nationals' willingness to help expatriates: The role of social categorization. *Thunderbird International Business Review, 53*(3), 353–364.

Wan-Huggins, V. N., Riordan, C. M., & Griffeth, R. W. (1998). The development and longitudinal test of a model of organizational identification. *Journal of Applied Social Psychology, 28*(8), 724–749.

Whitener, E. M. (2001). Do "high commitment" human resource practices affect employee commitment? *Journal of Management, 27*(5), 515–535.

Williams, L. J., Cote, J. A., & Buckley, M. R. (1989). Lack of method variance in self-reported affect and perceptions at work: Reality of artifact? *Journal of Applied Psychology, 74*(3), 462–468.

Wu, J., Chen, W., & Liu, Y. (2010). An IP/C model of employee-organization relationship: A dual perspective. *Frontiers of Business Research in China, 4*(4), 630–652.

Yoon, J., & Thye, S. (2000). Supervisor support in the work place: Legitimacy and positive affectivity. *The Journal of Social Psychology, 140*(3), 295–316.

Zeira, Y. (1979). Ethnocentrism in host-country organizations. *Business Horizons, 22*(3), 66–75.

Zhou, X., & Qin, J. (2009). A study on cross-cultural adjustment of Japanese and American expatriates in China. *International Journal of Business and Management, 4*(12), 197–206.

CHAPTER 9

Conclusions

Introduction

We have discussed in the previous chapters IHRM policies and practices (including international staffing, training and development, performance appraisal, and reward and compensation), the use and management of non-traditional expatriates, and the impact of IHRM on employees who work for South Korean MNEs in China. In this concluding chapter, we concentrate on this study's theoretical and practical implications. The chapter is structured as follows: first, the research questions will be revisited; and second, theoretical contributions of the research findings will be evaluated. This is followed by addressing the practical implications for MNEs. Subsequently, limitations of this research and suggested future research directions for this topic will be explored. Finally, this chapter finishes with an overall conclusion on the major themes covered here.

Research Questions Revisited

This book has aimed to explore how South Korean MNEs manage people in their Chinese subsidiaries. In particular, we have discussed international staffing, training and development, performance appraisal, reward and compensation, and the use and management of non-traditional expatriates. Furthermore, the book investigates the impacts of IHRM on employees' work outcomes, that is, HCNs' willingness to help expatriates. To achieve

H. Kang, J. Shen, *International Human Resource Management in South Korean Multinational Enterprises*,
DOI 10.1007/978-981-10-3093-2_9

the research objectives, the study firstly addresses the following question: *How do South Korean MNEs manage people in their Chinese subsidiaries?* This question relates to international recruitment and selection, training and development, performance appraisal, reward and compensation, and the use and management of non-traditional expatriates. Therefore, we have developed five sub-questions and they are presented in more detail below.

The first sub-question is: *What are the South Korean MNEs' approaches to international recruitment and selection and associated factors in their Chinese subsidiaries?* This question was addressed in Chap. 3. The research shows that the sample MNEs tended to adopt one-way selection by assigning international assignments to employees. The case study MNEs in general adopted the polycentric approach to international staffing in China. This finding does not support previous research, such as Paik and Sohn (1998), which suggested South Korean MNEs normally adopt the ethnocentric approach to international staffing. The case study South Korean MNEs used expatriates in their Chinese subsidiaries for a wide range of reasons, including control, communication and technology, and knowledge transfer. These reasons have been reported in previous international staffing studies (e.g. Shen 2006). The criteria for selecting expatriates in the case study South Korean MNEs focused on job expertise, job performance, communication skills, cultural empathy, and personality. Similarly, these criteria have been regarded as important, and utilized by American, European, Australian, and Chinese MNEs (e.g. Shen and Edwards 2004). Moreover, the sample MNEs provided some support for repatriates' relocation, but paid inadequate attention to repatriates' cultural adjustment and career development. Such negligence is often encountered in other national MNEs, such as those of Australia (Newton et al. 2007) and China (e.g. Shen and Edwards 2004).

The second sub-question is: *How do South Korean MNEs manage international training and development in their Chinese subsidiaries and what are the influencing factors?* Chapter 4 addresses this research question. Our study revealed that inadequate, low-rigor pre-departure CCT was provided to expatriates in the case of South Korean MNEs. This finding is consistent with the prevailing literature suggesting that MNEs worldwide fail to provide adequate pre-departure CCT (e.g. Baumgarten 1995; Dowling et al. 2013; Gamble 2000; Shen and Darby 2006; Tung 1982; Welch 1994). This research also suggests that the case study South Korean MNEs paid significant attention to language training, but provided limited post-arrival training to expatriates. This is due to the fact that there are cultural and institutional similarities between South Korean and China in any case, which made CCT less important. In addition, the case of South Korean MNEs preferred to recruit expatriates who either had previously lived in China or had some knowledge of or familiarity with the Chinese language and culture, thus making their adaptation much easier. The sample MNEs offered extensive safety training only to HCN production workers but not to non-production workers. This finding does not support previous research (e.g. Lansbury et al. 2006) reporting that South Korean MNEs provided extensive training to local employees. We further found there was a lack of career development planning for expatriates in the case study MNEs. It is important to note that past research is inconsistent on this issue. For example, while Lansbury et al. (2006) reported that South Korean MNEs do not pay adequate attention to employee career development, Kim and Slocum (2008) argued that South Korean MNEs in the US provided great opportunities for career development to expatriates. The national cultural view and relative strength effect, i.e. the relative economic strengths and contextual differences between China and South Korea, can explain why South Korean MNEs adopt such practices in China.

The third sub-question is: *How do South Korean MNEs manage international performance appraisal in their Chinese subsidiaries and what are the influencing factors?* Chapter 5 addresses this research question. It is found that the case study MNEs adopted home-based performance appraisal procedures and methods when evaluating expatriates' work. This finding receives some support from previous studies (e.g. Taylor et al. 2001). The results also show that an integrated approach (i.e. the integration of localization and ethnocentric approach) was used to evaluate HCNs' performance. This finding supports Zou and Lansbury's (2009) research. The major performance appraisal criteria for both expatriates and HCNs include work performance, work attitudes, and competence, which is consistent with Lansbury et al. (2006) and Taylor et al.'s (2001) research. Finally, we found that unlike Chinese MNEs, South Korean MNEs provided feedback including written feedback during appraisal interviews. This confirms that South Korean MNEs are ethnocentric in providing employee feedback and this lends some support to Zou and Lansbury's (2009) research. These approaches can be attributed to the previously mentioned relative strength effects.

The fourth sub-question is: *What are the South Korean MNEs' approaches to international reward and compensation, and associated factors in their Chinese subsidiaries?* As shown in Chap. 6, the compensation package for expatriates and HCNs included base pay, performance-based pay, allowances, and benefits. In particular, the sample MNEs transferred their home-oriented base salary, performance-related pay, and allowances and benefits practices for expatriates to their Chinese subsidiaries. For HCNs, the sample MNEs tended to adopt an integrative approach to their base salaries and performance-related pay, and a localized approach to allowances and benefits. It is argued in our study that the relative strength of home and host country's economy impacts on the international reward and compensation approaches adopted by the case of South Korean MNEs operating in China. That is, the transfer or localization is due to the relative dominance of home/host country's economic and technological advancement.

The fifth sub-question is: *How do South Korean MNEs manage non-traditional expatriates in China?* Chapter 7 addresses this research question, the results of which indicate that utilizing non-traditional expatriates has increased in the case study MNEs over the last decade. This finding is consistent with a number of industry surveys showing MNEs worldwide have increasingly used non-traditional expatriates (e.g. KPMG 2010). The reasons for doing this in the sample MNEs include: cost-effectiveness, flexibility, knowledge transfer, and management control, and these have been confirmed by previous research (e.g. Mayerhofer et al. 2004). Furthermore, the way the case South Korean MNEs manage expatriates is different from non-traditional expatriates. For example, the sample MNEs did not have formal and systematic recruitment and selection policies for non-traditional expatriates; however, they had formulated and designed written policies for traditional expatriates.

The second research question addresses the relationship between IHRM and HCNs' willingness to help expatriates and the underlying mechanisms. In order to answer research question 2, three hypotheses were developed. The hypotheses are linked to the relationships of high-commitment HRM and socially responsible HRM with HCNs' willingness to help expatriates in and outside of the workplace and the sequential mediation of POS and employee organizational identification. While Research Question 1 was addressed by analyzing the data collected through interviews, Research Question 2 was answered by examining the survey data. The results indicate that high-commitment HRM influences HCNs' willingness directly and indirectly through the mediation of POS. This finding has found support from previous research suggesting that high-commitment HRM which addresses employees' needs and interests leads to positive employee outcomes (Chiang et al. 2011; McClean and Collins 2011). Moreover, socially responsible HRM influences HCNs' willingness to help expatriates indirectly through the mediation of organizational identification. This finding is consistent with Shen and Benson (2014) who concluded that organizational identification mediates the relationship of socially responsible HRM with employees' work attitudes and behaviors. Furthermore, it emerged that high-commitment HRM and HCNs' willingness to help expatriates is sequentially mediated by POS and organizational identification. This is consistent with the literature regarding the relationship between POS and organizational identification.

Theoretical Contributions

There is limited research on examining IHRM policies and practices of South Korean MNEs (Kang and Shen 2014). Given their competitive status in the global market and the growing interest in exploring IHRM derived from emerging MNEs, there is a great need for more studies on the topic. Moreover, little is known about how IHRM affects employee outcomes. In particular, this research is pioneering in examining the effects of IHRM on HCNs' willingness to help expatriates who represent MNEs. As such, the current research makes several important theoretical contributions.

Firstly, there is limited research on how South Korean MNEs recruit and select expatriates and HCNs. To date only five studies have examined staffing issues in South Korean MNEs and they mostly concentrated on recruiting and selecting HCNs. Hence, the current research fills this important literature gap by exploring a number of important issues including the staffing approach and its associated factors, expatriates' selection criteria and procedures, and repatriation management. An analysis of South Korean MNEs' staffing practices in China is an important step toward understanding their global staffing practices and helps to understand how non-Western MNEs manage international staffing. This research therefore has the potential to contribute to the international staffing literature.

Secondly, international training and development is also an under-researched topic in the IHRM literature; hence, the current research adds to the knowledge base of the international HRM literature. The sample

South Korean MNEs provided limited, low-rigor CCT to expatriates. In alignment with the existing literature, it can be suggested that it has likely become commonplace for MNEs not to provide adequate, high-rigor CCT. A major reason for MNEs not providing adequate, high-rigor pre-departure CCT is the common belief among senior managers that such training is of little use, or it is simply lacking. However, academics insist that pre-departure CCT is important and they continue to advocate the provision of extensive, high-rigor pre-departure CCT. Based on the findings of this study and taking into account what the existing literature generally suggests, we tend to believe that choosing people who have prior knowledge and experience of host-country cultures and providing regular post-arrival training would make pre-departure training less necessary. In today's modern society, people have access to advanced information technology through which they learn about different cultures, customs, and traditions. This considerably reduces the significance of pre-departure CCT. We therefore call for more studies to re-examine the practices and importance of pre-departure CCT and the relative impact of pre-departure training, post-arrival training, and expatriates' selection criteria on expatriates' adjustment and work performance in international assignments. Therefore, our study provides some insight into the importance of pre-departure training.

This study helps to better understand the linkage between expatriation and management development. The sample MNEs did not develop formal career development plans for expatriates. We suspect that if this is the case, international experience may be regarded as less significant when expatriates work in developing or underdeveloped countries. However, this finding could be Korea-specific and needs to be further examined in studies conducted in cross-cultural contexts. Furthermore, our study provides a new perspective to understand MNEs' decisions on training for expatriates. The South Korean MNEs in our sample provided extensive language training to expatriates prior to departure and post-arrival. Hence, there is the possibility that, when the need for some training is not apparent, MNEs may allocate more resources to other training programs. This finding is worth further empirical exploration.

Thirdly, there is a paucity of research exploring international performance appraisals (Festing et al. 2012). By exploring international performance appraisals of both HCNs and expatriates, this research adds to the knowledge base on the international appraisal literature. Little research has thus far explored the international performance appraisal practices of

South Korean MNEs. A review of the literature has unearthed only three studies, namely Lansbury et al. (2006), Taylor et al. (2001), and Zou and Lansbury (2009), which provided some empirical data on appraisal practices of South Korean MNEs. However, none of the three studies extensively explored performance appraisal practices for expatriates. This research helps to fill this literature void. Most importantly, this study is one of the few that explores the approaches to international performance appraisal practices and analyzes the underlying factors. One interpretation of why South Korean MNEs adopt the ethnocentric approach to manage international performance appraisal practices is the relative strength effect. This finding provides some support to Pudelko and Harzing (2007), who advocated that MNEs originating from advanced economies, where the best management practices are supposed to exist (Smith and Meiksins 1995), and HCNs in underdeveloped or developing countries may be more likely to expect MNEs originating from advanced economies to manage people differently from local companies by bringing in the best practices. The Korean economy (i.e. a developed economy) enjoys relative strength over the Chinese economy (i.e. a developing economy). South Korean MNEs may believe their home appraisal practices to be superior to those of Chinese firms, and therefore, more suitable for their Chinese subsidiaries despite the apparent cultural and institutional differences between the two countries.

Fourthly, we investigated the international reward and compensation system of South Korean MNEs in China, and the empirical findings contribute to the literature in three ways. (1) International reward and compensation is under-researched; the extant literature is mostly derived from studies of MNEs originating from Western, developed economies. Little research has been devoted to non-Western MNEs. Therefore, by exploring international reward and compensation policies and practices of South Korean MNEs in China, this study extends the IHRM literature. (2) The existing IHRM literature does not differentiate the approaches to reward and compensation for different nationalities, and to different components of reward and compensation practices. This study revealed that the sample MNEs adopted differentiated approaches to managing reward and compensation for expatriates and for HCNs, and to different components of reward and compensation, for example, focal pay or peripheral pay. This finding helps to develop a better understanding of MNE approaches to international reward and compensation. (3) The extant literature is widely divided in relation to the reasons MNEs transfer or localize IHRM policies and practices, while the particular literature on international reward and compensation is largely lacking. Our study provides some support to, but does not entirely agree with, both the predominant views in the IHRM literature: the national culture model (Bloom et al. 2003; Vo and Stanton 2011) and the dominance effect model (Pudelko and Harzing 2007; Smith and Meiksins 1995). We suggest that: firstly, relative economic strength has a dominant effect on focal components of reward and compensation for expatriates; and secondly, cultural differences have a dominant effect on peripheral components for HCNs. Relative economic strength and cultural differences have an interactive effect on peripheral components of compensation practices for expatriates and on focal components for HCNs. Thus, our study extends institutional theory and sheds some new light on the factors influencing MNE decisions to transfer or localize IHRM practices.

Fifthly, we also explored the use and management of non-traditional expatriates of South Korean MNEs in China, which are the groups that been defined differently from traditional, long-term expatriates. The research contributes to the IHRM literature in three important ways. By focusing on non-traditional expatriates in South Korean MNEs, it has added significantly to the knowledge base of the IHRM literature as it is one of the first to examine MNEs in the rapidly expanding Asian region. By undertaking detailed interviews with representatives of South Korean MNEs operating in China, a rich source of data was obtained which is not normally possible with survey data. South Korean MNEs are structured quite differently from their Western counterparts and the findings that South Korean MNEs behave in a similar fashion to other MNEs with regard to managing expatriates suggest a convergence of managerial practices, at least in the management of FDI ventures. Moreover, there is limited research identifying the trend in using non-traditional expatriates in MNEs with research typically failing to make the distinction between non-traditional and the more traditional expatriates.

The current study demonstrated that there is an increasing reliance on using non-traditional expatriates in the sample South Korean MNEs. This suggests a convergence in MNE expatriates' practices. Furthermore, there is limited empirical research exploring the management of non-traditional expatriates (e.g. Tahvanainen et al. 2005). The current research investigated how South Korean MNEs manage non-traditional expatriates in China by examining the selection, training, performance appraisal, and reward and compensation perspectives. This addresses an important gap in the literature, and the findings suggest that little thought has been given to accommodating the unique aspects of this form of expatriation.

Finally, this study investigated the impacts of IHRM policies and practices on employee outcomes, in particular, HCNs' willingness to help expatriates. The derived empirical results contribute significantly to the IHRM literature. Previous studies on antecedents to HCNs' attitudes and behaviors toward expatriates focused on the predictive power of personal and intrapersonal factors, such as personality and social categorization (Arman and Aycan 2013; Caligiuri 2000; (Toh & DeNisi 2007); Varma et al. 2009, 2011). These predicting factors were conceptualized in contexts in which expatriates and HCNs were viewed more as co-workers (Toh and Srinivas 2012). This study nevertheless recognizes that, in addition to being co-workers, expatriates are also viewed by HCNs as representatives of the MNE. As such, HCNs' help provided to expatriates is not only helping co-worker behavior but also positive behavior toward the MNE. The finding that high-commitment HRM and socially responsible HRM predict HCNs' willingness to help expatriates through either HCNs' perceptions of organizational support or organizational identification sheds light on organizational antecedents of HCNs' attitudes and behaviors toward expatriates. It is evident that these go beyond personal and intrapersonal factors.

This study is innovative as it took into account the needs and interests of employees in the international business setting. The IHRM literature has advanced significantly during the last three decades (Dowling et al. 2013). The most important advance made to date is the development of strategic IHRM models that address MNEs' needs for strategic integration, local responsiveness, and global coordination simultaneously (De Cieri and Dowling 2012; Schuler et al. 1993; Taylor et al. 1996). However, the needs and interests of employees have been largely neglected in the IHRM literature (Shen 2011). The last few decades have witnessed the development of a broader view among HRM scholars which includes employees' interests, needs, and well-being beyond the basic business requirements for profits and growth (e.g. Chiang et al. 2011; McClean and Collins 2011). Comparatively, the IHRM literature has lagged behind in this regard (Shen 2011). This study helps to fill this gap by examining the effect of high-commitment HRM on the outcomes of HCNs in the international business setting.

The strategic IHRM literature has also neglected the interests and needs of external stakeholders (Shen 2011). The concept of socially responsible

HRM that addresses this limitation by integrating HRM with CSR has received growing research attention (Shen 2011). This is the first study to examine the employee outcomes of socially responsible HRM in the MNE context. In doing so, it adds to the knowledge base of the IHRM literature regarding the integration of IHRM and CSR. Moreover, there is a debate as to whether organizational social performance is at the cost of organizational financial and economic performance (Peloza and Shang 2011). This research provides evidence that socially responsible HRM is positively related to HCNs' willingness to help expatriates. Given that expatriates' success is crucial to an MNE's international business success, socially responsible HRM is likely to contribute to successful organizational financial and economic performance. This positive finding is a contribution to this debate.

Since the late 1980s, many HRM scholars have called for more studies to unlock the 'black box' of HRM due to its complex and changing nature (Mossholder et al. 2011; Jiang et al. 2012). More research is needed—especially in the MNE context. Building on social exchange theory (Blau 1964) and social identity theory (Tajfel 1978; Tajfel and Turner 1985), we explored the mediation of POS and organizational identification in the relationships of high-commitment HRM and socially responsible HRM with HCNs' willingness to help expatriates. These mediation relationships have not been previously studied in the IHRM literature and this study makes a contribution by developing a better understanding of social and psychological processes of IHRM in the MNE context.

Managerial Implications

The current research has significant implications for South Korean managers as well as for managers in other national MNEs. International staffing plays a key role in innovation, organizational learning, corporate integration, and management development in MNEs and therefore affects organizational performance and long-term sustainability (Collings et al. 2009). The findings of this study have significant implications for South Korean MNEs as well as for other national MNEs. MNEs need to consider employees' willingness to take up international assignments and family issues in expatriates' recruitment and selection. The 'two-way selection approach' would enable MNEs to recruit qualified and willing expatriates. Previous overseas experience should be considered as an important expatriate selection criterion as it is a key factor determining expatriates' success (Tung 1981; Harvey and Buckley 1998; Dowling et al. 2008). MNEs should pay more attention to repatriation management, especially with regard to career development. South Korean MNEs should take the advice offered by Lazarova and Cerdin (2007), who argued that it is to everyone's benefit to sign a repatriate agreement with the expatriate candidate to guarantee a suitable position upon his/her return, and provide realistic job previews for expatriates before they come home (Feldman and Thomas 1992). This practice will negate disappointment and unrealistic expectations.

The sample MNEs provided inadequate, low-rigor pre-departure CCT and leadership training to expatriates, inadequate on-the-job training to HCNs, and limited management development schemes and opportunities to both expatriates and HCNs. This deficiency has a negative impact on expatriates' adjustment to new working and living environments and on organizational commitment and retention among both expatriates and HCNs. To address this problem, MNEs should analyze the need for pre-departure training. If the need is identified, high-rigor training programs, for example, short-term assignments and host-country visits, may be offered. The current study shows that post-arrival training can reflect expatriates' experience and be effective when adjusting to new environments. MNEs hence should provide regular post-arrival training to expatriates. Given the linkage between management development practices and expatriates'/repatriates' retention (Dowling et al. 2013), MNEs should develop well-designed management development programs for expatriates, including mentoring during expatriation and position arrangement upon repatriation. Moreover, MNEs rely heavily on HCNs to manage business matters in foreign operations. With this in mind, MNEs should pay more attention to developing HCN managers by providing HCNs with more opportunities for promotion and individualized management development plans. This would help attract and retain high-caliber local talent.

In addition, MNEs always need to make critical decisions on approaches to their international performance appraisal practices. The overwhelming advice from academics so far is to localize, as localization is believed to have many benefits for MNEs. However, the findings of this study suggest that it is more important for MNEs originating from advanced economies to adopt international performance appraisal approaches with their own characteristics, reflecting the national institutional influences of their own home countries. For MNEs originating from less developed economies, it is important that they analyze their management strengths and the acceptability of their appraisal practices to HCNs when selecting approaches to international performance appraisals. However, it should be noted that the transfer of the home system may not be always successful due to the lack of local employees' support and high cultural discrepancies (e.g. Chen and Eldridge 2010; Pudelko and Harzing 2007; Vo and Stanton 2011). Hence, we suggest that MNEs consider adopting integrative approaches to managing international performance appraisals for both expatriates and HCNs.

Furthermore, international reward and compensation influences the work attitudes and behaviors of both expatriates and HCNs, and the international performance of MNEs. Accordingly, MNEs should formulate and implement effective international reward and compensation policies. Based on the findings of this study, MNEs should take into account a range of factors when making decisions about approaches to international reward and compensation. We suggest that when the home economy is relatively more dominant than the host economy, MNEs should consider adopting the home-oriented approach to focal reward and compensation for expatriates. Although MNEs may not have to pay HCNs at the same standards as for expatriates, they need to be aware of pay differentials between expatriates and HCNs due to the fact that large pay disparity is a major reason for job dissatisfaction among HCNs and HCNs' serious intentions to leave a company. We also suggest MNEs consider host contexts, such as traditions, when deciding their approach to managing peripheral components of reward and compensation for both expatriates and HCNs. For instance, in many Asian cultures, employers distribute presents to employees at traditional festivals. Chinese companies normally provide employees with transport allowances to compensate for commuting costs. Western MNEs operating in Asia should respect these traditions. Otherwise, job dissatisfaction may occur, resulting in talent losses and poorer company performance.

The current research also provides some suggestions for MNEs managing non-traditional expatriates. Consistent with the findings of Western studies (Suutari et al. 2013; Tahvanainen et al. 2005), our case study MNEs did not undertake a formal recruitment and selection process for non-traditional expatriates. As Suutari et al. (2013) suggested, a lack of formal recruitment and selection process has a negative impact on short-term expatriates and the company as a whole. At the very least, it would suggest that in many cases an inferior assignee would be appointed. We therefore recommend that MNEs should adopt a formal internal recruitment and selection system for non-traditional assignments. This will allow for interested candidates to compete for international assignments. In addition to expertise and experience, family issues should be considered in selection as they can be a major stressor for non-traditional expatriates (Dowling and Welch 2004). Many non-traditional expatriates were found to have no prior international experience and would thus benefit from programs such as pre-departure cross-cultural training. Whilst such programs are typically not available, we would suggest that MNEs consider introducing such training on a formal basis. Ideally, such programs would include families as they can help non-traditional expatriates to adjust to new cultures in a number of important and more subtle ways. Using managers in subsidiaries as raters for non-traditional expatriates and performance appraisals which are conducted on a project basis can increase appraisal accuracy and objectivity. As such, we recommend this practice to all MNEs who also should provide support to non-traditional expatriates while on international assignments. Our study along with the existing Western literature shows that non-traditional expatriates are all paid in the home country. Given the short nature of assignment durations, we believe this compensation practice is appropriate. However, allowances should vary according to the host country, assignment type, and duration. Support for family visits or relocation may also be a useful program for non-traditional expatriates, even where assignments may be relatively short, as this will help garner family support which in turn should improve the assignees' performance.

Finally, this research has demonstrated the predictive power of high commitment HRM and socially responsible HRM with regard to HCNs' willingness to help expatriates. This finding has significant implications for managers in MNEs. The assistance of HCNs within and outside the workplace is essential to expatriate success (Caligiuri et al. 1999; Farh et al. 2010; Varma et al. 2011). Therefore, to promote HCNs' willingness to help expatriates, MNEs should formulate and adopt appropriate IHRM policies and practices. MNEs should also adopt high-commitment HRM practices by addressing the interests and needs of both employees and external stakeholders, rather than focusing solely on strategic integration and financial performance.

MNEs also need to comply with both host-country labor laws and international labor laws with regard to the use of labor, working conditions (e.g. workplace health and safety), working hours, and pay. Moreover, MNEs should consider 'going beyond' local labor laws with regard to issues such as job security, work–life balance, equitable and competitive pay, and opportunities for personal development, training, and involvement in decision-making. These discretionary HRM practices should increase employees' POS and, consequently, increase employees' willingness to do extra for the MNE such as helping expatriates.

Given that CSR has become a social norm in the advanced economies, MNEs should also adopt socially responsible HRM by emphasizing personal CSR values in recruitment and selection, providing CSR training to improve employees' skills and awareness to engage in CSR activities and increase CSR cognition, properly appraising employees' social performance and linking social performance to promotion and financial rewards. These HRM practices will result in POS and organizational identification, which are positively related to HCNs' willingness to help expatriates as well as a wide range of other employee and organizational work outcomes, as many studies have suggested (Allen et al. 2003; Dukerich et al. 2002; Knight and Haslam 2010; Purcell and Hutchinson 2007).

Limitations and Future Research Directions

The current research has several limitations that should be addressed in future studies. First, the sample size in this study is small; only ten South Korean MNEs participated in this research. Future research should employ a larger sample of MNEs operating in many countries or regions to increase the generalizability of the research findings. Larger samples are also necessary for (e.g. more than 30 firms) conducting multi-level modeling which will enable researchers to aggregate socially responsible HRM to the organizational level so it takes into account the organizational contextual effects. This study is a first step to exploring the micro effects of CSR in the IB context. A range of employee consequences of CSR are worth exploring, such as employees' organizational commitment, job satisfaction, in-role and extra-role performance, ethical and social behavior, and creativity—all of which have a potentially significant effect on MNE performance. It has recently been argued that there is a need for multilevel conceptualization and analysis in CSR research (Aguinis and Glavas 2012). A similar call has been made with regard to HRM research (Ostroff and Bowen 2000; Shen 2016). In addition, future IB and IHRM studies should also consider multi-level modeling. More specifically, when exploring the effects of socially responsible HRM/high-commitment HRM, it should be conceptualized as an organization-level construct because

HCNs' attitudinal responses are not independent of MNEs' contextual effects.

Secondly, the interview data were collected mainly from managerial employees. However, non-managerial employees may have different insights into IHRM policies and practices. For this reason, future studies should consider collecting data from a wider range of employee sources.

Thirdly, the data were collected mainly from local subsidiaries. Due to the possible incongruence regarding goals between subsidiaries and headquarters (Dowling et al. 2008), the perceived HR practices (e.g. staffing) of subsidiary managers may differ from that of their company's headquarters. Hence, future studies should collect data from both subsidiaries' and headquarters' points of view toward IHRM policies and practices adopted by subsidiaries.

Fourthly, this research was conducted in two national contexts—South Korea and China. China is the only host country with a national culture that is very similar to South Korean culture. Although no theories or literature suggest that this study's findings may not be applicable in other national contexts, it would be helpful to replicate this research in other settings, such as with multiple foreign MNEs in a single host country, multiple foreign MNEs in multiple host countries, and MNEs from less-developed economies investing in developed economies. Furthermore, it would be useful to replicate this study in cross-cultural contexts where there are different CSR standards and employees' needs. Future research to test this assumption is recommended.

Finally, although common method bias was not a pervasive problem in this study, the risk of such bias still exists due to the use of self-report and single-sourced data. One way to resolve this issue is to collect data from multiple sources, including expatriates, HCNs, supervisors, and co-workers. This is especially important if the outcome variables are employees' work behaviors and performance. In addition, this study used cross-sectional data. As a result, potential reverse causality cannot be completely ruled out. We therefore suggest that future research utilize longitudinal data to explore the effect of change to HRM systems on HCNs' attitudes and behavior toward expatriates that may change over time.

Concluding Remarks

This study explores the IHRM policies and practices South Korean MNEs adopted in their Chinese subsidiaries and the effect of IHRM practices on the willingness of HCNs to help expatriates. The staffing practices that South Korean MNEs operated in China could be characterized as: a polycentric-tendency staffing approach, 'one-way selection' of expatriates, major selection criteria being job expertise, job performance, communication skills, cultural empathy and personality, and localized approach of recruiting and selection HCNs. There was a lack of repatriation management, little support has been provided to repatriates' relocation, and little attention has been paid to repatriates' career development.

The sample South Korean MNEs provided expatriates with extensive language training prior to departure and following arrival, but inadequate and low-rigor cross-cultural training. Limited training was provided to HCN production and office workers. The sample South Korean MNEs paid little attention to management development to both expatriates and HCNs, which had a negative effect on employees' organizational commitment and retention. South Korean MNEs tended to adopt an integrated approach to HCNs' training and development. This finding provides some support to the national cultural view and relative strength theory.

The sample South Korean MNEs standardized their performance appraisal practices in their Chinese subsidiaries, and that this approach can be attributed to the relative strength effect. Based on the findings of this study, the standardized approach may be most appropriate for MNEs originating from advanced economies for operations in less developed countries. The sample MNEs adopted different approaches to reward and compensation for expatriates and HCNs, and to focal and peripheral components of reward and compensation. The transfer of reward and compensation is due to the relative strength of the home economy over the host economy. In the meantime, the localization tendency of reward and compensation resulted from contextual differences such as economic development and cost of living.

Utilizing non-traditional expatriates has been on the rise in the sample MNEs, and they undertook similar roles to the long-term expatriates including control, problem-solving, management development, and knowledge transfer. It is evident that formal and systematic policies were lacking when it came to selecting, training, evaluating, and rewarding non-traditional expatriates.

High-commitment HRM directly and indirectly influences HCNs' willingness to help expatriates through the mediation of POS. Socially responsible HRM indirectly influences HCNs' willingness to help expatriates through the mediation of organizational identification. In addition, the relationship between high-commitment HRM and HCNs' willingness to help expatriates is sequentially mediated by POS and organizational identification.

Bibliography

Aguinis, H., & Glavas, A. (2012). What we know and don't know about corporate social responsibility: A review and research agenda. *Journal of Management, 38*(4), 932–968.

Allen, D. G., Shore, L. M., & Griffeth, R. W. (2003). The role of perceived organizational support and supportive human resource practices in the turnover process. *Journal of Management, 29*(1), 99–118.

Arman, G., & Aycan, Z. (2013). Host country nationals' attitudes toward expatriates: Development of a measure. *International Journal of Human Resource Management, 24*(15), 2927–2947.

Baumgarten, K. E. E. (1995). Training and development of international staff. In A. W. K. Harzing & J. van Ruysseveldt (Eds.), *International human resource management* (pp. 205–228). London: Sage.

Blau, P. (1964). *Exchange and power in social life*. New York: Wiley.

Bloom, M., Milkovich, G. T., & Mitra, A. (2003). International compensation: Learning from how managers respond to variations in local host contexts. *International Journal of Human Resource Management, 14*(8), 1350–1367.

Caligiuri, P. M. (2000). Selecting expatriates for personality characteristics: A moderating effect of personality on the relationship between host national contact and cross-cultural adjustment. *Management International Review, 40*(1), 61–80.

Caligiuri, P. M., Joshi, A., & Lazarova, M. (1999). Factors influencing the adjustment of women on global assignments. *International Journal of Human Resource Management, 10*(2), 163–179.

Chen, J., & Eldridge, D. (2010). Are "standardized performance appraisal practices" really preferred? A case study in China. *Chinese Management Studies, 4*(3), 244–257.

Chiang, H. H., Han, T. S., & Chuang, J. S. (2011). The relationship between high-commitment HRM and knowledge-sharing behavior and its mediators. *International Journal of Manpower, 32*(5/6), 604–622.

Collings, D. G., Scullion, H., & Dowling, P. J. (2009). Global staffing: A review and thematic research agenda. *The International Journal of Human Resource Management, 20*(6), 1253–1272.

De Cieri, H., & Dowling, P. J. (2012). Strategic human resource management in multinational enterprises: Developments and directions. In G. Stahl, I. Björkman, & S. Morris (Eds.), *Handbook of international HRM research*. Cheltenham: Edward Elgar.

Dowling, P. J., & Welch, D. E. (2004). *International human resource management. Managing people in a multinational context*. London: Thomson.

Dowling, P. J., Festing, M., & Engle, A. D. (2008). *International human resource management* (5th ed.). Stamford: Cengage Learning.

Dowling, P. J., Festing, M., & Engle, A. D. (2013). *International human resource management*. London: Cengage Learning.

Dukerich, J. M., Golden, B. R., & Shortell, S. M. (2002). Beauty is in the eye of the beholder: The impact of organizational identification, identity, and image on the cooperative behaviors of physicians. *Administrative Science Quarterly, 47*(3), 507–533.

Farh, C. I. C., Bartol, K. M., Shapiro, D. L., & Shin, J. (2010). Networking abroad: A process model of how expatriates form support ties to facilitate adjustment. *Academy of Management Review, 35*(3), 434–454.

Feldman, D. C., & Thomas, D. C. (1992). Career management issues facing expatriates. *Journal of International Business Studies, 23*(2), 271–293.

Festing, M., Knappert, L., Dowling, P. J., & Engle, A. D. (2012). Global performance management in MNEs: Conceptualization and profiles of country-specific characteristics in China, Germany, and the United States. *Thunderbird International Business Review, 54*, 825–843.

Gamble, J. (2000). Localizing management in foreign-invested enterprises in China: Practical, cultural and strategic perspectives. *International Journal of Human Resource Management, 11*, 883–903.

Harvey, M., & Buckley, M. R. (1998). The process for developing an international program for dual-career couples. *Human Resource Management Review, 8*(1), 99–123.

Jiang, K. F., Lepak, D., Hu, J., & Baer, J. C. (2012). How does human resource management influence organizational outcomes? A meta-analytical investigation of mediating mechanisms. *Academy of Management Journal, 55*(6), 1264–1294.

Kang, H. Y., & Shen, J. (2014). International human resource management policies and practices of South Korean MNEs: A review of the literature. *Asia Pacific Business Review, 20*(1), 42–58.

Kim, K. H., & Slocum, J. W. (2008). Individual differences and expatriate assignment effectiveness: The case of US-based Korean expatriates. *Journal of World Business, 43*(1), 109–126.

Knight, C., & Haslam, S. A. (2010). Your place or mine? Organizational identification and comfort as mediators of relationships between the managerial control of workspace and employees' satisfaction and wellbeing. *British Journal of Management, 21*(3), 717–735.

KPMG. (2010). *Global assignment policies and practices survey*. Retrieved March 10, 2014, from, https://www.kpmg.com/ZA/en/IssuesAndInsights/ArticlesPublications/Tax-and-Legal-Publications/Documents/GAPP-Survey-2010.pdf

Lansbury, D. R., Kwon, S. H., & Suh, C. S. (2006). Globalization and employment relations in the Korean auto industry: The case of the Hyundai Motor Company in Korea, Canada and India. *Asia Pacific Business Review, 12*(2), 131–147.

Lazarova, M. B., & Cerdin, J. L. (2007). Revisiting repatriation concerns: Organizational support versus career and contextual influences. *Journal of International Business Studies, 38*(3), 404–429.

Mayerhofer, H., Hartmann, L. C., Michelitsch-Riedl, G., & Kollinger, I. (2004). Flexpatriate assignments: A neglected issue in global staffing. *The International Journal of Human Resource Management, 15*(8), 1371–1389.

McClean, E., & Collins, C. J. (2011). High-commitment HR practices, employee effort, and firm performance: Investigating the effects of HR practices across employee groups within professional services firms. *Human Resource Management, 50*(3), 341–363.

Mossholder, K. W., Richardson, H. A., & Settoon, R. P. (2011). Human resource systems and helping in organizations: A relational perspective. *Academy of Management Review, 36*(1), 33–52.

Newton, S., Hutchings, K., & Kabanoff, B. (2007). Repatriation in Australian organisations: Effects of function and value of international assignment on program scope. *Asia Pacific Journal of Human Resources, 45*(3), 295–313.

Ostroff, C., & Bowen, D. E. (2000). Moving HR to a higher level: HR practices and organizational effectiveness. In K. J. Klein & S. W. J. Kozlowski (Eds.), *Multilevel theory, research, and methods in organizations: Foundations, extensions, and new directions* (pp. 211–266). San Francisco: Jossey-Bass.

Paik, Y. S., & Sohn, J. D. (1998). Confucius in Mexico: Korean MNEs and the maquiladoras. *Business Horizons, 41*(6), 25–33.

Peloza, J., & Shang, J. (2011). How can corporate social responsibility activities create value for stakeholders? A systematic review. *Journal of the Academy of Marketing Science, 39*(1), 117–135.

Pudelko, M., & Harzing, A. (2007). Country of origin, localization, or dominance effects? An empirical investigation of HRM practices in foreign subsidiaries. *Human Resource Management, 46*(4), 535–559.

Purcell, J., & Hutchinson, S. (2007). Front line managers as agents in the HRM performance causal chain: Theory, analysis and evidence. *Human Resource Management Journal, 17*(1), 3–20.

Schuler, R. S., Dowling, P. J., & De Cieri, H. (1993). An integrative framework of strategic international human resource management. *Journal of Management, 19*(2), 419–459.

Shen, J. (2006). Factors affecting international staffing in Chinese MNEs. *International Journal of Human Resource Management, 17*(2), 295–315.

Shen, J. (2011). Developing the concept of socially responsible international human resource management. *The International Journal of Human Resource Management, 22*(6), 1351–1363.

Shen, J. (2016). Multilevel analysis in HRM research using HLM: Principle and application. *Human Resource Management, 55*(6), 951–965

Shen, J., & Benson, J. (2014). When CSR is a social norm: How socially responsible human resource management affects employee work behavior. *Journal of Management*. p.0149206314522300.

Shen, J., & Darby, R. (2006). Training and management development in Chinese multinational enterprises. *Employee Relations, 28*(4), 342–362.

Shen, J., & Edwards, V. (2004). Recruitment and selection in Chinese MNEs. *The International Journal of Human Resource Management, 15*(4), 814–835.

Smith, C., & Meiksins, P. (1995). System, society and dominance effects in cross-national organisational analysis. *Work, Employment & Society, 9*(2), 241–267.

Suutari, V., Brewster, C., Riusala, K., & Syrjäkari, S. (2013). Managing non-standard international experience: Evidence from a Finnish company. *Journal of Global Mobility: The Home of Expatriate Management Research, 1*(2), 118–138.

Tahvanainen, M., Welch, D., & Worm, V. (2005). Implications of short-term international assignments. *European Management Journal, 23*(6), 663–673.

Tajfel, H. (1978). The achievement of group differentiation. In H. Tajfel (Ed.), *Differentiation between social groups: Studies in the social psychology of intergroup relations* (pp. 77–98). London: Academic Press.

Tajfel, H., & Turner, J. C. (1985). The social identity theory of intergroup behavior. In S. Worchel & W. G. Austin (Eds.), *Psychology of intergroup relations* (pp. 7–24). Chicago: Nelson-Hall.

Taylor, S., Beechler, S., & Napier, N. (1996). Toward an integrative model of strategic international human resource management. *Academy of Management Review, 21*(4), 959–985.

Taylor, R., Cho, D. Y., & Hyun, J. H. (2001). Korean companies in China: Strategies in the localisation of management. In C. Rowley, T. W. Sohn, & J. Bae (Eds.), *Managing Korean business: Organisation, culture, human resources and change* (pp. 161–181). London: Frank Cass.

Toh, S. M., & DeNisi, A. S. (2007). Host country nationals as socializing agents: A social identity approach. *Journal of Organizational Behavior, 28*(3), 281–301.

Toh, S. M., & Srinivas, E. S. (2012). Perceptions of task cohesiveness and organizational support increase trust and information sharing between host country nationals and expatriate coworkers in Oman. *Journal of World Business, 47*(4), 696–705.

Tung, R. L. (1981). Selecting and training of personnel for overseas assignments. *Colombia Journal of World Business, 16*(2), 67–78.

Tung, R. L. (1982). Selection and training procedures of US, European, and Japanese multinationals. *California Management Review, 25*, 57–71.

Varma, A., Pichler, S., Budhwar, P., & Biswas, S. (2009). Chinese host country nationals' willingness to support expatriates: The role of collectivism, interpersonal affect and guanxi. *International Journal of Cross Cultural Management, 9*(2), 199–216.

Varma, A., Budhwar, P., & Pichler, S. (2011). Chinese host country nationals' willingness to help expatriates: The role of social categorization. *Thunderbird International Business Review, 53*(3), 353–364.
Vo, A., & Stanton, P. (2011). The transfer of HRM policies and practices to a transnational system: The case of performance management practices of the US and Japanese MNEs operating in Vietnam. *International Journal of Human Resource Management, 22*(17), 3513–3527.
Welch, D. (1994). Determinants of international human resource management approaches and activities: A suggested framework. *Journal of Management Studies, 31*(2), 139–164.
Zou, M., & Lansbury, R. D. (2009). Multinational corporations and employment relations in the People's Republic of China: The case of Beijing Hyundai Motor Company. *International Journal of Human Resource Management, 20*(11), 2349–2369.

Bibliography

Adler, N. J., & Bartholomew, S. (1992). Managing globally competent people. *The Executive, 6*(3), 52–65.

Aguinis, H., & Glavas, A. (2012). What we know and don't know about corporate social responsibility: A review and research agenda. *Journal of Management, 38*(4), 932–968.

Ahn, Y. D. (1998). *Traditional Korean management systems as impediments to localization strategies on United States' subsidiaries*. Claremont: The Claremont Graduate University.

Akhtar, S., Ding, D. Z., & Ge, L. (2008). Strategic HRM practices and their impact on company performance in Chinese enterprises. *Human Resource Management, 47*(1), 15–32.

Allen, D. G., Shore, L. M., & Griffeth, R. W. (2003). The role of perceived organizational support and supportive human resource practices in the turnover process. *Journal of Management, 29*(1), 99–118.

Ancona, D. G., & Caldwell, D. F. (1992). Demography and design: Predictors of new product team performance. *Organization Science, 3*(3), 321–341.

Anderson, J. B. (1990). Compensating your overseas executives, part 2: Europe in 1992. *Compensation & Benefits Review, 22*(4), 25–35.

Anderson, B. A. (2005). Expatriate selection: Good management or good luck? *The International Journal of Human Resource Management, 16*(4), 567–583.

Anderson, J. C., & Gerbing, D. W. (1984). The effect of sampling error on convergence, improper solutions, and goodness-of-fit indices for maximum likelihood confirmatory factor analysis. *Psychometrika, 49*(2), 155–173.

H. Kang, J. Shen, *International Human Resource Management in South Korean Multinational Enterprises*,
DOI 10.1007/978-981-10-3093-2

Ando, N. (2011). Isomorphism and foreign subsidiary staffing policies. *Cross Cultural Management: An International Journal, 18*(2), 131–143.

Appelbaum, S. H., Roy, M., & Gilliland, T. (2011). Globalization of performance appraisals: Theory and applications. *Management Decision, 49*, 570–585.

Arman, G., & Aycan, Z. (2013). Host country nationals' attitudes toward expatriates: Development of a measure. *International Journal of Human Resource Management, 24*(15), 2927–2947.

Armstrong-Stassen, M., & Schlosser, F. (2010). When hospitals provide HR practices tailored to older nurses, will older nurses stay? It may depend on their supervisor. *Human Resource Management Journal, 20*(4), 375–390.

Ashforth, B. E., & Mael, F. (1989). Social identity theory and the organization. *Academy of Management Review, 14*(1), 20–39.

Atkinson, C., & Hall, L. (2011). Flexible working and happiness in the NHS. *Employee Relations, 33*(2), 88–105.

Average Salary Survey. (2013). *Average salary in South Korea*. Retrieved July 20, 2013, from http://www.averagesalarysurvey.com/article/average-salary-in-southkorea/12190513.aspx

Bae, J. S. (2004, June 23–26). *Globalization of human resource management: The cases of Korean MNCs in the UK and Thailand*. The IIRA Asian Regional Congress, Seoul.

Bae, J. S., & Lawler, J. J. (2000). Organizational and HRM strategies in Korea: Impact of firm performance in an emerging economy. *Academy of Management Journal, 43*(3), 502–517.

Bae, J. S., Chen, S. J., & Rowley, C. (2011). From a paternalistic model towards what? HRM trends in Korea and Taiwan. *Personnel Review, 40*(6), 700–722.

Bagozzi, R. P., & Yi, Y. (1990). Assessing method variance in multitrait-multimethod matrices: The case of self-reported affect and perceptions at work. *Journal of Applied Psychology, 75*(5), 547–560.

Barney, J. B. (1991). Firm resources and sustained competitive advantage. *Journal of Management, 17*(1), 99–120.

Basu, K., & Palazzo, G. (2008). Corporate social responsibility: A process model of sense making. *The Academy of Management Review Archive, 33*(1), 122–136.

Baumgarten, K. E. E. (1995). Training and development of international staff. In A. W. K. Harzing & J. van Ruysseveldt (Eds.), *International human resource management* (pp. 205–228). London: Sage.

Baxter, P., & Jack, S. (2008). Qualitative case study methodology: Study design and implementation for novice researchers. *The Qualitative Report, 13*(4), 544–559.

Bazeley, P., & Richards, L. (2000). *The NVIVO qualitative project book*. London: Sage.

Behrend, T. S., Baker, B. A., & Thompson, L. F. (2009). Effects of pro- environmental recruiting messages: The role of organizational reputation. *Journal of Business and Psychology, 24*(3), 341–350.

Benson, G. S., & Pattie, M. (2009). The comparative roles of home and host supervisors in the expatriate experience. *Human Resource Management, 48*(1), 49–68.

Berg, B. L. (2004). *Qualitative research methods.* Boston: Pearson Education.

Bernthal, P., Rogers, R., & Smith, A. (2003). *Managing performance: Building accountability for organizational success.* Pittsburgh: Development Dimensions International, Inc.

Björkman, I., & Gertsen, M. (1993). Selecting and training Scandinavian expatriates: Determinants of corporate practice. *Scandinavian Journal of Management, 9*(2), 145–164.

Björkman, I., & Lu, Y. (2000). Local or global? Human resource management in international joint ventures in China. In M. Warner (Ed.), *Changing workplace relations in the Chinese economy* (pp. 117–138). London: Palgrave Macmillan.

Black, J. S., & Gregersen, H. B. (1999). The right way to manage expats. *Harvard Business Review, 77*(2), 52–63.

Black, J. S., Gregersen, H. B., & Mendenhall, M. E. (1992). Toward a theoretical framework of repatriation adjustment. *Journal of International Business Studies, 23*, 737–760.

Black, J. S., Morrison, A., & Gregersen, H. B. (2000). *Global explorers: The next generation of leaders.* London: Routledge.

Blau, P. (1964). *Exchange and power in social life.* New York: Wiley.

Blau, G. (1999). Testing the longitudinal impact of work variables and performance appraisal satisfaction on subsequent overall job satisfaction. *Human Relations, 52*, 1099–1113.

Bloom, M., Milkovich, G. T., & Mitra, A. (2003). International compensation: Learning from how managers respond to variations in local host contexts. *International Journal of Human Resource Management, 14*(8), 1350–1367.

Bolino, M. C. (2007). Expatriate assignments and intra-organizational career success: Implications for individuals and organizations. *Journal of International Business Studies, 38*(5), 819–835.

Bonache, J. (2006). The compensation of expatriates: A review and future research agenda. In G. Stahl & I. Bjo rkman (Eds.), *Handbook of research in international human resource management* (pp. 158–175). Cheltenham: Edward Elgar.

Bonache, J., & Brewster, C. (2001). Knowledge transfer and the management of expatriation. *Thunderbird International Business Review, 43*(1), 145–168.

Bonache, J., & Noethen, D. (2014). The impact of individual performance on organizational success and its implications for the management of expatriates. *The International Journal of Human Resource Management, 25*(14), 1960–1977.

Bonache, J., Brewster, C., & Suutari, V. (2001). Expatriation: A developing research agenda. *Thunderbird International Business Review, 43*(1), 3–20.

Bossard, A. B., & Peterson, R. B. (2005). The repatriate experience as seen by American expatriates. *Journal of World Business, 40*(1), 9–28.

Brammer, S., Millington, A., & Rayton, B. (2007). The contribution of corporate social responsibility to organizational commitment. *The International Journal of Human Resource Management, 18*(10), 1701–1719.

Braun, W., & Warner, M. (2002). Strategic human resource management in western multinationals in China. *Personnel Review, 31*(5), 553–579.

Brewster, C. (1988). *The management of expatriates* (Human Resource Research Centre monograph, No. 2). Bedford: Cranfield School of Management.

Briscoe, D. R., & Claus, L. (2008). Employee performance management: Policies and practices in multinational enterprises. In A. Varma, P. S. Budhwar, & A. DeNisi (Eds.), *Performance management systems: A global perspective* (pp. 15–39). New York: Routledge.

Brookfield. (2015). Retrieved March 15, 2015, from http://globalmobilitytrends.brookfieldgrs.com/assets/downloads/Full-Report-Brookfield-GRS-2015-Global-Mobility-Trends-Survey.pdf

Brookfield Global Relocation Services. (2012). *Global relocation trends 2012 survey report.* Retrieved March 10, 2014, from http://espritgloballearning.com/wp-content/uploads/2011/03/2012-Brookfield-Global-Relocations-Trends-Survey.pdf

Browne, M. W., & Cudeck, R. (1989). Single sample cross validation indices for covariance Structures. *Multivariate Behavioral Research, 24*, 445–455.

Browne, M. W., & Cudeck, R. (1993). Alternative ways of assessing model fit. In K. Bollen & S. Long (Eds.), *Testing structural equation models* (pp. 136–162). Newbury Park: Sage.

Bruning, N. S., Bebenroth, R., & Pascha, W. (2011). Valuing Japan-based German expatriate and local manager's functions: Do subsidiary age and managerial perspectives matter? *The International Journal of Human Resource Management, 22*(4), 778–806.

Bryman, A., & Cassell, C. (2006). The researcher interview: A reflexive perspective. *Qualitative Research in Organizations and Management: An International Journal, 1*(1), 41–55.

Buckley, J. P., Clegg, J., & Tan, H. (2009a). Cultural awareness in knowledge transfer to China—The role of guanxi and mianzi. In J. P. Buckley (Ed.), *Foreign direct investment, China and the world economy* (pp. 165–191). Basingstoke: Palgrave Macmillan.

Buckley, J. P., Clegg, J., Cross, A., & Tan, H. (2009b). China's inward foreign direct investment success: Southeast Asia in the shadow of the dragon. In J. P. Buckley (Ed.), *Foreign direct investment, China and the world economy* (pp. 239–269). Basingstoke: Palgrave Macmillan.

Buckley, J. P., Wang, C. Q., & Clegg, J. (2009c). The impact of foreign ownership, local ownership and industry characteristics on spillover benefits from foreign direct investment in China. In J. P. Buckley (Ed.), *Foreign direct investment, China and the world economy* (pp. 305–326). Basingstoke: Palgrave Macmillan.

Budhwar, P. (2012). Management of human resources in foreign firms operating in India: The role of HR in country-specific headquarters. *The International Journal of Human Resource Management, 23*(12), 2514–2531.

Burnett, M., & Von Glinow, M. A. (2011). Total rewards in the international context. In A. W. Harzing & A. H. Pinnington (Eds.), *International human resource management* (pp. 468–496). London: Sage.

Burns, S. M. (2003). Flexible international assignee compensation plans. *Compensation & Benefits Review, 35*(3), 35–42.

Byrne, B. M. (2012). *Structural equation modeling with Mplus: Basic concepts, applications, and programming.* New York: Routledge.

Cai, Z., Morris, J. L., & Chen, J. (2011). Explaining the human resource management preferences of employees: A study of Chinese workers. *The International Journal of Human Resource Management, 22*(16), 3245–3269.

Caligiuri, P. M. (2000). Selecting expatriates for personality characteristics: A moderating effect of personality on the relationship between host national contact and cross-cultural adjustment. *Management International Review, 40*(1), 61–80.

Caligiuri, P. M., & Colakoglu, S. (2007). A strategic contingency approach to expatriate assignment management. *Human Resource Management Journal, 17*(4), 393–410.

Caligiuri, P. M., & Stroh, L. K. (1995). Multinational corporation management strategies and international human resources practices: Bringing IHRM to the bottom line. *The International Journal of Human Resource Management, 6*(3), 494–507.

Caligiuri, P. M., Joshi, A., & Lazarova, M. (1999). Factors influencing the adjustment of women on global assignments. *International Journal of Human Resource Management, 10*(2), 163–179.

Caplan, R. D., Cobb, S., French, J. R. P., Van Harrison, R., & Pinneau, S. R. (1980). *Job demands and worker health: Main effects and occupational differences.* Ann Arbor: University of Michigan Institute for Social Research.

Cardy, R. L., & Dobbins, G. H. (1994). *Performance appraisal: Alternative perspectives.* Cincinnati: South-Western Publishing.

Carver, C. S., & Scheier, M. F. (1982). Control theory: A useful conceptual framework for personality–social, clinical, and health psychology. *Psychological Bulletin, 92*, 111–135.

Cascio, W. F. (1998). *Managing human resources.* Boston: McGraw-Hill.

Cascio, W. F. (2006). Global performance management systems. In G. K. Stahl & I. Bjorkman (Eds.), *Handbook of research in international human resource management* (pp. 187–188). Cheltenham: Edward Elgar.

Cerdin, J. L., & Brewster, C. (2014). Talent management and expatriation: Bridging two streams of research and practice. *Journal of World Business, 49*(2), 245–252.

Chang, C. S., & Chang, N. J. (1994). *The Korean management system: Cultural, political, economic Foundations*. Westport: Quorum.

Charmaz, K. (2006). *Constructing grounded theory: A practical guide through qualitative analysis*. London: Sage.

Chen, M. (2004). *Asian management systems*. Hampshire: Cengage Learning EMEA.

Chen, H. A. (2006). *Recruitment and selection in China: An application to the case of Lenovo*. School of Management, University of Nottingham, Semenyih.

Chen, D. (2011). Research on performance management of Chinese SME. *International Journal of Business and Management, 6*(4), 263–265.

Chen, J., & Eldridge, D. (2010). Are "standardized performance appraisal practices" really preferred? A case study in China. *Chinese Management Studies, 4*(3), 244–257.

Cheng, M. J. (2015). *One belt, one road, one capital market*. Retrieved April 3, 2016, from http://www.financeasia.com/News/402733,one-belt-one-road--one-capital-market.aspx#reg-popup

Cheng, H. L., & Lin, C. Y. Y. (2009). Do as the large enterprises do? Expatriate selection and overseas performance in emerging markets: The case of Taiwan SMEs. *International Business Review, 18*(1), 60–75.

Chiang, F. F. T., & Birtch, T. A. (2010). Appraising performance across borders: An empirical examination of the purposes and practices of performance appraisal in a multi-country context. *Journal of Management Studies, 47*, 1365–1393.

Chiang, H. H., Han, T. S., & Chuang, J. S. (2011). The relationship between high-commitment HRM and knowledge-sharing behavior and its mediators. *International Journal of Manpower, 32*(5/6), 604–622.

China Labour Bulletin. (2013). *Wages in China*. Retrieved July 20, 2013, from http://www.clb.org.hk/en/content/wages-china

China Statistical Yearbook. (2012). *Average wage of employed persons in urban units by sector*. Retrieved August 15, 2013, from http://www.stats.gov.cn/tjsj/ndsj/2012/indexeh.htm

Chiu, R. K., Luk, V. W. M., & Tang, T. L. P. (2002). Retaining and motivating employees: Compensation preferences in Hong Kong and China. *Personnel Review, 31*(4), 402–431.

Cho, Y. J., Park, H. Y., & Wagner, S. (1999). Training in a changing Korea. *Training & Development, 53*(5), 98–100.

Cho, T., Hutchings, K., & Marchant, T. (2013). Key factors influencing Korean expatriates' and spouses' perceptions of expatriation and repatriation. *The International Journal of Human Resource Management, 24*(5), 1051–1075.

Choi, C. H. (2003). *The China strategies of Korea's winning companies* (Nomura Research Institute, No. 67, pp. 1–8). Tokyo: Nomura Research Institute.

Chow, H. S. (1995). An opinion survey of performance appraisal practices in Hong Kong and the People's Republic of China. *Asia Pacific Journal of Human Resources, 32*(3), 67–79.

Chu, C. M. (2003). *The study on related expatriate cross-cultural training and expatriate success: The example of Taiwanese enterprises in China*. National Science Council Project Research Planning Report. Taiwan: National Science Council.

Chung, K. T. (2008). Korea's shift to pay-for-performance. *SERI Quarterly, 1*(2), 9–17.

Chung, K. H., Lee, H. C., & Jung, K. H. (1997). *Korea management: Global strategy and cultural transformation*. Berlin/New York: Walter de Gruyter.

Clegg, B., & Gray, S. J. (2002). Australian expatriates in Thailand: Some insights for expatriate management policies. *International Journal of Human Resource Management, 13*, 598–623.

Cleveland, J. N., Murphy, K. R., & Williams, R. (1989). Multiple uses of performance appraisal: Prevalence and correlates. *Journal of Applied Psychology, 74*, 130–135.

Cleveland, J. N., Lim, A. S., & Murphy, K. R. (2007). Feedback phobia? Why employees do not want to give or receive performance feedback. In J. Langan-Fox, C. L. Cooper, & R. J. Klimoski (Eds.), *Research companion to the dysfunctional workplace: Management challenges and symptoms* (pp. 172–176). Cheltenham: Edward Elgar.

Colakoglu, S., & Caligiuri, P. (2008). Cultural distance, expatriate staffing and subsidiary performance: The case of US subsidiaries of multinational corporations'. *The International Journal of Human Resource Management, 19*(2), 223–239.

Colakoglu, S., Tarique, I., & Caligiuri, P. (2009). Towards a conceptual framework for the relationship between subsidiary staffing strategy and subsidiary performance. *The International Journal of Human Resource Management, 20*(6), 1291–1308.

Collings, D. G. (2014). Toward mature talent management: Beyond shareholder value. *Human Resource Development Quarterly, 25*(3), 301–319.

Collings, D. G., Scullion, H., & Morley, M. J. (2007). Changing patterns of global staffing in the multinational enterprise: Challenges to the conventional expatriate assignment and emerging alternatives. *Journal of World Business, 42*(2), 198–213.

Collings, D. G., Scullion, H., & Dowling, P. J. (2009). Global staffing: A review and thematic research agenda. *The International Journal of Human Resource Management, 20*(6), 1253–1272.

Collins, C. J., & Smith, K. G. (2006). Knowledge exchange and combination: The role of human resource management practices in the performance of high technology firms. *Academy of Management Journal, 40*(3), 544–560.

Cooke, F. L. (2004). *HRM, work and employment in China*. Oxon: Routledge.

Cooke, F. L. (2005a). *HRM, work and employment in China*. Oxon: Routledge.

Cooke, F. L. (2005b). Employment relations in small commercial businesses in China. *Industrial Relations Journal, 36*(1), 19–37.

Cooke, F. L. (2008). The changing dynamics of employment relations in China: An evaluation of theorising level of labour disputes. *Journal of Industrial Relations, 50*, 111–138.

Cooke, F. L. (2011). The role of the state and emergent actors in the development of human resource management in China. *The International Journal of Human Resource Management, 22*(18), 3830–3848.

Cooke, F. L. (2012). *Human resource management in China: New trends and practices.* New York: Routledge.

Coyle-Shapiro, J. A. M., & Shore, L. M. (2007). The employee-organization relationship: Where do we go from here? *Human Resource Management Review, 17*(2), 166–179.

Crano, W. D., & Brewer, M. B. (2002). Content analysis. In N. J. Mahwah (Ed.), *Principles and methods of social research* (pp. 245–263). Mahwah: Lawrence Erlbaum Associates.

Creswell, J. W. (1994). *Research design: Qualitative, quantitative and mixed methods approach.* London: Sage.

Creswell, J. W. (2003). *Research design: Qualitative, quantitative and mixed methods approaches.* Thousand Oaks: Sage.

Cropanzano, R., & Mitchell, M. S. (2005). Social exchange theory: An interdisciplinary review. *Journal of Management, 31*(6), 874–900.

Culpan, O., & Wright, G. H. (2002). Women abroad: Getting the best results from women managers. *The International Journal of Human Resource Management, 13*(5), 784–801.

Cunningham, L. X. (2010). Managing human resources in SMEs in a transition economy: Evidence from China. *The International Journal of Human Resource Management, 21*(12), 2120–2141.

Dasmalchian, A., Lee, S., & Ng, I. (2000). The interplay between organizational and national cultures: A comparison of organizational practices in Canada and South Korea using the competing values framework. *The International Journal of Human Resource Management, 11*(2), 388–412.

David, M., & Sutton, C. (2011). *Social research: An introduction.* London: Sage.

De Cieri, H., & Dowling, P. J. (2012). Strategic human resource management in multinational enterprises: Developments and directions. In G. Stahl, I. Björkman, & S. Morris (Eds.), *Handbook of international HRM research.* Cheltenham: Edward Elgar.

De Luque, M. F. S., & Sommer, S. M. (2000). The impact of culture on feedback-seeking behavior: An integrated model and propositions. *Academy of Management Review, 25*(4), 829–849.

De Vaus, D. A. (2001). *Research design in social research.* Thousand Oaks: Sage.

Debrah, Y. A., & Rees, C. J. (2011). The development of global leaders and expatriates. In A. W. Harzing & A. H. Pinnington (Eds.), *International human resource management* (3rd ed., pp. 377–414). London: Sage.

Demel, B., & Mayrhofer, W. (2010). Frequent business travelers across Europe: Career aspirations and implications. *Thunderbird International Business Review, 52*(4), 301–311.

Demirbag, M., Tatoglu, E., & Glaister, K. W. (2009). Equity-based entry modes of emerging country multinationals: Lessons from Turkey. *Journal of World Business, 44*(4), 445–462.

Dickmann, M., Doherty, N., Mills, T., & Brewster, C. (2008). Why do they go? Individual and corporate perspectives on the factors influencing the decision to accept an international assignment. *The International Journal of Human Resource Management, 19*(4), 731–751.

DiMaggio, P. J., & Powell, W. W. (1983). The iron cage revisited: Institutional isomorphism and collective rationality in organizational fields. *American Sociological Review, 48*, 147–160.

Ding, D., & Warner, M. (2001). China's labour–management system reforms: Breaking the 'three old irons' (1978–1999). *Asia Pacific Journal of Management, 18*(3), 315–334.

Ding, D., Fields, D., & Akhtar, S. (1997). An empirical study of human resource management policies and practices in foreign-invested enterprises in China: The case of Shenzen Special Economic Zone. *International Journal of Human Resource Management, 8*(5), 595–613.

Ding, D., Akhtar, S., & Ge, L. G. (2006). Organizational differences in managerial compensation and benefits in Chinese firms. *The International Journal of Human Resource Management, 17*(4), 693–715.

Dorrenbacher, C., & Geppert, M. (2010). Subsidiary staffing and initiative-taking in multinational corporations: A socio-political perspective. *Personnel Review, 39*(5), 600–621.

Dowling, P. J., & Welch, D. E. (1988). International human resource management: An Australian perspective. *Asia Pacific Journal of Management, 6*(1), 39–65.

Dowling, P. J., & Welch, D. E. (2004). *International human resource management. Managing people in a multinational context.* London: Thomson.

Dowling, P. J., Welch, D. E., & Schuler, R. S. (1999). *International human resource management.* Cincinnati: South-Western.

Dowling, P. J., Festing, M., & Engle, A. D. (2008). *International human resource management* (5th ed.). Stamford: Cengage Learning.

Dowling, P. J., Festing, M., & Engle, A. D. (2013). *International human resource management.* London: Cengage Learning.

Dukerich, J. M., Golden, B. R., & Shortell, S. M. (2002). Beauty is in the eye of the beholder: The impact of organizational identification, identity, and image on the cooperative behaviors of physicians. *Administrative Science Quarterly, 47*(3), 507–533.

Dutton, E. J., Dukerich, J. M., & Harquail, V. C. (1994). Organizational images and member identification. *Administrative Science Quarterly, 39*(2), 239–263.

Edström, A., & Galbraith, J. R. (1977). Transfer of managers as a coordination and control strategy in multinational organizations. *Administrative Science Quarterly, 22*, 248–263.

Edwards, M. R. (2009). HR, perceived organizational support and organizational identification: An analysis after organizational formation. *Human Resource Management Journal, 19*(1), 91–115.

Edwards, M. R., & Peccei, R. (2010). Perceived organizational support, organizational identification, and employee outcomes: Testing a simultaneous multifoci model. *Journal of Personnel Psychology, 9*(1), 17–26.

Eisenberger, R., Huntington, R., Hutchison, S., & Sowa, D. (1986). Perceived organizational support. *Journal of Applied Psychology, 71*(3), 500–507.

Eisenberger, R., Cummings, J., Armeli, S., & Lynch, P. (1997). Perceived organizational support, discretionary treatment, and job satisfaction. *Journal of Applied Psychology, 82*(5), 812–820.

Eisenberger, R., Stinglhamber, F., Vandenberghe, C., Sucharski, I. L., & Rhoades, L. (2002). Perceived supervisor support: Contributions to perceived organizational support and employee retention. *Journal of Applied Psychology, 87*(3), 565–573.

Eisenberger, R., Jones, J., Aselage, J., & Sucharski, I. (2004). Perceived organizational support. In J. Coyle-Shapiro, L. Shore, M. Taylor, & L. Tetrick (Eds.), *The employment relationship: Examining psychological and contextual perspectives* (pp. 206–225). Oxford, UK: Oxford University Press.

El Mansour, B., & Wood, E. (2010). Cross-cultural training of European and American managers in Morocco. *Journal of European Industrial Training, 34*(4), 381–392.

Eriksson, S., & Kobin, U. (2007). *International human resource training in Swedish MNCs.* Master's thesis, Department of Business Administration and Social Sciences, University of Technology, LuLea.

Eschbach, D. M., Parker, G. E., & Stoeberl, P. E. (2001). American repatriate employees' retrospective assessments of the effects of cross-cultural training on their adaptation to international assignments. *International Journal of Human Resource Management, 12*, 270–287.

Evans, P., & Lorange, P. (1989). The two logics behind human resource management. In P. Evans, Y. Doz, & A. Laurent (Eds.), *Human resource management in international firms: Change, globalization and innovation* (pp. 144–161). London: Macmillan.

Export-Import Bank of Korea. (2011). *Foreign investment statistics by country.* Retrieved May 6, 2011, from http://www.kexim.co.kr/en2/05_fdi/02_statistic/04.jsp

Farh, J., Dobbins, G. H., & Cheng, B. (1991). Cultural relativity in action: A comparison of self-ratings made by Chinese and US workers. *Personnel psychology, 44*(1), 129–147.

Farh, C. I. C., Bartol, K. M., Shapiro, D. L., & Shin, J. (2010). Networking abroad: A process model of how expatriates form support ties to facilitate adjustment. *Academy of Management Review, 35*(3), 434–454.

Farndale, E., Paauwe, J., Morris, S. S., Stahl, G. K., Stiles, P., Trevor, J., & Wright, P. M. (2010). Context-bound configurations of corporate HR functions in multinational corporations. *Human Resource Management, 49*(1), 45–66.

Feely, A. J., & Harzing, A. W. (2003). Language management in multinational companies. *Cross Cultural Management: An International Journal, 10*, 37–52.

Feldman, D. C., & Thomas, D. C. (1992). Career management issues facing expatriates. *Journal of International Business Studies, 23*(2), 271–293.

Fenwick, M. (2004). International compensation and performance management. In A. W. K. Harzing & J. Van Ruysseveldt (Eds.), *International HRM: Managing people across borders* (pp. 307–332). Newbury Park: Sage.

Ferner, A. (1997). Country of origin effects and HRM in multinational companies. *Human Resource Management Journal, 7*(1), 19–37.

Ferris, G. R., Liden, R. C., Munyon, T. P., Summers, J. K., Basik, K. J., & Buckley, M. R. (2009). Relationships at work: Toward a multidimensional conceptualization of dyadic work relationships. *Journal of Management, 35*(6), 1379–1403.

Festing, M., Knappert, L., Dowling, P. J., & Engle, A. D. (2012). Global performance management in MNEs: Conceptualization and profiles of country-specific characteristics in China, Germany, and the United States. *Thunderbird International Business Review, 54*, 825–843.

Fisher, C. D. (1989). Current and recurrent challenges in HRM. *Journal of Management, 15*(2), 157–180.

Fletcher, C., & Perry, P. (2002). Performance appraisal and feedback: A consideration of national culture and a review of contemporary and future trends. In N. Anderson, D. Ones, H. Sinangil, & C. Viswesvaran (Eds.), *International handbook of industrial, work and organizational psychology* (pp. 127–144). Beverly Hills: Sage.

Flick, U. W. E. (2006). *An introduction to qualitative research*. London: Sage.

Forster, N. (2000). Expatriates and the impact of cross cultural training. *Human Resource Management Journal, 10*(3), 63–78.

Fortune. (2016). *Global 500*. Retrieved March 27, 2016, from http://fortune.com/global500/

Furnham, A., & Stringfield, P. (1998). Congruence in job-performance ratings: A study of 360 feedback examining self, manager, peers, and consultant ratings. *Human Relations, 51*(4), 517–530.

Furuya, N., Stevens, M. J., Bird, A., Oddou, G., & Mendenhall, M. (2008). Managing the learning and transfer of global management competence: Antecedents and outcomes of Japanese repatriation effectiveness. *Journal of International Business Studies, 40*(2), 200–215.

Gabris, G. T., & Ihrke, D. M. (2001). Does performance appraisal contribute to heightened levels of employee burnout? The results of one study. *Public Personnel Management, 30*, 157–172.

Gamble, J. (2000). Localizing management in foreign-invested enterprises in China: Practical, cultural and strategic perspectives. *International Journal of Human Resource Management, 11*, 883–903.

Garavan, T. N., Morley, M., & Flynn, M. (1997). 360 degree feedback: Its role in employee development. *Journal of Management Development, 16*(2), 134–147.

General Motors Acceptance Corporation. (2004). *Global relocation trends 2003/2004 survey report.* Retrieved March 10, 2014, from http://www.nftc.org/default/hr/GRTS%202003-4.pdf

Ghafoor, S., Khan, U. F., Idrees, F., Javed, B., & Ahmed, F. (2011). Evaluation of expatriates performance and their training on international assignments. *Interdisciplinary Journal of Contemporary Research in Business, 3*(5), 335–351.

Gibney, R., Zagenczyk, T. J., Fuller, J. B., Hester, K., & Caner, T. (2011). Exploring organizational obstruction and the expanded model of organizational identification. *Journal of Applied Social Psychology, 41*(5), 1083–1109.

Glover, L., & Wilkinson, A. (2007). Worlds colliding: The translation of modern management practices within a UK based subsidiary of a Korean-owned MNC. *The International Journal of Human Resource Management, 18*(8), 1437–1455.

GMA News. (2013). *Korea hikes minimum wage for workers—DOLE.* Retrieved July 20, 2013, from http://www.gmanetwork.com/news/story/292870/economy/companies/korea-hikesminimumwage-for-workers-dole

Gong, Y. (2003). Toward a dynamic process model of staffing composition and subsidiary outcomes in multinational enterprises. *Journal of Management, 29*(2), 259–280.

Gong, Y., & Chang, S. (2008). Institutional antecedents and performance consequences of employment security and career advancement practices: Evidence from the People's Republic of China. *Human Resource Management, 47*(1), 33–48.

Gong, Y., & Yang, W. G. (2012). Performance management at Shenhua Guohua Electric Power. In J. C. Hayton, M. Byron, L. C. Christiansen, & B. Kuvaas (Eds.), *Global HRM case book* (pp. 253–265). New York: Routledge.

Gosling, S. D., Rentfrow, P. J., & Swann Jr., W. B. (2003). A very brief measure of the Big-Five personality domains. *Journal of Research in Personality, 37*(6), 504–528.

Gregersen, H. B., Hite, J. M., & Black, J. S. (1996). Expatriate performance appraisal in US multinational firms. *Journal of International Business Studies, 27*, 711–738.

Gudykunst, W. B. (2004). *Bridging differences: Effective intergroup communication.* Thousand Oaks: Sage.

Hamill, J. (1989). Expatriate policies in British multinationals. *Journal of General Management, 14*(4), 18–33.

Han, J., & Han, J. (2009). Network-based recruiting and applicant attraction in China: Insights from both organizational and individual perspectives. *The International Journal of Human Resource Management, 20*(11), 2228–2249.

Hana Financial Group. (2013). *2013 Hana Financial Group sustainability report.* Retrieved April 11, 2016, from, http://www.hanafn.com/eng/csr/sustainability/sustainabilityFileDown.do?fileName=report_2013_english.pdf

Harris, H., & Brewster, C. (1999). The coffee-machine system: How international selection really works. *The International Journal of Human Resource Management, 10*(3), 488–500.

Harris, H., & Kumra, S. (2000). International manager development—Cross-cultural training in highly diverse environments. *Journal of Management Development, 19*, 602–614.

Harris, M. M., & Schaubroeck, J. (1988). A meta-analysis of self-supervisor, self-peer, and peer-supervisor ratings. *Personnel Psychology, 41*, 43–62.

Harrison, D. A., & Shaffer, M. A. (2005). Mapping the criterion space for expatriate success: Task- and relationship-based performance, effort and adaptation. *The International Journal of Human Resource Management, 16*(8), 1454–1474.

Hart-Landsberg, M. (2004). The South Korean economy and US policy. *Asian Perspective, 28*, 89–117.

Hartmann, E., Feisel, E., & Schober, H. (2010). Talent management of western MNCs in China: Balancing global integration and local responsiveness. *Journal of World Business, 45*, 169–178.

Harvey, M., & Buckley, M. R. (1998). The process for developing an international program for dual-career couples. *Human Resource Management Review, 8*(1), 99–123.

Harvey, M., Speier, C., & Novicevic, M. M. (1999). The role of inpatriation in global staffing. *International Journal of Human Resource Management, 10*, 459–476.

Harzing, A. W. (1999). *Managing the multinationals: An international study of control mechanisms.* Cheltenham: Edward Elgar.

Harzing, A. W. (2001). Of bears, bumble-bees, and spiders: The role of expatriates in controlling foreign subsidiaries. *Journal of World Business, 36*(4), 366–379.

Harzing, A. W., & Christensen, C. (2004). Expatriate failure: Time to abandon the concept? *Career Development International, 9*(7), 616–626.

Herrmann, P., & Werbel, J. (2007). Promotability of host country nationals: A cross cultural study. *British Journal of Management, 18*, 281–293.

Hlasny, V., & Jiang, M. (2014). *Discrimination in recruitment in China: An employer-level analysis of applicant screening.* Available at SSRN 2226238.

Hofstede, G. (1980). Culture and organizations. *International Studies of Management and Organization, 10*(4), 15–41.

Horak, S. (2015). The informal dimension of human resource management in Korea: Yongo, recruiting practices and career progression. *The International*

Journal of Human Resource Management, 1–24. doi:10.1080/09585192.2015.1089062.

Horwich, G. (1993). The role of the for-profit private sector in disaster mitigation and response. *International Journal of Mass Emergences and Disasters, 11*(2), 189–205.

Hu, F., & Leung, C. M. (2010). *Top management turnover, firm performance and government control: Evidence from China's listed state-owned enterprises*. http://papers.ssrn.com/sol3/papers.cfm?abstract_id=1532724

Huang, S. C. (2002). *The overseas adaptation of Taiwanese expatriates working at Taiwanese subsidiary companies in Malaysia*. Nantou: National Chi Nan University.

Huo, Y. P., & Von Glinow, M. A. (1995). On transplanting human resource practices to China: A culture-driven approach. *International Journal of Manpower, 16*(9), 3–15.

Hutchings, K. (2003). Cross-cultural preparation of Australian expatriates in organisations in China: The need for greater attention to training. *Asia Pacific Journal of Management, 20*(3), 375–396.

Hutchings, K. (2005). Koalas in the land of the pandas: Reviewing Australian expatriates' China preparation. *International Journal of Human Resource Management, 16*, 553–566.

Hyde, K. F. (2000). Recognising deductive processes in qualitative research. *Qualitative market research: An International Journal, 3*(2), 82–90.

Ilies, R., Nahrgang, J. D., & Morgeson, F. P. (2007). Leader-member exchange and citizenship behaviors: A meta-analysis. *Journal of Applied Psychology, 92*(1), 269–277.

Jackson, S., & Littler, C. R. (1991). Wage trends and policies in China: Dynamics and contradictions. *Industrial Relations Journal, 22*(1), 5–19.

Jackson, S., & Schuler, R. S. (2003). *Managing human resources through strategic partnerships*. Cincinnati: South-Western.

Jang, I. C. (2015). Language learning as a struggle for distinction in today's corporate recruitment culture: An ethnographic study of English study abroad practices among South Korean undergraduates. *L2 Journal, 7*(3), 57–77.

Jang, S. Y., & Merriam, S. (2004). Korean culture and the reentry motivations of university-graduated women. *Adult Education Quarterly, 54*(4), 273–290.

Janssens, M. (1994). Evaluating international managers' performance: Parent company standards as control mechanism. *The International Journal of Human Resource Management, 5*, 853–873.

Janssens, M. (2002). Developing a culturally synergistic approach to international human resource management. *Journal of World Business, 36*(4), 429–450.

Jaussaud, J., & Liu, X. (2011). When in China… The HRM practices of Chinese and foreign-owned enterprises during a global crisis. *Asia Pacific Business Review, 17*(4), 473–491.

Jawahar, I. M. (2006). An investigation of potential consequences of satisfaction with appraisal feedback. *Journal of Leadership & Organizational Studies, 13*, 14–28.

Jenkins, R. (2005). Globalization, corporate social responsibility and poverty. *International Affairs, 81*(3), 525–540.

Jhun, S., Bae, Z. T., & Rhee, S. Y. (2012). Performance change of managers in two different uses of upward feedback: A longitudinal study in Korea. *The International Journal of Human Resource Management, 23*, 4246–4264.

Jiang, K. F., Lepak, D., Hu, J., & Baer, J. C. (2012). How does human resource management influence organizational outcomes? A meta-analytical investigation of mediating mechanisms. *Academy of Management Journal, 55*(6), 1264–1294.

Johnson, R. B., & Onwuegbuzie, A. J. (2004). Mixed methods research: A research paradigm whose time has come. *Educational Researcher, 33*(7), 14–26.

Johnson, E. C., Kristof-brown, A. L., Van Vianen, A. E. M., De Pater, I. E., & Klein, M. R. (2003). Expatriate social ties: Personality antecedents and consequences for adjustment. *International Journal of Selection and Assessment, 11*(4), 277–288.

Judge, T. A., & Piccolo, R. F. (2004). Transformational and transactional leadership: A meta-analytic test of their relative validity. *Journal of Applied Psychology, 89*(5), 755–768.

Kang, H. Y., & Shen, J. (2013). International recruitment and selection practices of South Korean multinationals in China. *The International Journal of Human Resource Management, 24*(17), 3325–3342.

Kang, H. Y., & Shen, J. (2014). International human resource management policies and practices of South Korean MNEs: A review of the literature. *Asia Pacific Business Review, 20*(1), 42–58.

Kang, H. Y., Shen, J., & Xu, G. (2015). International training and management development policies and practices of South Korean MNEs in China. *Thunderbird International Business Review, 57*(3), 229–240.

Kearney, R. P. (1991). *The warrior worker: The history and challenge of South Korea's economic miracle*. New York: Henry Holt & Co.

Kerr, J. L., & Slocum, J. W. (1987). Managing corporate cultures through reward systems. *Academy of Management Executive, 1*(2), 3–15.

Kim, C. S. (1992). *The culture of Korean industry: An ethnography of Poongsan Corporation*. Tucson: The University of Arizona Press.

Kim, L. (1997). The dynamics of Samsung's technological learning in semiconductors. *California Management Review, 39*(3), 86–100.

Kim, P. S. (2001). Utilising 360-degree feedback in the public sector: A case study of the Korean central government. *Asian Journal of Political Science, 9*, 95–108.

Kim, S., & Briscoe, D. R. (1997). Globalization and a new human resource policy in Korea: Transformation to a performance-based HRM'. *Employee Relations, 19*(4), 298–308.

Kim, Y., & Gao, F. Y. (2010). An empirical study of human resource management practices in family firms in China. *The International Journal of Human Resource Management, 21*(12), 2095–2119.

Kim, Y., & Gray, S. J. (2005). Strategic factors influencing international human resource management practices: An empirical study of Australian multinational corporations. *The International Journal of Human Resource Management, 16*(5), 809–830.

Kim, J. M., & Rhe, D. K. (2009). Trends and determinants of South Korean outward foreign direct investment. *The Copenhagen Journal of Asian Studies, 27*(1), 126–154.

Kim, J. W., & Rowley, C. (2001). Managerial problems in Korea-Evidence from the nationalized industries. *International Journal of Public Sector Management, 14*(2), 129–149.

Kim, K. H., & Slocum, J. W. (2008). Individual differences and expatriate assignment effectiveness: The case of US-based Korean expatriates. *Journal of World Business, 43*(1), 109–126.

Kim, D. H., Pan, Y. G., & Park, H. S. (1998). High- versus low-context culture: A comparison of Chinese, Korean, and American cultures. *Psychology & Marketing, 15*(6), 507–521.

Kim, H., Kwon, D. B., & Pyun, C. (2008). Korean corporate HRD in transition: Issues and challenges. *Human Resource Development International, 11*(1), 81–89.

Kim, H. R., Lee, M., Lee, H. T., & Kim, N. M. (2010). Corporate social responsibility and employee–company identification. *Journal of Business Ethics, 95*(4), 557–569.

Kim, H. D., Sutton, K. L., & Gong, Y. P. (2013). Group-based pay-for-performance plans and firm performance: The moderating role of empowerment practices. *Asia Pacific Journal of Management, 30*(1), 31–52.

Kim, M., Chai, D. S., Kim, S., & Park, S. (2015). New employee orientation: Cases of Korean corporations. *Human Resource Development International, 18*(5), 481–498.

Knight, C., & Haslam, S. A. (2010). Your place or mine? Organizational identification and comfort as mediators of relationships between the managerial control of workspace and employees' satisfaction and wellbeing. *British Journal of Management, 21*(3), 717–735.

Kobrin, S. J. (1988). Expatriate reduction and strategic control in American multinational corporations. *Human Resource Management, 27*(1), 63–75.

Koch, M., Nam, S. H., & Steers, R. M. (1995). Human resource management in South Korea. In L. F. Moore & P. D. Jennings (Eds.), *Human resource management on the Pacific Rim* (pp. 217–242). New York: De Gmyter.

Kong, D., Kim, S., & Yang, S. B. (2013). *Individual performance appraisal in the government of Korea, Knowledge Sharing Program: KSP Modularization*. Seoul: KDI School of Public Policy and Management.

Kopp, R. (1994). International human resource policies and practices in Japanese, European, and United States multinationals. *Human Resource Management, 33*(4), 581–599.

Korea Eximbank. (2013). *Investment statistics by country*. Retrieved April 10, 2013, from http://211.171.208.92/odisas_eng.html

Korea Eximbank. (2016a). *By region*. Retrived March 15, 2016, from http://211.171.208.92/odisas_eng.html?type=03

Korea Eximbank. (2016b). *By industry*. Retrieved March 15, 2016, from http://211.171.208.92/odisas_eng.html?type=03

Korea Eximbank. (2016c). *Investment statistics by country*. Retrieved April 10, 2016, from http://211.171.208.92/odisas_eng.html

Korean Air. (2014). *Who we are*. Retrieved April 13, 2016, from https://www.koreanair.com/global/zh_cn/about/who-we-are2.html

Korzec, M. (1992). *Labour and the failure of reform in China*. London/New York: Macmillan/St. Martin's Press.

KPMG. (2010). *Global assignment policies and practices survey*. Retrieved March 10, 2014, from, https://www.kpmg.com/ZA/en/IssuesAndInsights/Articles Publications/Tax-and-Legal-Publications/Documents/GAPP-Survey-2010.pdf

Kreiner, G. E., & Ashforth, B. E. (2004). Evidence toward an expanded model of organizational identification. *Journal of Organizational Behavior, 25*(1), 1–27.

Kuhlmann, T., & Hutchings, K. (2010). Expatriate assignments vs localization of management in China: Staffing choices of Australian and German companies. *Career Development International, 15*(1), 20–38.

Kulkarni, M., Lengnick-Hall, M. L., & Valk, R. (2010). Employee perceptions of repatriation in an emerging economy: The Indian experience. *Human Resource Management, 49*(3), 531–548.

Kwon, O. Y., & Oh, I. (2001). *Korean direct investment in Australia: Issues and prospects*. Brisbane: Griffith University: Australian Centre for Korean Studies.

Lane, C. (1998). European companies between globalization and localization: A comparison of internationalization strategies of British and German MNCs. *Economy and Society, 27*(4), 462–485.

Lansbury, D. R., Kwon, S. H., & Suh, C. S. (2006). Globalization and employment relations in the Korean auto industry: The case of the Hyundai Motor Company in Korea, Canada and India. *Asia Pacific Business Review, 12*(2), 131–147.

Lasserre, P., & Ching, P. S. (1997). Human resources management in China and the localization challenge. *Journal of Asian Business, 13*(4), 85–99.

Lazarova, M., & Caligiuri, P. (2001). Retaining repatriates: The role of organizational support practices. *Journal of World Business, 36*, 389–401.

Lazarova, M. B., & Cerdin, J. L. (2007). Revisiting repatriation concerns: Organizational support versus career and contextual influences. *Journal of International Business Studies, 38*(3), 404–429.

Lee, S. H. (1998a). Organizational flexibility in Korean companies: Rules and procedures on managerial discretion and employee behaviour. *The International Journal of Human Resource Management, 9*(3), 478–493.

Lee, H. C. (1998b). Transformation of employment practices in Korean businesses. *International Studies of Management & Organization, 28*(4), 26–39.

Lee, C. W. (2003). Changing labor relations and human resources management of Korean Businesses in China and future challenges. *e-Labor News*, 21. Retrieved August 21, 2013, from http://unpan1.un.org/intradoc/groups/public/documents/APCITY/UNPAN020894.pdf

Lee, T. Z. (2004a). *A study on related factors expatriate human resource management affecting cross-cultural adjustment and organizational involvement.* National Science Council project research planning report. Taiwan: National Science Council.

Lee, Y. I. (2004b). South Korean companies in transition: An evolving strategic management style. *Strategic Change, 13*(1), 29–35.

Lee, K. W. (2005). *Training by small and medium scale enterprises in the knowledge economy: A case study of Korea.* Seoul: Ewha Womans Univerisity Press.

Lee, C. H., & Bruvold, N. T. (2003). Creating value for employees: Investment in employee development. *The International Journal of Human Resource Management, 14*(6), 981–1000.

Lee, E., & Kim, S. (2006). Best practices and performance-based HR system in Korea. *Seoul Journal of Business, 12*(1), 3–17.

Legewie, J. (2002). Control and co-ordination of Japanese subsidiaries in China: Problems of an expatriate-based management system. *International Journal of Human Resource Management, 13*, 901–919.

Lertxundi, A., & Landeta, J. (2012). The dilemma facing multinational enterprises: Transfer or adaptation of their human resource management systems. *The International Journal of Human Resource Management, 23*(9), 1788–1807.

Leung, A., & Smith, C. (2005, December 4–7). *Chinese human resource practices at the firm level: The migrant worker issue.* Asia-Pacific Researchers in Organization Studies, 11th International Colloquium, Melbourne.

LG. (2016). *Fair evaluation.* Retrieved March 15, 2016, from http://www.lg.com/global/sustainability/employee/fair-evaluation

Li, J. (2003). Strategic human resource management and MNEs' performance in China. *International Journal of Human Resource Management, 14*(2), 157–173.

Li, Y. Q., Sheldon, P., & Sun, J. M. (2011). Education, training and skills China's changing workplace. In P. Sheldon, S. H. Kim, Y. Q. Li, & M. Warner (Eds.), *China's changing workplace* (pp. 111–128). Oxon: Routledge.

Lin, S. Y. (2009). *Experiences and reflections on industrial needs orientation of vocational technical high school education in the Republic of Korea (South Korea) in linking vocational training with the enterprises—Asian perspectives.* Retrieved March 12, 2016, from http://www.unevoc.unesco.org/up/Link_Voc_End.pdf

Lin, C. Y. Y., & Wei, Y. C. (2005). An Eastern and SME version of expatriate management: An empirical study of small and medium enterprises in Taiwan. *International Journal of Human Resource Management, 16*, 1431–1453.

Lindholm, N. (1999). Performance management in MNC subsidiaries in China: A study of host country managers and professionals. *Asia Pacific Journal of Human Resources, 37*, 18–35.

Littrell, L. N., & Salas, E. (2005). A review of cross-cultural training: Best practices, guidelines, and research needs. *Human Resource Development Review, 4*, 305–334.

Liu, E., & Wu, J. (1999). *Minimun wage systems.* Retrieved April 15, 2016, from http://www.legco.gov.hk/yr98-99/english/sec/library/989rp08.pdf

Locke, E. A., & Latham, G. P. (1990). *A theory of goal setting & task performance.* Eaglewood Cliffs: Prentice- Hall.

Logger, E., & Vinke, R. (1995). Compensation and appraisal of international staff. In A. Harzing & J. Ruysseveldt (Eds.), *International human resource management* (pp. 252–269). London: Sage.

Lowe, K. B., Milliman, J., De Cieri, H., & Dowling, P. J. (2002). International compensation practices: A ten-country comparative analysis. *Human Resource Management, 41*(1), 45–66.

Luo, Y. D., & Tung, R. L. (2007). International expansion of emerging market enterprises: A springboard perspective. *Journal of International Business Studies, 38*(4), 481–498.

MacCallum, R. (1986). Specification searches in covariance structure modeling. *Psychological Bulletin, 100*(1), 107–120.

MacVaugh, J., & Evans, J. (2012). A re-examination of flexible employment practices in Japan. *The International Journal of Human Resource Management, 23*(6), 1245–1258.

Mahajan, A. (2011). Host country national's reactions to expatriate pay policies: Making a case for a cultural alignment pay model. *International Journal of Human Resource Management, 22*(1), 121–137.

Mahajan, A., & Toh, S. M. (2014). Facilitating expatriate adjustment: The role of advice-seeking from host country nationals. *Journal of World Business, 49*(4), 476–487.

Maley, J. F. (2009). The influence of performance appraisal on the psychological contract of the inpatriate manager. *SA Journal of Human Resource Management, 7*(1), 100–109.

Maley, J. F., & Kramar, R. (2007). International performance appraisal: Policies, practices and processes in Australian subsidiaries of healthcare MNCs. *Research and Practice in Human Resource Management, 15*, 21–40.

Manolopoulos, D., Dimitratos, P., & Sapouna, P. (2011). An investigation into international assignment directions of R&D MNE employees: Evidence from Greece. *The International Journal of Human Resource Management, 22*(05), 1093–1108.

Maon, F., Lindgreen, A., & Swaen, V. (2009). Designing and implementing corporate social responsibility: An integrative framework grounded in theory and practice. *Journal of Business Ethics, 87*(1), 71–89.

Marczyk, G., DeMatteo, D., & Festinger, D. (2005). *Essentials of research design and methodology*. Hoboken: Wiley.

Marshall, C., & Rossman, G. B. (2006). *Designing qualitative research* (4th ed.). London: Sage.

Martin, D. C., & Bartol, K. M. (2003). Factors influencing expatriate performance appraisal system success: An organizational perspective. *Journal of International Management, 9*, 115–132.

Martins, D., & Diaconescu, L. M. (2014). Expatriates recruitment and selection for long-term international assignments in Portuguese companies. *Tékhne, 12*, 48–57.

Mayerhofer, H., Hartmann, L. C., Michelitsch-Riedl, G., & Kollinger, I. (2004). Flexpatriate assignments: A neglected issue in global staffing. *The International Journal of Human Resource Management, 15*(8), 1371–1389.

Mayerhofer, H., Schmidt, A., Hartmann, L., & Bendl, R. (2011). Recognising diversity in managing work life issues of flexpatriates. *Equality, Diversity and Inclusion: An International Journal, 30*(7), 589–609.

Maylor, H., & Blackmon, K. (2005). *Researching business and management: A roadmap for success*. Basingstoke: Palgrave Macmillan.

Mayrhofer, W., & Brewster, C. (1996). In praise of ethnocentricity: Expatriate policies in European multinationals. *The International Executive, 38*(6), 749–778.

McClean, E., & Collins, C. J. (2011). High-commitment HR practices, employee effort, and firm performance: Investigating the effects of HR practices across employee groups within professional services firms. *Human Resource Management, 50*(3), 341–363.

McGovern, P. (1999). HRM policies and management practices. In L. Govern, V. Hope Hailey, P. Stiles, & C. Truss (Eds.), *Strategic human resource management*. Oxford: Oxford University Press.

McPherson, A. H., & Roche, W. K. (1997). Peripheral location equals localized labour? Multinationals and the internationalization of training and development in Ireland. *International Journal of Human Resource Management, 8*, 369–384.

Mehegan, P. (2003). *Cross-cultural awareness training in Australian organizations.* IDP Australian International Education Conference, Melbourne.

Mendenhall, M., & Oddou, G. (1991). Expatriate performance appraisal: Problems and solutions. In M. Mendenhall & G. Oddou (Eds.), *Readings and cases in international human resource management.* Boston: PWS-Kent.

Mendenhall, M. E., & Wiley, C. (1994). Strangers in a strange land: The relationship between expatriate adjustment and impression management. *American Behavioral Scientist, 37*(5), 605–620.

Mendenhall, M., Kuhlmann, T. M., Stahl, G. K., & Osland, J. S. (2002). *Employee development and expatriate assignments.* London: Blackwell.

Meng, X., & Kidd, M. P. (1997). Labor market reform and the changing structure of wage determination in China's state sector during the 1980s. *Journal of Comparative Economics, 25*(3), 403–421.

Mercer. (2013). *Mercer's Worldwide International Assignments Policies and Practices report.* Retrieved March 10, 2014, from http://m.mercer.com/press-releases/1521435?detail=D

Meyer, J. P., & Smith, C. A. (2000). HRM practices and organizational commitment: Test of a mediation model. *Canadian Journal of Administrative Sciences, 17*(4), 319–331.

Meyer, K. E., Mudambi, R., & Narula, R. (2011). Multinational enterprises and local contexts: The opportunities and challenges of multiple embeddedness. *Journal of Management Studies, 48*(2), 235–252.

Mezias, J. M., & Scandura, T. A. (2005). A needs-driven approach to expatriate adjustment and career development: A multiple mentoring perspective. *Journal of International Business Studies, 36*, 519–538.

Milliman, J., Taylor, S., & Czaplewski, A. (2000). Performance feedback in MNC: Opportunities for organizational learning. *Human Resource Planning, 25*, 29–44.

Minbaeva, D. B., & Michailova, S. (2004). Knowledge transfer and expatriation in multinational corporations: The role of disseminative capacity. *Employee Relations, 26*(6), 663–679.

Mitrev, S., & Culpepper, R. (2012). Expatriation in Europe: Factor and insights. *Journal of International Management Studies, 7*, 158–167.

Mol, S. T., Born, M. P., & van der Molen, H. T. (2005). Developing criteria for expatriate effectiveness: Time to jump off the adjustment bandwagon. *International Journal of Intercultural Relations, 29*(3), 339–353.

Morgan, G., Kelly, B., Sharpe, D., & Whitley, R. (2003). Global managers and Japanese multinationals: Internationalization and management in Japanese financial institutions. *The International Journal of Human Resource Management, 14*(3), 389–407.

Morley, M. J., & Flynn, M. (2003). The relationship between work-role characteristics and intercultural transitional adjustment domain patterns among a sample of US and Canadian expatriates on assignment in Ireland. *Cross Cultural Management: An International Journal, 10*(3), 42–57.

Morris, R. (1994). Computerized content analysis in management research: A demonstration of advantages & limitations. *Journal of Management, 20*(4), 903–931.

Morris, M., & Robie, C. (2002). A meta-analysis of the effects of cross cultural training on expatriate performance and adjustment. *International Journal of Training and Development, 5*, 112–125.

Morrison, E. W. (1993). A longitudinal study of the effects of information seeking on newcomer socialization. *Journal of Applied Psychology, 78*(2), 173–183.

Mossholder, K. W., Richardson, H. A., & Settoon, R. P. (2011). Human resource systems and helping in organizations: A relational perspective. *Academy of Management Review, 36*(1), 33–52.

Muchinsky, P. M. (2002). *Psychology applied to work* (6th ed.). Wadsworth: Belmont.

Muratbekova-Touron, M. (2008). From an ethnocentric to a geocentric approach to IHRM. *Cross Cultural Management: An International Journal, 15*(4), 335–352.

Murphy, K. R., & Cleveland, J. N. (1991). *Performance appraisal: An organizational perspective.* Needham Heights: Allyn & Bacon.

Murray, T. R. (2003). *Blending qualitative and quantitative research methods in theses and dissertations.* Thousand Oaks: Corwin Press.

Myers, M. D. (2009). *Qualitative research in business & management.* London: Sage.

Myers, M. D. (2013). *Qualitative research in business and management.* London: Sage.

Myloni, B. (2002). *The transfer of human resource management practices within multinational companies in Greece—A comparative analysis of human resource management practices in subsidiaries of European and US multinationals and Greek companies.* Unpublished doctoral dissertation, University of Bradford, Bradford.

Nathan, B. R., Mohrman Jr., A. M., & Milliman, J. (1991). Interpersonal relations as a context for the effects of appraisal interviews on performance and satisfaction: A longitudinal study. *Academy of Management Journal, 34*, 352–369.

Neuman, W. L. (2003). *Social research method: Qualitative and quantitative methods.* Boston: Allyn and Bacon.

Newman, A., & Sheikh, A. Z. (2014). Determinants of best HR practices in Chinese SMEs. *Journal of Small Business and Enterprise Development, 21*(3), 414–430.

Newton, S., Hutchings, K., & Kabanoff, B. (2007). Repatriation in Australian organisations: Effects of function and value of international assignment on program scope. *Asia Pacific Journal of Human Resources, 45*(3), 295–313.

Ng, S. H., & Warner, M. (2000). Industrial relations versus human resource management in the PRC: Collective bargaining 'with Chinese characteristics'. In *Changing workplace relations in the Chinese economy* (pp. 100–116). London: Palgrave Macmillan.

Ngo, H. Y., Turban, D., Lau, C. M., & Lui, S. Y. (1998). Human resource practices and firm performance of multinational corporations: Influences of country origin. *International Journal of Human Resource Management, 9*(4), 632–652.

Nguyen, T. N., Truong, Q., & Buyens, D. (2011). Training and firm performance in economies in transition: A comparison between Vietnam and China. *Asia Pacific Business Review, 17*(1), 103–119.

Nigam, R., & Su, Z. (2010). Climbing up the performance ladder: A conceptual framework for emerging country multinationals. *International Journal of Business and Management, 5*(4), 13–25.

Nishii, L. H., Lepak, D. P., & Schneider, B. (2008). Employee attributions of the "why" of HR practices: Their effects on employee attitudes and behaviors, and customer satisfaction. *Personnel Psychology, 61*(3), 503–545.

OECD. (2013). *FDI in figures.* Retrieved 21, July 2013, from www.oecd.org/investment/statistics.htm

Orlitzky, M., & Swanson, D. L. (2006). Socially responsible human resource management. In J. R. Deckop (Ed.), *Human resource management ethics* (pp. 3–25). Charlotte: Information Age Publishing.

Osland, A., & Osland, J. S. (2005). Contextualization and strategic international human resource management approaches: The case of Central America and Panama. *The International Journal of Human Resource Management, 16*(12), 2218–2236.

Ostroff, C., & Bowen, D. E. (2000). Moving HR to a higher level: HR practices and organizational effectiveness. In K. J. Klein & S. W. J. Kozlowski (Eds.), *Multilevel theory, research, and methods in organizations: Foundations, extensions, and new directions* (pp. 211–266). San Francisco: Jossey-Bass.

Paauwe, J., & Dewe, P. (1995). Human resource management in multinational corporations: Theories and models'. In A. Harzing & J. Ruysseveldt (Eds.), *International human resource management* (pp. 75–98). London: Sage.

Paik, Y. S., & Sohn, J. D. (1998). Confucius in Mexico: Korean MNEs and the maquiladoras. *Business Horizons, 41*(6), 25–33.

Paik, Y. S., & Sohn, J. D. (2004). Expatriate managers and MNC's ability to control international subsidiaries: The case of Japanese MNCs. *Journal of World Business, 39*, 61–71.

Paik, Y. S., Parboteeah, P. K., & Shim, W. S. (2007). The relationship between perceived compensation, organizational commitment and job satisfaction: The case of Mexican workers in the Korean Maquiladoras. *International Journal of Human Resource Management, 18*(10), 1768–1781.

Pan, Q. H., & Zhang, X. F. (2011). *New changes and effects of Korean investment in China.* Retrieved March 16, 2014, from http://ieeexplore.ieee.org/stamp/stamp.jsp?arnumber=05998548

Park, W. W. (2004). *Human resource management in developing countries.* New York: Routledge.

Park, W. S., & Yu, G. C. (2000). *Transformation and new patterns of HRM in Korea.* Michigan: Citeseer.

Park, H. J., Mitsuhashi, H., Fey, C. F., & Björkman, I. (2003). The effect of human resource management practices on Japanese MNC subsidiary performance: A partial mediating model. *The International Journal of Human Resource Management, 14*(8), 1391–1406.

Park, B. S., Kim, J. W., Park, S. B., Kao, J. S., Liu, Y. J., Lin, H. Y., & Sun, M. T. (2008). *Study on Korean and Taiwanese investment patterns in China.* Seoul: Samsung Economic Research Institute.

Pattie, M., White, M. M., & Tansky, J. (2010). The homecoming: A review of support practices for repatriates. *Career Development International, 15*(4), 359–377.

Peloza, J., & Shang, J. (2011). How can corporate social responsibility activities create value for stakeholders? A systematic review. *Journal of the Academy of Marketing Science, 39*(1), 117–135.

Perlmutter, H. V. (1969). The tortuous evolution of the multinational corporation. *Columbia Journal of World Business, 4*(1), 9–18.

Perlmutter, H. V., & Heenan, D. A. (1974). How multinational should your top managers be? *Harvard Business Review, 52*(6), 121–132.

Perlmutter, H. V., & Heenan, D. A. (1979). *Multinational organizational development.* Reading: Addison-Wesley.

Perrin, S. (1999). The emergence of Korean multinational enterprises in European manufacturing. In S. G. Lee & P. B. Ruffini (Eds.), *The global integration of Europe and East Asia: Studies of international trade and investment* (pp. 187–199). Cheltenham: Edward Elgar Publishing.

Petrovic, J., Harris, H., & Brewster, C. (2000). *New forms of international working CReME research report.* Retrieved October 18, 2014, from https://dspace.lib.cranfield.ac.uk/bitstream/1826/3702/3/New_forms_of_international_working-2000.pdf

Pfeffer, J. (2005). Changing mental models: HR's most important task. *Human Resource Management, 44*(2), 123–128.

Pfeffer, J. (2010). Building sustainable organizations: The human factor. *Academy of Management Perspectives, 24*(1), 34–45.

Ployhart, R. E., & Weekley, J. A. (2014). Recruitment and selection in global organizations. In D. G. Collings, G. T. Wood, & P. M. Caligiuri (Eds.), *The*

Routledge companion to international human resource management (pp. 155–171). Oxon: Routledge.

Podsakoff, P. M., MacKenzie, S. B., Lee, J. Y., & Podsakoff, N. P. (2003). Common method biases in behavioral research: A critical review of the literature and recommended remedies. *Journal of Applied Psychology, 88*(5), 879–903.

Poon, H. F., Wei, Q., & Rowley, C. (2010). The changing face of performance management in China. In C. Rowley & F. L. Cooke (Eds.), *The changing face of management in China* (pp. 149–169). Oxon: Routledge.

Porter, M. E., & Kramer, M. R. (2011). Creating shared value. *Harvard Business Review, 89*(1/2), 62–77.

POSCO. (2008). *Home*. Retrieved April 12, 2016, from http://www.poscoenc.com.cn/

Pratt, M. G. (1998). To be or not to be: Central questions in organizational identification'. In D. Whetten & P. Godfrey (Eds.), *Identity in organizations: Developing theory through conversations* (pp. 171–207). Thousand Oaks: Sage.

PricewaterhouseCoopers. (2000). *Managing in a virtual world*. London: PricewaterhouseCoopers.

PricewaterhouseCoopers. (2005). *International assignments: Global policy and practice: Key trends 2005*. Retrived October 18, 2014, from http://www.pwc.lu/en_LU/lu/hr/docs/hrs062005.pdf?q=assignments

Pucik, V., & Lim, J. C. (2001). Transforming human resource management in a Korean Chaebol: A case study of Samsung. *Asia Pacific Business Review, 7*(4), 137–160.

Pudelko, M., & Harzing, A. (2007). Country of origin, localization, or dominance effects? An empirical investigation of HRM practices in foreign subsidiaries. *Human Resource Management, 46*(4), 535–559.

Punch, K. F. (2005). *Introduction to social research: Quantitative and qualitative approaches*. New Delhi: Sage.

Purcell, J., & Hutchinson, S. (2007). Front line managers as agents in the HRM performance causal chain: Theory, analysis and evidence. *Human Resource Management Journal, 17*(1), 3–20.

Qiao, J. S., & Wang, W. (2009). Managerial competencies for middle managers: Some empirical findings from China. *Journal of European Industrial Training, 33*(1), 69–81.

Qiao, K., Khilji, S., & Wang, X. Y. (2009). High-performance work systems, organizational commitment, and the role of demographic features in the People's Republic of China. *The International Journal of Human Resource Management, 20*(11), 2311–2330.

Ragin, C. C. (1994). *Constructing social research*. Thousand Oaks: Pine Forge Press.

Reiche, B. S. (2007). The effect of international staffing practices on subsidiary staff retention in multinational corporations. *The International Journal of Human Resource Management, 18*(4), 523–536.

Reiche, B. S., & Harzing, A. W. (2009). International assignments. In A. W. K. Harzing & A. Pinnington (Eds.), *International human resource management*. London: Sage.

Reiche, B. S., Harzing, A. W., & Kraimer, M. L. (2008). The role of international assignees' social capital in creating inter-unit intellectual capital: A cross-level model. *Journal of International Business Studies, 40*(3), 509–526.

Reynolds, C. (1986). Compensation of overseas personnel. In J. J. Famularo (Ed.), *Handbook of human resources administration* (pp. 47–61). New York: McGraw-Hill.

Reynolds, C. (1997). Expatriate compensation in historical perspective. *Journal of World Business, 32*(2), 118–132.

Rhoades, L., & Eisenberger, R. (2002). Perceived organizational support: A review of the literature. *Journal of Applied Psychology, 87*(4), 698–714.

Richard, O. C., Ismail, K. M., Bhuian, S. N., & Taylor, E. C. (2009). Mentoring in supervisor subordinate dyads: Antecedents, consequences, and test of a mediation model of mentorship. *Journal of Business Research, 62*(11), 1110–1118.

Rienda, L., Claver, E., & Quer, D. (2013). The internationalisation of Indian multinationals: Determinants of expansion through acquisitions. *Journal of the Asia Pacific Economy, 18*(1), 115–132.

Rosenzweig, P. M., & Singh, J. V. (1991). Organizational environments and the multinational enterprises. *The Academy of Management Review, 16*(2), 340–361.

Rousseau, D. M. (1989). Psychological and implied contracts in organizations. *Employee Responsibilities and Rights Journal, 2*(2), 121–139.

Rousseau, D. M. (1995). *Psychological contracts in organizations: Understanding written and unwritten agreements*. Thousand Oaks: Sage.

Rowley, C. (2005). Context, developments and interactions in the HRM system in South Korea: Between rigidity and flexibility. *Journal of Comparative Asian Development, 4*(1), 105–133.

Rowley, C., & Bae, J. S. (2002). Globalization and transformation of human resource management in South Korea. *International Journal of Human Resource Management, 13*(3), 522–549.

Rowley, C., & Bae, J. S. (2004). Human resource management in South Korea after the Asian financial crisis: Emerging patterns from the labyrinth. *International Studies of Management & Organization, 34*(1), 52–82.

Rowley, C., & Yang, H. S. (2009). The development of Asian performance management systems: The example of South Korea. Performance management in

South Korea. In A. Varma et al. (Eds.), *Performance management systems: A global perspective*. Abingdon: Routledge.

Rowley, C., & Yoo, K. S. (2013). Workforce development in South Korea: A driving force in the korean miracle'. In J. Benson, H. Gospel, & Y. Zhu (Eds.), *Workforce development and skill formation in China* (pp. 67–88). Routledge: London.

Rupp, D., Ganapathi, E. J., Aguilera, R. V., & Williams, C. A. (2006). Employee reactions to corporate social responsibility: An organizational justice framework. *Journal of Organizational Behavior, 27*(4), 537–543.

Samnani, A. K., & Singh, P. (2013). Exploring the fit perspective: An ethnographic approach. *Human Resource Management, 52*(1), 123–144.

Sanchez, J. I., Spector, P. E., & Cooper, C. L. (2000). Adapting to a boundaryless world: A developmental expatriate model. *Academy of Management Executive, 14*, 96–106.

Sanchez Vidal, E. M., Sanz Valle, R., Barba Aragon, I. M., & Brewster, C. (2007). Repatriation adjustment process of business employees: Evidence from Spanish workers. *International Journal of Intercultural Relations, 31*(3), 317–337.

Santoso, J., & Loosemore, M. (2013). Expatriate management in Australian multinational enterprises. *Construction Management and Economics, 31*(11), 1098–1109.

Sayim, K. Z. (2010). Pushed or pulled? Transfer of reward management policies in MNCs. *International Journal of Human Resource Management, 21*(14), 2631–2658.

Schaaper, J., Amann, B., Jaussaud, J., Nakamura, H., & Mizoguchi, S. (2013). Human resource management in Asian subsidiaries: Comparison of French and Japanese MNCs. *International Journal of Human Resource Management, 24*(7), 1454–1470.

Schell, M. S., & Solomon, C. M. (1997). *Capitalizing on the global workforce: A strategic guide to expatriate management*. New York: McGraw Hill.

Schensul, J. J. (2012). Methodology, methods and tools in qualitative research. In S. D. Lapan, M. Y. Quartaroli, & F. J. Reimer (Eds.), *Qualitative research an introduction to methods and designs* (p. 70). San Francisco: Jossey-Bass.

Schroeder, D. A., & Graziano, W. G. (2015). *The Oxford handbook of prosocial behaviors*. Oxford: Oxford University Press.

Schuh, A. (2007). Regionalization in Central and Eastern Europe: Searching for regiocentric orientations in MNC strategies. *Journal of East-West Business, 13*(2–3), 143–166.

Schuler, R. S., Dowling, P. J., & De Cieri, H. (1993). An integrative framework of strategic international human resource management. *Journal of Management, 19*(2), 419–459.

Schuler, S. R., Budhwar, S. P., & Florkowski, W. G. (2002). International human resource management: Review and critique. *International Journal of Management Review, 4*(1), 41–70.

Scott, W. R. (1995). *Institutions and organizations*. Thousand Oaks: Sage.

Scullion, H. (1994). Staffing policies and strategic control in British multinationals. *International Studies of Management and Organization, 3*(4), 86–104.

Scullion, H. (1995). International human resource management. In J. Storey (Ed.), *Human resource management: A critical text* (pp. 352–382). London: Routledge.

Scullion, H., & Brewster, C. (2002). The management of expatriates: Messages from Europe. *Journal of World Business, 36*, 346–365.

Scullion, H., & Collings, D. G. (2006). Introduction. In H. Scullion & D. G. Collings (Eds.), *Global staffing* (pp. 1–13). London: Routledge.

Scullion, H., & Lenihan, M. (2005). *International human resource management: A critical text*. Basingstoke: Palgrave.

Seak, N., & Enderwick, P. (2008). The management of New Zealand expatriates in China. *International Journal of Human Resource Management, 19*, 1298–1313.

Selmer, J. (1999). Career issues and international adjustment of business expatriates. *Career Development International, 4*(2), 77–87.

Selmer, J. (2002). To train or not to train? European expatriate managers in China. *International Journal of Cross Cultural Management, 2*(1), 37–51.

Selmer, J., Torbiorn, I., & de Leon, C. T. (1998). Sequential cross-cultural training for expatriate business managers: Pre-departure and post-arrival. *International Journal of Human Resource Management, 9*, 831–840.

SERI. (2008). *Study on Korean and Taiwanese investment patterns in China*. Retrieved May 5, 2010, from http://www.seriworld.org/04/wldBookV.html?mn¼E&natcd¼&mncd¼0301&key¼20080808000001&pPage¼1&listopt¼FL

Shaffer, M. A., Kraimer, M. L., Chen, Y. P., & Bolino, M. C. (2012). Choices, challenges, and career consequences of global work experiences: A review and future agenda. *Journal of Management, 38*(4), 1282–1327.

Sharma, S., Sharma, J., & Devi, A. (2009). Corporate social responsibility: The key role of human resources management. *Human Resource Management: Issues, Challenges and Opportunities, 2*(1), 205–213.

Shay, J. P., & Baack, S. (2006). An empirical investigation of the relationships between modes and degree of expatriate adjustment and multiple measures of performance. *International Journal of Cross Cultural Management, 6*(3), 275–294.

Sheehan, C., Fenwick, M., & Dowling, P. J. (2010). An investigation of paradigm choice in Australian international human resource management research. *International Journal of Human Resource Management, 21*(11), 1816–1836.

Shelton, T. (2008). Global compensation strategies: Managing and administering split pay for an expatriate workforce. *Compensation & Benefits Review, 40*(1), 56–60.

Shen, J. (2004a). International performance appraisals. *International Journal of Manpower, 25*, 547–563.

Shen, J. (2004b). Compensation in Chinese multinationals. *Compensation & Benefits Review, 36*(1), 15–25.

Shen, J. (2005a). Effective international performance appraisals: Easily said, hard to do. *Compensation & Benefits Review, 37*, 70–79.

Shen, J. (2005b). Towards a generic IHRM model. *Journal of Organisational Transformation & Social Change, 2*(2), 83–102.

Shen, J. (2005c). International training and management development: Theory and reality. *Journal of Management Development, 24*, 656–666.

Shen, J. (2006). Factors affecting international staffing in Chinese MNEs. *International Journal of Human Resource Management, 17*(2), 295–315.

Shen, J. (2007). *Labour disputes and their resolution in China*. Oxford: Chandos Publishing.

Shen, J. (2008). HRM in Chinese privatised enterprises. *Thunderbird International Business Review, 50*(2), 91–104.

Shen, J. (2010). Employees' satisfaction with HRM in Chinese privately-owned enterprises. *Asia Pacific Business Review, 16*(3), 339–354.

Shen, J. (2011). Developing the concept of socially responsible international human resource management. *The International Journal of Human Resource Management, 22*(6), 1351–1363.

Shen, J. (2016). Multilevel analysis in HRM research using HLM: Principle and application. *Human Resource Management, 55*(6), 951–965.

Shen, J., & Benson, J. (2014). When CSR is a social norm: How socially responsible human resource management affects employee work behavior. *Journal of Management*. p.0149206314522300.

Shen, J., & Darby, R. (2006). Training and management development in Chinese multinational enterprises. *Employee Relations, 28*(4), 342–362.

Shen, J., & Edwards, V. (2004). Recruitment and selection in Chinese MNEs. *The International Journal of Human Resource Management, 15*(4), 814–835.

Shen, Y., & Hall, D. T. T. (2009). When expatriates explore other options: Retaining talent through greater job embeddedness and repatriation adjustment. *Human Resource Management, 48*(5), 793–816.

Shen, J., & Lang, B. (2009). Cross-cultural training and its impact on expatriate performance in Australian MNEs. *Human Resource Development International, 12*(4), 371–386.

Shen, J., & Zhu, C. J. (2011). Effects of socially responsible human resource management on employee organizational commitment. *The International Journal of Human Resource Management, 22*(15), 3020–3035.

Shen, J., Edwards, V., & Lee, G. (2005). Developing an integrative international human resource model: The contribution of Chinese multinational enterprises. *Asia Pacific Business Review, 11*(3), 369–388.

Shen, J., Tang, N., & D'Netto, B. (2014). A multilevel analysis of the effects of HR diversity management on employee knowledge sharing: The case of Chinese employees. *The International Journal of Human Resource Management, 25*(12), 1720–1738.

Shore, L. M., & Shore, T. M. (1995). Perceived organizational support and organizational justice. In R. S. Cropanzano & K. M. Kacmar (Eds.), *Organizational politics, justice, and support: Managing the social climate of the workplace* (pp. 149–164). Westport: Quorum.

Siders, M. A., George, G., & Dharwadkar, R. (2001). The relationship of internal and external commitment foci to objective job performance measures. *Academy of Management Journal, 44*, 570–579.

SK. (2013). *SK Telecom annual report.* Retrieved April 15, 2016, from http://www.sktelecom.com/img/kor/persist_report/20140806/SUSTAIN_REPORT_2013_ENG.pdf

Sluss, D. M., Klimchak, M., & Holmes, J. J. (2008). Perceived organizational support as a mediator between relational exchange and organizational identification. *Journal of Vocational Behavior, 73*(3), 457–464.

Smith, M. A., & Canger, J. M. (2004). Effects of supervisor "big five" personality on subordinate attitudes. *Journal of Business and Psychology, 18*(4), 465–481.

Smith, D., & Langfield-Smith, K. (2004). Structural equation modeling in management accounting research: Critical analysis and opportunities. *Journal of Accounting Literature, 23*(1), 49–86.

Smith, C., & Meiksins, P. (1995). System, society and dominance effects in cross-national organisational analysis. *Work, Employment & Society, 9*(2), 241–267.

Snape, E., & Redman, T. (2010). HRM practices, organizational citizenship behaviour, and performance: A multi-level analysis. *Journal of Management Studies, 47*(7), 1219–1247.

Solutions Consultant. (2014). *Tips for performance appraisal.* Retried March 12, 2016, from http://china.smetoolkit.org/china/zh/content/en/376/Tips-for-Performance-Appraisal

South Korea Government. (2012). *Economy.* Retrieved March 30, 2016, from http://www.southkoreagovernment.com/economy.htm

Sparrow, P. R., Schuler, R. S., & Jackson, S. E. (1994). Convergence of divergence: Human resource practices and policies for competitive advantage worldwide. *The International Journal of Human Resource Management, 5*(2), 267–300.

Sparrow, P., Brewster, C., & Harris, H. (2004). *Globalizing human resource management.* London: Routledge.

Stahl, G. K., Miller, E. L., & Tung, R. L. (2002). Toward the boundaryless career: A closer look at the expatriate career concept and the perceived implications of an international assignment. *Journal of World Business, 37*(3), 216–227.

Starr, T. L., & Currie, G. (2009). 'Out of sight but still in the picture': Short-term international assignments and the influential role of family. *The International Journal of Human Resource Management, 20*(6), 1421–1438.

Stone, J. R. (2008). *Managing human resource.* Milton: Wiley.

Stroh, L. K., & Caligiuri, P. M. (1998). Increasing global competitiveness through effective people management. *Journal of World Business, 33*(1), 1–16.

Sun, B. (2000). Pay and motivation in Chinese enterprises. In M. Warner (Ed.), *Changing workplace relations in the Chinese economy* (pp. 205–223). London: Palgrave Macmillan.

Suutari, V., & Brewster, C. (2001). Making their own way: International experience through self-initiated foreign assignments. *Journal of World Business, 35*, 417–436.

Suutari, V., & Ma kela, K. (2007). The career capital of managers with global careers. *Journal of Managerial Psychology, 22*(7), 628–648.

Suutari, V., & Tahvanainen, M. (2002). The antecedents of performance management among Finnish expatriates. *The International Journal of Human Resource Management, 13*, 55–75.

Suutari, V., & Tornikoski, C. (2001). The challenge of expatriate compensation: The sources of satisfaction and dissatisfaction among expatriates. *International Journal of Human Resource Management, 12*(3), 389–404.

Suutari, V., Raharjo, K., & Riikkilä, T. (2002). The challenge of cross-cultural leadership interaction: Finnish expatriates in Indonesia. *Career Development International, 7*, 415–429.

Suutari, V., Brewster, C., Riusala, K., & Syrjäkari, S. (2013). Managing non-standard international experience: Evidence from a Finnish company. *Journal of Global Mobility: The Home of Expatriate Management Research, 1*(2), 118–138.

Tahvanainen, M., Welch, D., & Worm, V. (2005). Implications of short-term international assignments. *European Management Journal, 23*(6), 663–673.

Tajfel, H. (1978). The achievement of group differentiation. In H. Tajfel (Ed.), *Differentiation between social groups: Studies in the social psychology of intergroup relations* (pp. 77–98). London: Academic Press.

Tajfel, H., & Turner, J. C. (1985). The social identity theory of intergroup behavior. In S. Worchel & W. G. Austin (Eds.), *Psychology of intergroup relations* (pp. 7–24). Chicago: Nelson-Hall.

Tan, D., & Mahoney, J. T. (2006). Why a multinational firms chooses expatriates: Integrating resource-based, agency and transaction costs perspectives. *Journal of Management Studies, 43*(3), 457–484.

Tan, C. H., & Torrington, D. (1998). *Human resource management for Southeast Asia and Hong Kong.* Singapore: Prentice Hall.

Tarique, I., & Schuler, R. S. (2010). Global talent management: Literature review, integrative framework, and suggestions for future research. *Journal of World Business, 45*(2), 122–133.

Taylor, S., Beechler, S., & Napier, N. (1996). Toward an integrative model of strategic international human resource management. *Academy of Management Review, 21*(4), 959–985.

Taylor, R., Cho, D. Y., & Hyun, J. H. (2001). Korean companies in China: Strategies in the localisation of management. In C. Rowley, T. W. Sohn, & J. Bae (Eds.), *Managing Korean business: Organisation, culture, human resources and change* (pp. 161–181). London: Frank Cass.

Templer, K. J. (2010). Personal attributes of expatriate managers, subordinate ethnocentrism, and expatriate success: A host-country perspective. *The International Journal of Human Resource Management, 21*(10), 1754–1768.

Tepper, B. J., & Taylor, E. C. (2003). Relationships among supervisors and subordinates' procedural justice perceptions and organizational citizenship behaviors. *Academy of Management Journal, 46*(1), 97–105.

Thakur, R.. (2015). *One belt, one road: China's new strategic and trade policy.* Retrieved March 30, 2016, from http://www.delhipolicygroup.com/publications-detail/one-belt-one-road- chinas-new-strategic-and-trade-policy.html

Tharenou, P., & Harvey, M. (2006). Examining the overseas staffing options utilized by Australian headquartered multinational corporations. *The International Journal of Human Resource Management, 17*(6), 1095–1114.

The Bank of Korea. (2016). *A sixty-year history.* Retrieved April 4, 2016, from http://dl.bok.or.kr/viewer/MediaViewer.ax?cid=180415&rid=5&moi=0&infoID=67115

Tian, X., Harvey, M., & Slocum, J. W. (2014). The retention of Chinese managers: The Chinese puzzle box. *Organizational Dynamics, 43*(1), 44–52.

Tjosvold, D., & Chia, L. C. (1989). Conflict between managers and workers: The role of cooperation and competition. *The Journal of Social Psychology, 129*(2), 235–247.

Toh, S. M., & DeNisi, A. S. (2003). Host country national reactions to expatriate pay policies: A model and implications. *Academy of Management Review, 28*(4), 606–621.

Toh, S. M., & DeNisi, A. S. (2005). A local perspective to expatriate success. *Academy of Management Executive, 19*(1), 132–146.

Toh, S. M., & DeNisi, A. S. (2007). Host country nationals as socializing agents: A social identity approach. *Journal of Organizational Behavior, 28*(3), 281–301.

Toh, S. M., & Srinivas, E. S. (2012). Perceptions of task cohesiveness and organizational support increase trust and information sharing between host country nationals and expatriate coworkers in Oman. *Journal of World Business, 47*(4), 696–705.

Tolentino, P. E. (2000). *Multinational corporations: Emergence and evolution.* London: Routledge.

Torrington, D. (1994). *International human resource management: Think globally, act locally.* London: Prentice-Hall.

Tsai, C. J., & Wang, W. L. (2013). Exploring the factors associated with employees' perceived appraisal accuracy: A study of Chinese state-owned enterprises. *The International Journal of Human Resource Management, 24*(11), 2197–2220.

Tsang, E. W. K. (1994). Human resource management problems in Sino-foreign joint ventures. *International Journal of Manpower, 15*(9), 4–21.

Tsang, E. W. K. (2001). Adjustment of mainland Chinese academics and students to Singapore. *International Journal of Intercultural Relations, 25*(4), 347–372.

Tsui, A., Wang, D., & Zhang, Y. (2002). Employment relationships with Chinese managers: Exploring differences between state-owned and non–state-owned firms. In A. Tsui & C. Lau (Eds.), *The management of enterprises in the People's Republic of China* (pp. 347–374). Boston: Kluwer Academic.

Tung, R. L. (1981). Selecting and training of personnel for overseas assignments. *Colombia Journal of World Business, 16*(2), 67–78.

Tung, R. L. (1982). Selection and training procedures of US, European, and Japanese multinationals. *California Management Review, 25*, 57–71.

Tung, R. L. (1984). Strategic management of human resources in the multinational enterprise. *Human Resource Management, 23*(2), 120–143.

Tung, R. L. (1987). Expatriate assignments: Enhancing success and minimizing failure. *Academy of Management Executive, 1*(2), 117–125.

Tung, R. L., Paik, Y. S., & Bae, J. S. (2013). Korean human resource management in the global context. *International Journal of Human Resource Management, 24*(5), 905–921.

Tungli, Z., & Peiperl, M. (2009). Expatriate practices in German, Japanese, UK, and US multinational companies: A comparative survey of changes. *Human Resource Management, 48*(1), 153–171.

Turban, D. B., & Greening, D. W. (1997). Corporate social performance and organizational attractiveness to prospective employees. *Academy of Management Journal, 40*(3), 658–672.

Tziner, A., Murphy, K. R., Cleveland, J. N., & Roberts-Thompson, G. P. (2001). Relationships between attitudes toward organizations and performance appraisal systems and rating behavior. *International Journal of Selection and Assessment, 9*, 226–239.

United Nations Conference on Trade and Development (UNCTAD). (2005). *World investment report 2005.* Geneva: United Nations.

United Nations Conference on Trade and Development (UNCTAD). (2012). *World investment report 2012: Towards a new generation of investment policies.* Retrieved June 20, 2013, from http://www.unctad-docs.org/ files/UNCTAD-WIR2012-Full-en.pdf

United Nations Conference on Trade and Development (UNCTAD). (2013). *Inward and outward foreign direct investment stock, annual, 1980–2011.* Retrieved May 1, 2013, from http://unctadstat.unctad.org/TableViewer/tableView.aspx

Van den Born, F., & Peltokorpi, V. (2010). Language policies and communication in multinational companies. *Journal of Business Communication, 47*(2), 97–118.

Van den Hove, S., Le Menestrel, M., & de Bettignies, H. C. (2002). The oil industry and climate change: Strategies and ethical dilemmas. *Climate Policy, 2*(1), 3–18.

Van Dick, R., Wagner, U., Stellmacher, J., & Christ, O. (2004). The utility of a broader conceptualization of organizational identification: Which aspects really matter? *Journal of Occupational and Organizational Psychology, 77*(2), 171–191.

Van Maanen, J. (2000). *Qualitative methods in management research.* Thousand Oaks: Sage.

van Teijlingen, E., & Hundley, V. (2001). The importance of pilot studies. *Social Research Update, 35*, 1–4.

Vance, C. M., & Paik, Y. S. (2002). One size fits all in expatriate pre-departure training? Comparing the host country voices of Mexican, Indonesian and US workers. *Journal of Management Development, 21*(7), 557–571.

Vance, C. M., & Paik, Y. S. (2005). Forms of host-country national learning for enhanced MNC absorptive capacity. *Journal of Managerial Psychology, 20*, 590–606.

Vance, C. M., & Ring, P. S. (1994). Preparing the host country workforce for expatriate managers: The neglected other side of the coin. *Human Resource Development Quarterly, 5*(4), 337–352.

Vance, C. M., Chow, I. H. S., Paik, Y. S., & Shin, K. U. (2013). Analysis of Korean expatriate congruence with Chinese labor perceptions on training method importance: Implications for global talent management. *The International Journal of Human Resource Management, 24*(5), 985–1005.

Varma, A., Pichler, S., Budhwar, P., & Biswas, S. (2009). Chinese host country nationals' willingness to support expatriates: The role of collectivism, interpersonal affect and guanxi. *International Journal of Cross Cultural Management, 9*(2), 199–216.

Varma, A., Budhwar, P., & Pichler, S. (2011). Chinese host country nationals' willingness to help expatriates: The role of social categorization. *Thunderbird International Business Review, 53*(3), 353–364.

Vo, A. N. (2009). Career development for host country nationals: A case of American and Japanese multinational companies in Vietnam. *The International Journal of Human Resource Management, 20*(6), 1402–1420.

Vo, A., & Stanton, P. (2011). The transfer of HRM policies and practices to a transnational system: The case of performance management practices of the US and Japanese MNEs operating in Vietnam. *International Journal of Human Resource Management, 22*(17), 3513–3527.

Walsham, G. (2006). Doing interpretive research. *European Journal of Information Systems, 15*(3), 320–330.

Wang, Y. L., & Tran, E. (2012). Effects of cross-cultural and language training on expatriates' adjustment and job performance in Vietnam. *Asia Pacific Journal of Human Resources, 50*, 327–350.

Wang, J., & Wang, G. G. (2006). Exploring national human resource development: A case of China management development in a transitional context. *Human Resource Development Review, 5*(2), 176–201.

Wang, X., Bruning, N. S., & Peng, S. (2007). Western high-performance HR practices in China: A comparison among public-owned, private and foreign-invested enterprises. *The International Journal of Human Resource Management, 18*(4), 684–701.

Wang, L. H., Nicholson, J., & Zhu, J. (2009). Pay systems in Chinese state-owned enterprises: A review. *Chinese Management Studies, 3*(4), 328–355.

Wan-Huggins, V. N., Riordan, C. M., & Griffeth, R. W. (1998). The development and longitudinal test of a model of organizational identification. *Journal of Applied Social Psychology, 28*(8), 724–749.

Warner, M. (1995). *The management of human resources in Chinese industry*. New York: St. Martin's Press.

Warner, M. (2010). In search of Confucian HRM: Theory and practice in Greater China and beyond. *The International Journal of Human Resource Management, 21*(12), 2053–2078.

Warner, M., & Goodall, K. (2009). *Management training and development in China: Educating managers in a globalized economy*. Abingdon/New York: Routledge.

Warner, M., Goodall, K., & Ding, D. Z. (1999). The 'myth'of human resource management in Chinese enterprises. *Asia Pacific Business Review, 5*(3–4), 223–237.

Weathington, B. L., Cunningham, C. J. L., & Pittenger, D. J. (2012). *Understanding business research*. Hoboken: Wiley.

Weber, R. P. (1990). *Basic content analysis*. Newbury Park: Sage.

Wei, Q., & Rowley, C. (2009). Pay for performance in China's non-public sector enterprises. *Asia-Pacific Journal of Business Administration, 1*(2), 119–143.

Welch, D. (1994). Determinants of international human resource management approaches and activities: A suggested framework. *Journal of Management Studies, 31*(2), 139–164.

Welch, D. E., & Worm, V. (2006). International business travellers: A challenge for IHRM. In G. K. Stahl & I. Björkman (Eds.), *Handbook of research in international human resource management* (pp. 283–301). Cheltenham: Edward Elgar.

Welch, D. E., Worm, V., & Fenwick, M. (2003). Are virtual international assignments feasible? *Management International Review, 43*(1), 95–114.

Welch, D. E., Welch, L. S., & Worm, V. (2007). The international business traveller: A neglected but strategic human resource. *International Journal of Human Resource Management, 18*(2), 173–183.

Wentland, D. M. (2003). A new practical guide for determining expatriate compensation: The comprehensive model. *Compensation & Benefits Review, 35*(3), 45–50.

Whitener, E. M. (2001). Do "high commitment" human resource practices affect employee commitment? *Journal of Management, 27*(5), 515–535.

Whitford, C. M., & Coetsee, W. J. (2007). A model of the underlying philosophy and criteria for effective implementation of performance management. *SA Journal of Human Resource Management, 4*(1), 63–73.

Whitley, R. (1992). *Business systems in East Asia: Firms, markets and societies.* London: Sage.

William, N. (2006). *Social research methods.* London/Thousand Oaks: Sage.

Williams, R. S. (2002). *Managing employee performance: Design and implementation in organizations.* London: Thompson Learning.

Willing, C. (2013). *Introducing qualitative research in psychology.* Maidenhead: Open University Press.

Wittig-Berman, U., & Beutel, N. J. (2009). International assignments and the career management of repatriates: The boundaryless career concept. *International Journal of Management, 26*(1), 77–88.

Wong, C. S., & Law, K. S. (1999). Managing localization of human resources in the PRC: A practical model. *Journal of World Business, 34*(1), 26–40.

Wong, L. Y., & Slater, J. R. (2011). Executive development in China: Is there any in a Western sense? *International Journal of Human Resource Management, 13*(2), 338–360.

Wood, E. D. (2011). *Post-arrival performance interventions that assist expatriates' adjustment and performance.* PhD thesis, The College of Graduate and Professional Studies, Indiana State University, Terre Haute.

Wood, S. J., & De Menezes, L. M. (2010). Family-friendly management, organizational performance and social legitimacy. *International Journal of Human Resource Management, 21*(10), 1575–1597.

Woods, P. (2003). Performance management of Australian and Singaporean expatriates. *International Journal of Manpower, 24*(5), 517–534.

Wu, W. Y., Chen, C. P., & Gan, P. S. (2000). An empirical research on the effectiveness of cross-cultural training for expatriate managers. *NTU Management Review, 10*(2), 167–203.

Wu, J., Chen, W., & Liu, Y. (2010). An IP/C model of employee-organization relationship: A dual perspective. *Frontiers of Business Research in China, 4*(4), 630–652.

Xiu, L., & Gunderson, M. (2011). Performance pay in China: Gender aspects. *British Journal of Industrial Relations, 51*(1), 124–147.

Yamazaki, Y., & Kayes, D. C. (2007). Expatriate learning: Exploring how Japanese managers adapt in the United States. *International Journal of Human Resource Management, 18*, 1373–1395.

Yan, A., Zhu, G., & Hall, D. T. (2002). International assignments for career building: A model of agency relationships and psychological contracts. *Academy of Management Review, 27*(3), 373–391.

Yang, I., & Kelly, A. (2009). Assumptions in Korean organizations and their implications in a cross-cultural setting. *Advances in Global Leadership, 5*, 297–320.

Yang, H. S., & Rowley, C. (2008). Performance management in South Korea. In A. Varma, P. S. Budhwar, & A. DeNisi (Eds.), *Performance management systems: A global perspective* (pp. 211–270). New York: Routledge.

Yao, S. (1999). Economic growth, income inequality and poverty in China under economic reforms. *The Journal of Development Studies, 35*(6), 104–130.

Ye, L., & Ni, X. (2013). *Performance management in China: In pursuit of accountability and legitimacy*. Retrieved April 10, 2016, from http://www.umdcipe.org/conferences/GovernmentCollaborationShanghai/Submitted%20Papers/Ye_Ni_Paper.pdf

Yeung, A., Xin, K., Pfoertsch, W., & Liu, S. (2011). *The globalization of Chinese companies: Strategies for conquering international markets*. Singapore: Wiley.

Yin, R. K. (2009). *Case study research: Design and methods*. Thousand Oaks: Sage.

Yin, R. K. (2011). *Qualitative research from start to finish*. New York: Guilford Press.

Yoon, D. R. (2007, April 25–26). *Korea's outward FDI in Asia: Characteristics and prospects*. ICRIER Workshop, at Casurina Hall, India Habitat Centre, Lodhi Road New Delhi.

Yoon, J., & Thye, S. (2000). Supervisor support in the work place: Legitimacy and positive affectivity. *The Journal of Social Psychology, 140*(3), 295–316.

Yu, G. C., & Rowley, C. (2009). The changing face of Korean human resource management. In C. Rowley & Y. S. Paik (Eds.), *The changing face of Korean management* (pp. 29–51). London: Routledge.

Yueh, L. Y. (2004). Wage reforms in China during the 1990s. *Asian Economic Journal, 18*(2), 149–164.

Zappalà, G. (2004). Corporate citizenship and human resource management: A new tool or a missed opportunity? *Asia Pacific Journal of Human Resources, 42*(2), 185–201.

Zeira, Y. (1979). Ethnocentrism in host-country organizations. *Business Horizons, 22*(3), 66–75.

Zhang, M., Nyland, C., & Zhu, C. J. (2010). Hukou-based HRM in contemporary China: The case of Jiangsu and Shanghai. *Asia Pacific Business Review, 16*(3), 377–393.

Zhao, H. (2006). Expectations of recruiters and applicants in large cities of China. *Journal of Managerial Psychology, 21*(5), 459–475.

Zhao, S. M., & Chen, W. S. (2011). Human resource management and employment relations in state-owned enterprises. In P. Sheldon, S. Kim, Y. Li, & M. Warner (Eds.), *China's changing workplace* (pp. 163–179). Oxon: Routledge.

Zhao, W., & Zhou, X. G. (2004). Chinese organizations in transition: Changing promotion patterns in the reform source. *Organization Science, 15*(2), 186–199.

Zhou, X., & Qin, J. (2009). A study on cross-cultural adjustment of Japanese and American expatriates in China. *International Journal of Business and Management, 4*(12), 197–206.

Zhu, C. J. (1997). Human resource development in China during the transition to a new economic system. *Asia Pacific Journal of Human Resources, 35*, 19–44.

Zhu, C. J., & Dowling, P. J. (1998). Performance appraisal in China. In J. Selmer (Ed.), *International management in China: Cross-cultural issues* (p. 115). London: Routledge.

Zhu, C. J., & Dowling, P. J. (2000). Managing people during economic transition: The development of HR practices in China. *Asia Pacific Journal of Human Resources, 38*(2), 84–106.

Zhu, C. J., De Cieri, H., & Dowling, P. J. (1998). The reform of employee compensation in China's industrial enterprises. In *Management and international review* (pp. 65–87). Wiesbaden: Gabler Verlag.

Zou, M., & Lansbury, R. D. (2009). Multinational corporations and employment relations in the People's Republic of China: The case of Beijing Hyundai Motor Company. *International Journal of Human Resource Management, 20*(11), 2349–2369.

Index

H. Kang, J. Shen, *International Human Resource Management in South Korean Multinational Enterprises*,
DOI 10.1007/978-981-10-3093-2

C

Kolibri 360 GmbH
Ferdinand-Jühlke-Straße 7
99095 Erfurt, Deutschland
produktsicherheit@kolibri360.de